Masculinities in Theory

Masculinities in Theory

An Introduction

Todd W. Reeser

A John Wiley & Sons, Ltd., Publication

This edition first published 2010
© 2010 Todd W. Reeser

Blackwell Publishing was acquired by John Wiley & Sons in February 2007. Blackwell's publishing program has been merged with Wiley's global Scientific, Technical, and Medical business to form Wiley-Blackwell.

Registered Office
John Wiley & Sons Ltd, The Atrium, Southern Gate, Chichester, West Sussex, PO19 8SQ, United Kingdom

Editorial Offices
350 Main Street, Malden, MA 02148–5020, USA
9600 Garsington Road, Oxford, OX4 2DQ, UK
The Atrium, Southern Gate, Chichester, West Sussex, PO19 8SQ, UK

For details of our global editorial offices, for customer services, and for information about how to apply for permission to reuse the copyright material in this book please see our website at www.wiley.com/wiley-blackwell.

The right of Todd W. Reeser to be identified as the author of this work has been asserted in accordance with the Copyright, Designs and Patents Act 1988.

Wiley also publishes its books in a variety of electronic formats. Some content that appears in print may not be available in electronic books.

Designations used by companies to distinguish their products are often claimed as trademarks. All brand names and product names used in this book are trade names, service marks, trademarks or registered trademarks of their respective owners. The publisher is not associated with any product or vendor mentioned in this book. This publication is designed to provide accurate and authoritative information in regard to the subject matter covered. It is sold on the understanding that the publisher is not engaged in rendering professional services. If professional advice or other expert assistance is required, the services of a competent professional should be sought.

Library of Congress Cataloging-in-Publication Data

Reeser, Todd W., 1967–
    Masculinities in theory : an introduction / Todd W. Reeser.
      p.   cm.
    Includes bibliographical references and index.
    ISBN 978-1-4051-6859-5 (hardcover : alk. paper) – ISBN 978-1-4051-6860-1 (pbk. : alk. paper)
    1. Masculinity. I. Title.
    BF175.5.M37R44 2010
    305.31–dc22

                                                        2009023584

A catalogue record for this book is available from the British Library.

Set in Galliard 10.5/13 pt by SPi Publisher Services, Pondicherry, India
Printed in Singapore by Ho Printing Singapore Pte Ltd

001   2010

Contents

Acknowledgments

This book is the outcome of countless discussions with countless people in countless places about masculinity. If I have learned one thing while writing this book, it is that few are those who have nothing to say on the topic. One of my great academic pleasures over the last five years has been the dialogic relation between teaching and composing *Masculinities in Theory*. I owe a special intellectual debt to the students from my gender and sexuality courses, especially those from my graduate seminar "Masculinities in Theory and Practice." Watching them think so intelligently about gender has been a constant source of inspiration. Thus their dissemination throughout my text. Portions of this book were also conceived on the front porch over pastis and antipasto with Thomas McWhorter whose care and guidance over the past decade has been my greatest personal pleasure. For this reason and innumerable others, it is to him that this book is lovingly dedicated. Though she lives 2,000 miles away, Thérèse De Raedt remains as interactive and warm as she was on that fateful day when we first talked over cognac. I thank her for commenting on the manuscript. I thank Lewis Seifert for his faithful academic partnership and for his intellectual feedback on the project. The wonderfully collegial staff and faculty in the Department of French and Italian at the University of Pittsburgh have directly and indirectly helped me write this book, as have my sister and the rest of my family. I am greatly indebted to the four external readers of the manuscript who helped improve the text immensely (though all remaining flaws belong to me). My thanks to the staff at Wiley-Blackwell and to Jayne Fargnoli who first took on the project, and to my friend Paul Bowden for having sculpted the perfect men for the cover. Finally, I gratefully acknowledge support from the Richard D. and Mary Jane Edwards Endowed Publication Fund at the University of Pittsburgh.

Introduction: The Study of Masculinity

Why Masculinities?

It might seem odd to some to devote an entire book to the study of masculinity. After all, masculinity seems like an obvious thing, something we can and do take for granted. We know what it is when we see it: it is commonsensical, produced by testosterone or by nature. We can easily ascribe a series of characteristics to masculinity: "muscular," "strong," "hard," "brave," and "in control" are words that come to mind. We know that it is the opposite of femininity. We can also make a list of adjectives that do not describe masculinity, such as "weak," "soft," and "emotional."

Even if many of us would agree what masculinity is when asked, we may not necessarily think about it consciously as it passes by us invisibly and we take it for granted in our everyday lives. It may be only when something goes wrong or when it goes into excessive overdrive that we really notice it. A crying man might seem like such an oddity that we cannot help but think about his masculinity (or lack thereof). We all know certain men whom we would not label as "masculine" or whom we might call "effeminate" or something else denoting an absence of masculinity. When we see such men, masculinity becomes visible because of its perceived absence. On the other hand, we might become aware of masculinity when we see a very muscular bodybuilder or a man eager for a fight. The excess of masculinity in these kinds of cases makes us aware of it. Yet, even when we notice these types of masculinity, we may still perceive them as natural: the bodybuilder is taking the male body to its natural extreme and the effeminate man is naturally unmasculine.

Our assumptions of a natural masculinity are greatly complicated, however, when we begin to think more deeply and more broadly about the topic. By going back in time and by looking at definitions of what a man used to be, it becomes clear very quickly that masculinity has a history that does not always affirm our own modern ideas about what a man is. Students of the European Renaissance, for instance, are often struck when they read heterosexual men's writings about their intimate love for other men. They are even more struck when they learn that this writing does not make male writers seem effeminate or homosexual in their socio-historical context, but that, quite the contrary, expressions of male–male intimacy are more likely to reaffirm their masculinity. The nineteenth-century dandy is an important figure of masculinity which, to modern eyes, might seem odd: a man who makes the male body into a work of art might appear to many in the twenty-first century as an incarnation of the made-up, anti-masculine man. Yet, for people of the time, this would not necessarily have been the case, and the dandy was one figure of what a man could or should possibly be.

The concept of masculinity as natural is problematized by moving across cultures and looking at examples different from our own. There is such wide cultural variation in masculinity that considering various cases leads to the inevitable conclusion that it is something that is very difficult to ascertain. While some French men might appear effeminate by other cultures' standards, in context this is usually not the case. American students who travel to India are often surprised to see men walking arm in arm together. While this might not be a standard masculine behavior in most segments of modern American culture, it may not make sense to people used to a certain way of thinking about masculinity.

With innumerable variations in time and in space, masculinity is more complicated than we might first believe and, consequently, masculinity can be studied not as a single definition, but as variety and complexity. The range of masculinities comes into particular relief when someone used to one definition goes somewhere else, whether on an actual trip or whether they travel by reading texts, surfing the web, watching films, or viewing paintings from another time period or cultural context. Such cross-cultural or cross-temporal differences make us aware of masculinity as particularly relative, since we come to see that what is taken for granted is not at all a given, but a fabrication or a construct of a given historical and cultural context.

Yet even within a single cultural and temporal context, ideas of masculinity are far from stable and fixed. While there may be some agreement among some people about a given definition, such a definition is never entirely agreed upon, and it is always contested in some way. A construct of masculinity might be challenged through explicit external critique of the model or through another construct presented as more valid. A male college professor may be viewed as unmasculine by a factory worker, for whom the idea of masculinity is closely linked to physical labor. But equally importantly for this book, any construct of masculinity is already challenged on its own, before any external critique. Because masculinity requires constant work to be maintained and because it can never fully remain at rest, it cannot be maintained in the way that men way want it to appear. The confident, successful Wall Street businessman suffers from anxiety on some level and, if one looks closely, he can be read as faltering and not always confident and successful. Even the most courageous soldier falters in some way in his masculinity, whether on the battlefield itself or in his psyche.

Masculinity appears even less stable once what is perhaps the most basic assumption about masculinity is stripped away, namely that masculinity belongs to men. What does masculinity look like when we do not assume that masculinity and men are directly related? What happens when masculinity is disassociated from the male body altogether and the possibility of female masculinity is considered? Masculinity might suddenly become very visible because it is seen to reside somewhere it is not normally or naturally housed or somewhere it should not be. In this case, it may be the threat of women appropriating masculinity that makes it seem so visible, as a cultural anxiety about men losing masculinity to women is expressed. An even more radical way to strip away natural assumptions about masculinity is to consider what happens to masculinity in an age in which the body can be altered and a woman can acquire masculinity hormonally. How can masculinity be natural if a woman can become a man?

We might also notice masculinity when it starts to take unexpected shapes, when it morphs into something unfamiliar or ambiguous. What does it mean about masculinity when a heterosexual late-night talk-show host makes homoerotic jokes about himself and his male guests night after night? We might wonder what masculinity means while watching football players in their tight pants slapping each other on the butt. What happens to masculinity when a heterosexual man puts on female clothing or dresses as a woman for Halloween? The cross-dressed man might call attention to himself because men do not appear in this state very often, but the situation also calls attention to masculinity itself. These kinds of ambiguous gender manifestations might make us laugh, but their unexpectedness calls attention to masculinity as more unstable and more complex than we may have originally thought.

Why Masculinities in Theory?

Masculinities in Theory is intended to help readers make masculinity an explicit and visible object of analysis, when situations call for explanation as well as when they do not seem to need analysis at all. It will not, however, focus on describing actual or ideal definitions or constructs of masculinity, nor will it do a history of masculinity. Rather, the central goal of this book is to discuss how masculinity can be conceived, how it can be theorized, and how it can be studied. Certain texts (whether literary, cinematic, digital, or artistic) take as their principal subject matter the phenomenon of masculinity, but at other moments, when masculinity passes as more invisible or unnoticed, we have to work a little harder and read between the lines, interpreting what we see, hear, or read. For, as we go about our daily lives, we come into repeated and frequent contact with less obvious forms of masculinity: in meetings, in class, on the television, on the web, on the street, at the movies, and in advertisements. Whether visible or invisible to the observer, masculinity is so varied and complex that this book will not discuss so much what it *is* or how it is something stable that can be easily understood.

Consequently, this book reveals how complicated masculinity is as a cultural and theoretical phenomenon. I am particularly interested in how masculinity functions in ways that might not be obvious to the naked eye, how various thinkers have thought about this functioning, and how various literary and cultural theories can be employed to think about the traditional invisibility of masculinity. I am also interested in how masculinity is a changing phenomenon, how it is fluid, how it morphs, and how we can think about and study it as something ever changing and in movement. What does it mean to think about masculinity as something that cannot easily be located or pinned down, or ever really defined in any simple or coherent way? We may think of masculinity as hard, solid, stable, or reliable, but that illusion may simply be part of the way in which it functions. The goal of this book, then, is to present key models of masculinity in order to avoid a simplistic or purely descriptive approach to masculinity, even as the models that it presents will and should be questioned and interrogated as to their limits. This book is not a study of versions of masculinity across time and across space. I will not discuss the construct of masculinity in a socio-historical context such as ancient Rome or twenty-first-century Mexico, nor will I analyze literary images of masculinity such as those in Homer or Jane Austen. I will not take a category or morphology of masculinity, such as the businessman or the bachelor, and study its evolving role across time or across cultures. Numerous books on masculinity have now been written from the perspective of a defined place or time. Rather, instead of doing a literary, historical, sociological, or anthropological study of masculinity or of a certain definition of masculinity, this book treats approaches to the study of masculinity. I aim to think about how masculinity has been or can be approached in theoretical terms, while never forgetting about the specific and about relations between the theoretical and the specific. Some of these approaches have been previously discussed by various scholars and theorists, whereas others can be discussed only by considering the gendered implications of given theories. Still others are articulated here for the first time.

A second, more practical reason for *Masculinities in Theory* is to provide readers with ways in which they can study masculinity from an academic point of view. As a book of approaches, *Masculinities in Theory* could be taken as the first step in an academic process of the study of masculinity. Readers interested in thinking about some aspect of the study of masculinity, perhaps in some particular socio-historical context (e.g., the Italian Renaissance, Victorian England, twenty-first-century Cuba) or in some medium (e.g., literature, film, painting, digital media) may take this book as a starting point, as a place to locate models of masculinity that might lend themselves to their own texts or contexts and provide a jumping-off point for further study and analysis. These models can also be rejected as unworkable in a given context, and the reasons for their unworkability can provide greater understanding of that context and of gender itself. The model articulated in chapter 2, for example, is predicated on basic cultural assumptions of homophobia and sexism. So what happens to the model when a culture is less homophobic or has a greater degree of gender equality than most others? What happens in a culture in which the concept of homophobia is not articulated at all? The theoretical basis for the models in this book is Western, and largely French and Anglo-American. So what happens to these models in non-Western contexts? Are they unusable or can they be fully or partially adapted to other contexts? Can we even talk about masculinity in the first place in cultures that lack a word for masculinity or the concept itself?

My inquiry into categories used to make sense of masculinity in the study of gender and sexuality may not employ categories that the general populace uses to understand or to define masculinity, despite the fact that for me these categories are central to the task of thinking through masculinity. Even though most people would agree that sport and work are closely linked to masculinity, I do not have a chapter on how they define masculinity, for instance. Rather, I look at theoretical, hard-to-locate, often invisible, ways in which masculinity functions, and I show how these categories, upon close examination, reveal more aspects at work than might be immediately obvious on the basketball court or in the office. For example, I will discuss in chapter 1 how the concept of discourse relates to masculinity, and readers interested in the discourse of masculinity around sport or work may take the analytic techniques that I outline and apply them to their texts or contexts. Some of this book's categories do, however, overlap with widespread notions of masculinity (e.g., race, the male body), while others can be applied to conceptions of masculinity not discussed here.

Roughly speaking, the book is divided into two parts. In the first section of the book (chapters 1–3), I lay out some key theoretical models that have been or can be used in the study of masculinity. The approaches discussed in chapter 1 are adapted from the work of theorists who do not directly articulate ways in which masculinity can be thought about within their framework. By virtue of their theoretical nature, most of the models in these first three chapters are more abstract than concrete, and part of the task of theorizing masculinity is to consider how these models filter down into the concrete. I will provide some concrete examples in my discussions, but I anticipate that readers will do this on their own, based on their own interests and backgrounds, and that this book will serve as a springboard to discussions about gender. In the rest of the book (chapters 4–10), I examine key categories in the study of masculinity that often rely on those theoretical models.

Thus, the concept of gendered triangulation is discussed in chapter 2, and then in chapter 9 I think about various ways in which the model of triangulation relates to race and racialized masculinities. In chapter 3, I discuss the idea that gender creates sex, and in chapter 4, I bring this idea to bear on the study of the male body.

Presenting a series of important approaches to masculinity does not mean that this book will provide all the answers or all the keys to crack the code of what masculinity is, or of how it can be studied. On the contrary, one of the ultimate goals of *Masculinities in Theory* is to complicate the study of masculinity, to make masculinity seem even more complex than the beginning student of masculinity may ever have imagined. When I teach courses on masculinity, I tell my students on the first day of class that if they do not have more questions about masculinity on the last day of class than they did on the first, then I have not taught them properly. Indeed, having worked and published on masculinity for a number of years, I have found that masculinity has only become more complicated and opaque to me over the years, and that the more I study it the more questions I have and the more slippery it becomes. For these reasons, one way to imagine this book is as a series of possible theoretical questions, instead of definitive responses, that can be posed around the phenomenon of masculinity.

While it may often be perceived as invisible or men may try to make it invisible, masculinity has a determining effect on many or most aspects of culture. A number of the problems of modern society could be thought of as a result of various elements of masculinity: violence, war, sexism, rape, and homophobia all have some connection to masculinity. Masculinity is very often tied to power, whether in government, the household, or the military. One of the recurring features of masculinity – as opposed to femininity – is that men go to great pain to hide it and, by extension, to hide the way that it functions and operates. Hiding can allow masculinity to function without challenge or question. Masculinity is not always about an obvious use of power and muscle to overcome an enemy, and can work by detours in insidious ways. While the president of a country might not announce that he is invading a foreign country to reaffirm his or his country's masculinity, it still factors in to the military equation, but it may not be articulated as such for fear that it be critiqued or challenged. Masculinity also functions by detour when men talk about those against whom they define themselves (e.g., women or gay men) instead of by talking about masculinity itself. Male misogyny and homophobia are, in part, forms of masculinity in disguise. Consequently, to understand some of the ways in which masculinity functions or the techniques employed to maintain masculine hegemony is an important aspect of thinking about oppression, power, and subjection in a larger sense.

Even as questions of power are central to the study of gender and should never be forgotten, the study of masculinity should not assume that all men have power or hegemony at all times. One reason not to make masculinity monolithic in this way is that it can be oppressive to those that wield it. The French sociologist Pierre Bourdieu talks about how men are "dominated by their domination," how masculinity can cause internal problems for men who deploy it for various ends.[1] Thinking about ways in which masculinity tends to function, then, is a way to better understand how men also do physical or psychological harm to themselves. If masculinity is a factor contributing to war, then it easily doubles back on to the men fighting that war, causing them pain in the process. Another important consideration in this book is to bring out positive models of masculinity in which masculinity operates in a non-hegemonic way, moments in which men break or attempt to break their own hold over power and ways in which purely critical views of masculinity can be supplemented by more positive ones. If masculinity's hegemonic operations can be hidden, they can also be subverted, male power can be destabilized, and experiences outside hegemony can be created. To understand the subtleties of masculinity, then, helps us to understand important elements of culture and of individuals, ones that affect everyone in some way.

To talk about this invisibility in academic terms, I might say that masculinity tends to function as "unmarked." Because meaning is made through opposition (e.g., the word "man" and the concept behind it make sense because they are assumed to be not "woman"), theorists often consider "masculinity" as one element of a binary opposition with "femininity." In the opposition of two elements, one element can be considered unmarked – more frequent or less noticed than its marked counterpoint. Heterosexuality is unmarked because we tend not to think about it while homosexuality is marked, and whiteness is unmarked while blackness is marked. If masculinity is

---

[1]   Pierre Bourdieu, *Masculine Domination*, trans. Richard Nice (Stanford: Stanford University Press, 2001), 69.

unmarked because it is taken to be the norm and not thought about unless in opposition to something else, femininity is the marked category because people tend to think about it more often when they see it. Traditionally in Western culture, women are considered to have a gender, while men are more often considered genderless. But as the French theorist Roland Barthes writes, the unmarked term is not simply and purely absence of meaning, but what he calls "a significant absence."[2] Precisely because a term is unmarked, its silence speaks. In other words, the fact that masculinity has tended not to be thought of as gendered is a hole that should draw attention to its very absence. Because masculinity has traditionally not been taken to be a gender to be studied, its invisibility can be studied as one of its elements. So it is not just that masculinity is something that must be studied, but rather attempts to keep masculinity quiet – without a mark, without a gender – is one of its recurring characteristics that can and should be studied. How, precisely, has masculinity attempted to keep itself under cover of darkness and to pass unnoticed? How has masculinity created distractions to keep attention away from itself as gendered? How is masculinity's absence significant? And how does masculinity's silence speak? The covering-up process can be studied and discussed in specific contexts. By marking masculinity and by taking it as an explicit object of analysis, then, we can begin the process of better understanding what masculinity is and how it functions.

In twenty-first-century academic settings, marking masculinity has become an increasingly important goal, a fast-growing approach to gender studies in a number of different domains across the disciplines. There are various ways to go about a book that treats ways of thinking about masculinity: it could be discipline-specific, it could be social-science-based, it could be scientific, or it could be interdisciplinary. This book takes an interdisciplinary, humanities-based approach to the study of masculinity and, as such, aims to make a contribution to the field of gender studies. Because I will not take a scientific or a social science approach, I will not talk about methodology based on experiments, interviews, studies, statistics, or facts and figures. There will be no charts with statistics on stay-at-home dads over the past 20 years. My approach is to focus on masculinity as it is often studied

[2]   Roland Barthes, *Elements of Semiology*, trans. Annette Lavers and Colin Smith (New York: Hill and Wang, 1967), 77.

in the Humanities, as representational or depicted in a way that we can contemplate and study, with language and signs as the prime object of analysis. Reading critically between the lines and behind the signs is central to my book, as I will provide interpretive models that can be employed, revised, and reworked for various questions. I will take into account select but important ways in which masculinity has been thought about in scholarship in the Humanities, and thus provide some element of what might be called disciplinary coverage. At the same time, I include many of my own ideas and thoughts on the topic and thus aim to expand the scope of gender studies.

Why Masculinities in Post-Structuralist Theory?

My humanities-based approach will be inflected with literary and cultural theory, and particularly with theory that comes out of post-structuralist thought. I will think about how theoretical models can be lent to the study of masculinity and what this kind of approach can help us understand about masculinity. In many ways, post-structuralism provides a language that can be of great use in gender studies. This book, however, is meant for readers who may or may not have a firm basis in various approaches that the way of thinking provides. I will discuss various theoretical concepts as needed to explain the aspects of masculinity presented. This book will not cover post-structuralism (which would be impossible given the length and scope of my project), but will employ some of its key tools and techniques in order to think about what masculinity is and how it functions.

One inevitable question that must be answered is: what is it about post-structuralism that makes it appropriate as an intellectual basis for the study of masculinity? One response is that many of its concerns and premises (e.g., discourse, power, instability, representation) have direct application to gender studies. With post-structuralism, one tends to look behind the signs that one sees in order to find meaning that might not seem immediately apparent or might not seem to correspond to the visible sign. Because what one sees is often not what one gets, if we can take theoretical techniques for looking behind the sign, we might be able to look behind the signs, the images, and the discussions of masculinity that we see at first glance. This approach is especially important for masculinity, because of a tendency to present it as a stable and impermeable surface that hides meaning and hides its functioning so that it can work seamlessly. Post-structuralism is also helpful to a discussion of masculinity because it tends to consider that there is no essence or ontology for any given sign. For my purposes, I might say that it assumes that masculinity has no natural, inherent, or given meaning, that it does not have to mean something predetermined, and that whatever meaning it has is in constant movement. Masculinity's resistance to interpretation is alleviated, at least in part, with the aid of post-structuralism's interpretive tools. One of the things that we will see when we begin to look behind what is visible, for instance, is that masculinity is in fact connected with numerous other forms of identity or subjectivity, even if men claim or assume that it is not connected to or dependent on them for its definition. Masculinity is in dialogue; it is dependent on the very others that are defined as different from it (as we will see in chapter 1). Relations between masculinity and its others, or relations among types of masculinities, will thus be one focus in this book. These relations and instabilities are so definitional to masculinity that, while writing this book, I often found myself wondering if there was such a thing as masculinity at all, if it is not a contradiction in terms to write a whole book from this point of view. It often seemed to me that masculinity's slipperiness made it difficult, if not impossible, to discuss. While this intellectual lens underlies much of the book, there is no unified school or method in post-structuralism, so a constant and systematic application of its theories is impossible. I will thus bring out various aspects of post-structuralism as needed, as a kind of theoretical bag of tricks, within gendered categories that are not necessarily endemic to the approach but are logical extensions of it.

With this purpose, my book aims to bring out some of the tensions and contradictions inherent in masculinity, and to show how the study of masculinity might reveal that masculinity does not always make coherent or intuitive sense and is in fact often predicated on incoherencies. The male body, for instance, can be thought of as a contradiction in terms. On the one hand, the male body can stand in for masculinity. The body-builder is a key morphology of masculinity, an ideal of masculinity followed by many young boys who wish to have a bigger, better body. Other aspects of the male body could also be factored in here: chest hair or a large penis, for instance. These aspects of the male body put masculinity on display as masculine, their visual qualities a key aspect of how they function as signs. But on the other hand, masculinity is also predicated on hiding the male body, as ignoring the male body can reaffirm one's masculinity. The man who ignores and overcomes his sickness or illness can be seen as masculine, or certain potentially sexual aspects of the male body may be considered something to avoid (e.g., nipples or the prostate). So how can we think about masculinity's relation to the male body if the relation between masculinity and masculinity's most common corporal home is neither direct nor clear? What do these kinds of contradictions mean about how we go about studying masculinity? I will not try to flatten out these contradictions within masculinity, but rather I will try to bring them out and make them explicit objects of study. My assumption is that tensions and contradictions are one of the most important elements of what masculinity is and another indicator that masculinity is never a stable or monolithic phenomenon. It is not that masculinity requires hiding the male body, nor that it requires displaying it either. Rather, masculinity could be defined through both of these approaches and ultimately be about the movement of the male body between hiding and displaying. While the contradictory character of masculinity might be hidden to make it appear stable and to maintain its traditional hegemony, in fact it may very well not be that way at all. I aim, then, not to smooth over these contradictions, but rather to place them at the center of masculinity which is in part defined by tension and contestation.

Although post-structuralism often counters the idea of nature or the natural as given and immutable categories, it is not the case that there is no biological relation to masculinity, that testosterone or genetics or the male body do not influence masculinity. But a biological approach to masculinity is best left to other books to discuss. In my approach, culture and representation are considered so pervasive that they cannot be separated from nature and the natural and that they necessarily have an influence on what nature is assumed to be. The very dividing line between nature and nurture is so unclear and so unstable that it makes sense, for my purposes, to think solely about the cultural and how the cultural constructs the natural. I leave it to others to consider how nature constructs culture. When we think about the supposed natural aspects of masculinity, we usually employ language, but because language already contains so much cultural baggage, it is impossible to think about masculinity without wondering what kind of cultural assumptions are already at play just by talking about the seemingly natural. Someone might say that having a penis is a natural element of masculinity, but definitions of what the penis is – including the ways in which it is described and the importance attributed to it – are so bound up with cultural assumptions about masculinity that any purely natural approach to the penis as outside culture is impossible. So even seemingly objective medical studies of male impotence or premature ejaculation are necessarily already bound up in a whole set of cultural and linguistic assumptions about the penis.

My choice of terminology is largely dictated by the intellectual approach taken here. Whereas for me the terms "masculinity" and "male subjectivity" imply instability and a whole host of tensions and complications that this book will discuss, terms such as "manhood," "male identity," "masculine identity," and "male gender role" tend to connote a more stable approach to gender, and perhaps even a biologically based one (it is no accident, for instance, that "manhood" can also refer to the male member). Throughout my book, I will employ the terms "masculinity," "masculine subjectivity," and "male subjectivity" interchangeably, with the sole difference that the last two terms suggest masculinity within the context of the male body while "masculinity" allows for the possibility of a non-male subjectivity (especially with respect to female or transsexual masculinities). Because "subjectivity" is often taken as a less stable equivalent of "identity" and suggests complications and a closer relation to cultural and psychological influences, I avoid the term "identity" in this book (unless I mean to evoke stability) and use other terms (such as "male subject") to suggest these kinds of instabilities and influences.

Another way to articulate why post-structuralism is an appropriate analytical tool for this book is by opposing it to its predecessor, structuralism. A classic example of structural masculinity is the coming-of-age ritual. In this approach to gender, one is born a boy and then becomes a man through various symbolic and non-symbolic processes. The coming-of-age novel (the *Bildungsroman*) in Western culture, for instance, would be read as a series of transitions to masculinity, which could be discussed as a series of steps that a boy must go through in order to achieve masculinity. One could delineate, then, what the necessary steps are in the process and how masculinity is unlike its opposite, boyhood (or femininity, or whatever else it is defined against). A post-structuralist approach to this question, however, would not allow for a linear move from one type of identity (a boy) to another (a man), nor would it allow for strict delineation of identities. Rather, the notion of a man would already be considered implicit in the boy: he would, in part, be a man even before he goes through this rite. The boy would also still be implicit in the man: he cannot actually *become* and then *be* a man since subjectivity is too unstable simply to *be* a man. The man would have to continue repeatedly to become a man at many points of his daily life. He might slip in and out of masculinity, never able simply to remain a man without constant help and effort. In short, in a post-structuralist approach one cannot simply *be* a man, and masculinity cannot simply *be* defined in a certain way since structures do not underlie a male identity and since masculinity is inherently unstable.

My approach can also be juxtaposed with approaches based on thinking about stable categories of masculinity. For instance, in his well-known and ground-breaking book *Masculinities*, R. W. Connell presents four "patterns of masculinity in the current Western gender order": hegemony, subordination, complicity, and marginalization.[3] The first category is "the configuration of gender practice which embodies the currently accepted answer to the problem of the legitimacy of patriarchy, which guarantees (or is taken to guarantee) the dominant position of men and the subordination of women" (p. 77). There is no doubt that these kinds of relations circulate in culture, that some people conceive of dominant models of masculinity in a given cultural and temporal context (e.g., the bodybuilder or the father-provider), that other models are marginal to the hegemonic (e.g., Asian-American or gay male masculinity), and that one could define what those models are in a given context (e.g., what are the qualities of a knight in twelfth-century France?). My approach here, however, tends to focus not on articulating what these relations are or how masculine hegemony functions (though these qualities are crucial to my discussion), but on the fluidity or the instability of these relations, on the cracks and fissures in these relations, or on the successful and unsuccessful attempts by hegemony to hide itself as dominant. In this way, hegemonic masculinity is thought of as a model not only inextricable from subordination, but also very much dependent on it for its own definition. I focus, too, on ways in which a man oscillates between various relations of masculinity, how he is never really simply in any one position in any relation, but often somewhere in between. Thus, a successful businessman who might look like Western hegemony embodied may in fact be defined by his location

[3]   R. W. Connell, *Masculinities* (Berkeley: University of California Press, 1995), 77–81.

between hegemony and subordination if he is examined very closely. I am interested in how hegemonic masculinity employs subordination for various ends, how it is indistinguishable from it from time to time. How, for instance, does one explain that the most hegemonic of male subjects can take on certain aspects of subordinate masculinities, as when they joke about being gay, dress as women, or appropriate African-American masculine traits? So while I will employ relations of masculinity such as Connell's and am greatly indebted to them, they will not be expressed in stable terms, even as many of the concepts behind these kinds of stable categories will be implicit in my discussion. In my view, a post-structuralist approach better reflects the actual experiences of masculinity and reveals gender in its full complexity. In this sense, *Masculinities in Theory* is an extension of previous work in masculinity or in "Men's Studies," a field of inquiry largely social science in origin that often takes male hegemony and identities as its objects of study with the practical aim of reversing sexism and homophobia and of transforming men. This book takes a different approach by focusing on the instabilities of those categories, providing a concise and comprehensive discussion of such an approach.

One advantage to this way of examining masculinity is that it helps to destabilize stereotypes of masculinity. It is often said that stereotypes do not come from nowhere, that they cannot simply be disbanded with a wave of a magic wand. The jock, the macho man, the knight in shining armor, the man who runs from commitment, the drifter, the action-movie hero, the Marlboro man, the cowboy, and the butch lesbian are all masculine stereotypes that circulate widely in US culture. While it may be true that certain elements of these stereotypes can hold (cowboys may tend to be independent), the stability of the characteristics that these stereotypes imply (the cowboy is always independent; the jock cannot be intellectual or intelligent, and never has anxiety dreams about sports) cannot always hold. Stereotypes of masculinity do not point to a reality: few cowboys always act or dress the way the stereotype suggests. A stereotype of masculinity is an attempt to stabilize a subjectivity that can never ultimately be stabilized, to create a brand of masculinity as not in movement, and as such stands as proof of the unstable nature of masculinity. To think about masculinity as in movement, as fluid, and as unstable, then, necessarily keeps us from thinking in these culturally sanctioned molds that do not correspond to the complexity of masculinity.

Bibliography

On marked and unmarked categories, see Roland Barthes, *Elements of Semiology*, trans. Annette Lavers and Colin Smith (New York: Hill and Wang, 1967), 76–7; Sally Robinson, *Marked Men: White Masculinity in Crisis* (New York: Columbia University Press, 2000); Naomi Schor, "Dreaming Dissymmetry: Barthes, Foucault, and Sexual Difference," in *Men in Feminism*, ed. Alice Jardine and Paul Smith (New York: Methuen, 1987), 98–110.

On the *Bildungsroman* and gender, see Marc Redfield, *Phantom Formations: Aesthetic Ideology and the Bildungsroman* (Ithaca, NY: Cornell University Press, 1996).

For a basic introduction to post-structuralism, see Jonathan Culler, *Literary Theory: A Very Short Introduction* (Oxford: Oxford University Press, 1997); Terry Eagleton, *Literary Theory: An Introduction* (Minneapolis: University of Minnesota Press, 1983); R. Selden, ed., *The Cambridge History of Literary Criticism*, vol. 8: *From Formalism to Poststructuralism* (New York: Cambridge University Press, 1995); Madan Sarup, *An Introductory Guide to Post-Structuralism and Postmodernism* (Athens: University of Georgia Press, 1993).

1

Theorizing Masculinity

The Origins of Masculinity

In order to begin to think about theoretical approaches to masculinity, I might begin with one of the most central questions about masculinity: who creates it and where does it come from? If we assume that masculinity is not simply produced naturally or biologically, how does it come about? No identifiable person or group of people creates masculinity and then forces people to follow it. Masculinity is far too widespread, diffuse, and complicated for any single person or group to create it. Because it infuses everything, one cannot ultimately determine its origin. To say that it is created by the family, by media, by sports, or by another means only oversimplifies the complexity of the issue. A boy is influenced by so many brands of masculinity that it is very difficult to isolate a single source. In the end, we can only try to determine as best we can what it is and how it functions.

Clearly, men tend to have more of a vested interest in the propagation of many types of masculinity than women do, since they more often benefit from its advantages (or at least think they benefit from them). The male body is the most common purveyor of masculinity, but that does not mean that masculinity is entirely contained within the male body nor that non-men cannot profit from its advantages. Men may aid its propagation more than women, but other groups often considered outside the field of hegemonic masculinity can and do participate in its spread as well, including women, gay men, and lesbians. In fact, the very desire to have masculinity, when one perceives oneself as a member of a group not possessing it, can be a motivating factor in attempts to obtain it and in the value attached to it. One might imagine a female business executive who feels that she needs more masculinity because she lacks it or perceives herself as lacking it, whether because she is a woman in a male-dominated world or because culture does not automatically accord her the possibility of having masculinity. Female-to-male transsexuals might also have a vested interest in the masculinity that they desire in order to obtain a greater sense of wholeness. A further reason why men cannot simply be considered the inventors of masculinity is that many are critical of masculinity, while on the other hand some gay men and heterosexual women like it and may in fact find it erotic and attractive in themselves or in others. In short, although men may have more to gain from masculinity than other groups, the cause or the origin of masculinity cannot be directly linked to the male body in any simple or stable way.

A basic tenet of this chapter is that there is no single or simple origin to masculinity, and that it cannot be isolated as beginning in a single place or at a single point. Rather, it is constantly created and challenged in numerous ways. This chapter will outline many of those ways, with a focus on questions related to ideology, discourse, and signs. A second tenet of this chapter – and a corollary of the first – is that not only is there no single creator of masculinity, but there is no originary form of masculinity either. There is no single model that everyone turns to in order to define masculinity and to imitate it when they want to be or to act masculine. There are only innumerable copies of masculinities floating around in culture, copies that can never be brought back to an originary masculinity that invented them. Even if one takes what seems to be an origin of some key definition of masculinity, upon examination it cannot be considered the sole origin of that brand of masculinity since other copies of that origin end up taking over the definition. The construct of the bodybuilder is a case in point. Many consider Arnold Schwarzenegger the origin of the modern image of the muscular bodybuilder and, in a larger sense, of a certain influential idea of what the ideal male body should look like. Teenage boys or other bodybuilders interested in weightlifting might pin photos of him up on their walls, consider him legendary, and imitate other aspects of his brand of masculinity (perhaps from his films). The bodybuilders who are influenced by his example might imitate him and consider him a model, but they themselves then become new copies of Schwarzeneggerian masculinity that are necessarily different from the originary form, each different in its own hybrid way. One man might become a Latino version of Schwarzenegger, another a gay male version, another a female version, etc. Those men (or women) in turn influence the masculinity of others, whether because they too become famous or because they influence other men or boys that they encounter in their day-to-day interactions. That brand of masculinity also leaves the realm of the flesh and becomes representational, in film, TV, posters, magazines, etc. As a result, the original form of masculinity, based on Schwarzenegger himself, is widely disseminated throughout culture, and turned into a series of new originals that in turn influence other people and other texts. The documentary about Schwarzenegger's career *Pumping Iron* (1977), for instance, influences bodybuilding and then the documentary *Pumping Iron II: The Women* (1985), while influenced by the figure of Schwarzenegger, portrays a form of masculinity in a new form, which in turn has an influence on other bodybuilders. The Schwarzeneggerian form of masculinity is not absent, however, from these new versions of masculinity (quite the contrary in fact), but the new forms do not exist in the same originary forms in which they had existed before. One way to express this kind of approach to gender, then, is to say that copies of masculinity come to replace what might be considered the original. A given definition of masculinity, I might say, functions in complicated ways as it spreads throughout culture, influencing other definitions even as it is constantly transformed during its spread. This approach does not imply that gendered points of origin or various definitions of masculinity cannot be isolated, or that their influence cannot be isolated. One could still study the influence of *Pumping Iron* on the representation of the muscular male body. But those origins must be thought of as plural, as ultimately unlocalizable in a single relationship of influence.

Even the seemingly original models of masculinity themselves are not pure forms, but are already hybrid forms based on a mixture of other previous forms. Schwarzenegger's masculinity, for instance, relies on precedents, images of masculinity such as early twentieth-century photos of the male body or the idealized artistic male body of Renaissance and ancient art. Even seemingly stable masculinity, such as Schwarzenegger's, refers to other forms of masculinity, in an endless chain of linked but different masculinities. The necessary hybridity of masculinity might be considered more acute in a media-dominated era like the present in which masculinities can very easily circulate via TV, film, and the Internet.

Masculinity as Ideology

One way to understand the concept of masculinity as not created by any one person or by any single group is to consider masculinity as an ideology, a series of beliefs that a group of people buy into and that influences how they go about their lives. The concept of ideology is more traditionally associated with class and with politics (we talk about a "bourgeois ideology" or a "communist ideology"), but it is possible to think about masculinity as an ideology too. One reason to think in these terms is that ideology as a concept is often aligned with those in power: we talk about a "dominant ideology" as the political ideology that prevails in a given context. To consider masculinity as an ideology makes sense since it often is, or is often perceived of as, a subjectivity linked to power. A further parallel between masculinity and ideology is that, in the same way as no single class or single group can be considered to create ideology (though some groups are more major forces in its articulation and its propagation), no single group can be seen as responsible for constructing masculinity. Various institutions clearly have a self-interest in masculinity: the government needs soldiers to defend itself, so it promotes a military version of masculinity; the business world needs a capitalistic masculinity to make money, so it makes its version of gender appear ideal. But it is not possible to isolate any given institution as the origin of masculinity. Military masculinity is also produced, for instance, by cinema and by corporations (such as by marketing military toys to young boys). Several institutions may function together to build masculinity: sport and the military might have a mutual interest in a certain brand of muscular or fit masculinity, but neither creates masculinity from scratch. Another issue with seeing institutions as creating masculinity is that masculinity is not simply created by institutions, for masculinity itself also contributes to creating institutions. The military might try to create a military form of masculinity, but masculinity has already inflected the creation of the institution of the military in the first place, as well as the desire to propagate that genre of masculinity. So masculinity can be thought of both as created by institutions and as creating them, and the process of the construction of masculinity as a constant back-and-forth movement between masculinity and institutions.

One offshoot of thinking about masculinity as an ideology is the idea that one may buy into it without thinking about it, that it appears so natural within a given cultural and historical context that it is not questioned. In the United States, a large percentage of the population takes capitalism for granted or considers it a normal part of everyday life. Similarly, a large percentage of people take masculinity for granted as part of everyday life (if they think about it at all). Various groups tend to have different relations to the invisibility of masculinity. Men might be more prone not to see it as ideology, and women less so since they are often closed out of it, in the same way that a communist might see capitalism as far from natural because he or she functions in another economic system. Masculinity might be seen as ideological by men at times, of course, in the same way that someone living under capitalism might at times see capitalism from a distance and as one possible economic system among many. In the same way as one becomes conscious of the capitalist system when it does not function well for them, one may be more likely to view masculinity from a distance when there is a snag, a man who is unable to maintain his masculinity or a woman who is hurt by it.

Although a single origin to an ideology cannot be located, ideologies are often assumed to be created and propagated through various social forms, especially through images, myths, discourses, and practices. By virtue of their constant and unavoidable repetition throughout culture, these tools of ideology are eventually made to seem natural and thus to keep themselves from being questioned or interrogated, and they each have their own specific function in the large-scale process of constructing masculinity as ideology. We might be most familiar with the images of masculinity that pervade us: film, TV, and billboards would be some common examples of how we are given the message that a certain kind of masculinity is valid or more valid than another. Images related to advertising are particularly important in this context since they are one social form of masculinity in which capitalism and masculinity can function in tandem, as two ideologies can work together and buttress each other's propagation. A Calvin Klein underwear advertisement, for instance, may put forward a certain image of masculinity with great force because it is putting its products forward with great zeal, and some viewers' desire to possess or to be around the form of masculinity represented is inseparable (or is made to seem inseparable) from their desire to have the product pushed. These images might not be direct representations of actual or frequent masculinity, but symbolic images that require interpretation in order to be ideologically effective. Such symbols might function directly with readily available meanings that a culture has effectively already agreed on, as in the case of phallic symbols. On the other hand, the lack of culturally agreed-on meaning in these images can paradoxically make them more available to the ideology of masculinity since symbols or signs might be so subtle that one is less aware of their functioning than widely accepted signs like the penis.

Similar to images, myths also function as a way to make certain forms of masculinity seem eternal and unchanging, not open to change or variation, and not ideological in nature. Mythopoetic or Jungian approaches to masculinity that assume an inner core or essence of masculinity with which modern society has lost touch would fit into this category. Those who see masculinity as ideological are often skeptical and critical of such approaches, which tend to assume that there is a core of masculinity that all men can or should share and that myths put that core into an expression that explains their universality. In this approach, myths have the effect of retroactively reading a given idea of masculinity back onto all masculinity in order to make it appear universal when in fact it is fabricated. This idea is closely related to the idea that there are no underlying structures of masculinity: without such structures, myths themselves are not possible. Such myths might refer to actual myths or to narratives taken as universal that play a role similar to myths, such as Adam's creation in Genesis or Odysseus' epic journey in *The Odyssey*, whose elements are considered to represent a universal masculinity that links all men. Religious stories that explain elements of human existence might be purer examples of a myth because of their widespread cultural status, often taken as truth, meaning they can explain mythologically how aspects of masculinity come to be. The common understanding of Adam's creation, for example, makes the original man a heterosexual victim of a woman's seduction, and some believe that these aspects of Adam's creation apply to all men. Certain scientific ideas on masculinity can also become mythological in this sense when they are taken to be essential truth about men, including genetic explanations for violence or warfare, biological explanations for male sexuality, or studies about how boys are biologically more or less something than girls.

Images can be turned into myths when they become so widespread that culture takes them for granted as a narrative of masculinity. When such images are so widespread, they are taken as universal and, on a cultural level, come to appear as mythological. The cowboy's popularity as American cultural icon means that he represents an ideal of masculinity that appeals to so many boys that it effectively becomes an American myth. Male superheroes (Superman perhaps most famously) could be considered mythological figures in this sense: it is not that the creators of the Superman story necessarily set out to create a universal image of masculinity, but elements of that image appeal to so many boys (and grown men) that American culture has come to view Superman as universal and foundational to US masculinity. Cultural images not directly about men can also be related to masculinity. The hamburger has become an American myth, an essential aspect of American identity, but part of its mythological status derives from beef's link to masculinity (we talk about "beefy" men for instance). So the cultural myth of the hamburger is buttressed by masculinity and affirms, in turn, the recurring connection between meat and masculinity.

More influential than myths, discourse constructs the ideology of masculinity as well: groups of texts around a given topic with a similar function contain certain presuppositions about masculinity that are propagated among children and adults. Key examples of cultural discourses (e.g., medical, legal, psychoanalytic, religious, pedagogical, political) include official and unofficial types in written and oral forms. Pedagogical discourse, for instance, might include textbooks, teacher-training materials and courses, official publications by the government or school districts that have implicit or explicit representations of masculinity, but it also includes unofficial forms of discourse, particularly oral forms such as conversations among teachers in the teachers' lounge, actual verbal interactions between teachers and students in the classroom, or even conversations about teaching between students themselves.

Other less common, less categorical, or less official forms of discourse also create and propagate ideologies of masculinity: there might be a discourse around men's locker rooms, for instance. While there may not be much of an official collection of written texts to serve as a foundation to study the discourse on locker rooms (though there may in fact be some), there is an oral discourse on this topic that constructs masculinity, whether it is the actual discourse that men have in the locker rooms themselves, discussions or jokes among women about men's locker rooms, or gay male pornography that takes place in locker rooms. One could undertake, for example, a study of how a discourse around locker rooms constructs or destabilizes a certain idea of masculinity or the male body. Discourse serves as a particularly important organizing format for masculinity since language is central to masculinity (more on this later), and, because it is linguistically defined, it lends itself well to study and analysis.

A fourth way in which masculinity is propagated as ideology, one less language-based than discourse and the two other categories discussed above (images and myths), is through practices. When men perform various actions on a regular basis, they may be held within an ideology of masculinity. These actions might include sport, for instance, as men play football (and do not do gymnastics); they might include games, as boys play with toy guns (and not dolls); or they might include clothing, as men dress in jackets and ties (and not in dresses). With these practices, an ideological materiality becomes inscribed in daily life and transcends language and signs. The boy may be influenced by images or discourses around guns, and then change what he does on a daily basis (buy a toy gun, play with it, go hunting with his dad, vote for a pro-NRA political candidate). As these aspects of ideology influence practices, these practices in turn also serve to construct masculinity: the more I practice football, the more I believe that sport and masculinity are related, and the more I convey that belief to others (whether directly or indirectly). And the more American boys play football, the more American masculinity seems linked to football. Abstract ideology can never really be disassociated from the physicality of practice, and the dividing line between what I believe and what I do is never really clear or stable. To return to the question of origin, I might say that masculinity's origin cannot be isolated entirely within the realm of the abstract or of the physical either. The physical and the abstract constantly interact with each other in ways that are complicated and not easily determined.

Practices cannot be totally separated from images, myths, or discourse either. In fact, despite the distinctness of these four categories of ideology, they can all overlap with one another. Images of a militarized masculinity might pervade American film, and those images might encourage (or be reinforced by) the boyhood practice of playing with guns. The reverse can certainly be true as well: practice can influence image. The cultural practice of playing with or using guns might mean that Hollywood is more likely to make films with guns to sell films. Consequently, representations of masculinity (on TV, for instance) should be seen as having a double nature: on the one hand, they reveal a form of masculinity that already exists in culture, but on the other hand, they construct (or help construct) the masculinity that they depict in culture. Conversely, a representation might depict a critique of masculinity already in culture, or it might invent a new critique. In both cases, however, the representation of masculinity exists in a back-and-forth relation with culture.

The prevalence of these social forms suggests that masculinity is at least largely imposed via these forms. Practices of masculinity, for example, leave the boy with little choice of how to act. But oddly, masculinity is often perceived to be free, unlike femininity and its imagined constraints. One paradox of masculinity as ideological is that it often gives the illusion of freedom, the illusion that masculinity itself can be defined as freedom, whereas in fact it is this very imagined freedom that insures subjugation and hides its own arbitrary functioning. The only freedom, in actuality, is the freedom to accept or to reject forms of masculinity. Thinking along these lines, one might reconsider widespread constructs of masculinity that are dependent on an image of freedom, such as the cowboy, the Marlboro man, or the swinging bachelor. Because I imagine my masculinity as a single man who is not married and does not want or need a wife or children and can sleep with a number of different women for one night only, I may think that my gender subjectivity embodies freedom, but the very buying into these images or ideologies of masculinity suggests that these kinds of gender formations are not outside ideology. Rather, they are very much implicated in their own subjugation. The idea of freedom and solitude and of the man who needs no one is part and parcel of the illusion of freedom, an illusion that helps insure its own subjugation to a larger and more powerful ideology of masculinity in the first place. In this sense, masculinity resembles capitalism, which also seems to be predicated on the idea of freedom – whether to earn as much money as one wants, to change class status through hard work, to buy what one wants, or to select the product desired from among a large selection of products at the store. But in fact, we are subjugated by the very desire to earn money and to buy products while convinced that we are free.

At the same time as I am subjugated by masculinity, however, understanding masculinity as ideological does not mean that I am outside consciousness of my gender or outside consciousness that I am subjugated by it. Ideology is not seamlessly accepted nor is it never experienced

as imposed. It does not necessarily function as something invisible that I buy into on a daily basis without reflection. Men can and do realize that something that they are doing without thinking is a result of the ideological imposition of masculinity. At one moment, I might perform various gendered practices without thinking about them, because I blindly buy into that ideology, but at other times, I might become very aware that I am being invited or even coerced into a given ideology of masculinity. Consequently, masculinity can be experienced in two ways. On the one hand, masculinity can be viewed as an objective phenomenon: my own masculinity makes me part of a group of men who possess masculinity, such that I am simply following masculinity and the traits that normally accompany it. When I watch a football game, for instance, I am one spectator amongst many, and it is the experience of watching that game that creates my masculinity. I thus understand my own participation in a certain aspect of masculinity as one element of a larger organizing matrix, mediated in this example by a collectively imagined experience of watching a sports match. On the other hand, however, I experience my masculinity as an individual phenomenon. As a masculine man, I do not sit around all day long and imagine myself as part of a group defined by masculinity. Instead, I operate through a series of individual acts that I individually experience as part of masculinity but that do in fact relate (if I were to reflect on the topic) to the larger ideology of masculinity. So while watching a football game, I might at moments be aware of my participation in a larger community of masculinity, but at other moments (and probably more of them), I would see my own actions as perhaps masculine, but as individually defined. My masculinity would be coming from me, or more precisely, my masculinity would be experienced as coming from me as an individual. If I sit in front of the television and scream when one team scores a goal, I might be expressing a culturally defined aspect of masculinity and if someone asked me about it, I might be able to make that link between me and my culture, but, in the moment, I am unaware of that link and feel that my masculinity is coming from me. So it is not that my experience of masculinity is purely ideological, nor that it is purely individual either: it is defined by a continual move or oscillation between the idea of masculinity as part of me and as part of an ideology.

The relation between the subjective and the objective does not have to be a harmonious one. Rather, that relation might be defined as a tension between the subjective and the objective. I might go to the movies on Friday night, watch a James Bond film, and imagine that male figure as incarnating masculinity (he is stealthy, sexy, free, and desired by women), but if I try to apply some of the principles of masculinity from that fantasy figure to my own life, I might find that I am simply unable to put them into practice. The whole idea of Bond's masculinity is predicated on his seductiveness to women, but if I do not possess the qualities necessary for seduction and am unable to put Bond's masculinity into practice in my daily life, I might experience masculinity as a tension between this image of masculinity and my actual life in which I cannot quite reproduce the image or in which I can only recreate it in minor ways. Or I might delude myself into thinking that I am a flesh-and-blood copy of Bond's masculinity, fantasizing that I can or have become like him. But that delusion or fantasy is indicative of an impossibility of ever reaching the image that I see at the movies. It is, therefore, not exactly the case that masculinity in this situation is defined by James Bond, or that it is defined only by my desire to put Bond's masculine qualities into practice in my daily life. Instead, it is the relation between that desire for a certain masculine ideology in my life and the impossibility or the difficulty of that desire that defines my male subjectivity. The relation between masculine ideologies and the actual experience of those ideologies is a key way to consider and study masculinity.

The tension between the objective and subjective can be articulated as a crisis of masculinity, a way of thinking in broad, cultural terms about a split between men's subjective experience and larger ideologies that pervade culture. Masculinity might be in crisis when many men in a given context feel tension with larger ideologies that dominate or begin to dominate that context. The late nineteenth century in the United States, for example, is often seen as a historical moment in which shifting definitions of masculinity, from agriculturally based to industrially defined, led to widespread anxieties as the subjective did not correspond to the ideology of masculinity that was spreading via industrialization. Numerous other periods have been seen as crises of masculinity. A growing feminist discourse and a growing gay discourse can provoke a masculinity crisis as they transform cultural ideologies of masculinity into something that does not yet conform to individual experiences. Some say that feminism in the 1970s and 1980s precipitated a crisis in masculinity, and some believe that the visibility of male homosexuality in the last decade or so has put heterosexual masculinity into crisis because ideologies of masculinity cannot be easily defined in opposition to women or gay men. The idea of crisis implies that there are periods of little or no crisis when ideologies of masculinity and the male individual more or less correspond without tension. But some would say that the relation between masculine ideology and the subjective is always based in crisis, that the split between the objective and the subjective can only cause anxiety for men.

In addition to the mutation of ideologies, the complexity of ideology can end up confusing men and constantly making them wonder if they correspond to masculine ideology. For ideologies of masculinity are not only complicated when they are placed in relation with an actual man. Rather, ideologies of masculinity are already complicated on their own terms because of their own internal contradictions. Ideologies may, however, present themselves as clear, simple, and straightforward, and they may present seemingly widespread agreement on what they are. Institutions that propagate masculinity as ideology might buttress and reinforce each other, putting forth similar ideas of gender. The educational system's focus on the image of sport and masculinity might dovetail well with popular media's emphasis on televising sport. On the other hand, two institutions might put forward contrasting definitions of masculinity. A teenager might go to the movies on Friday night and see one image of masculinity, such as a war film, and then go to church on Sunday and see another very different image. That teenage boy might experience masculinity as a contradiction or as some kind of relation between those kinds of masculinities, or he might try to contextualize them by acting one way on the (imagined) battlefield and another way in church. Or he may try to reconcile them, as for instance by going to war both for religion and for a reaffirmation of his masculinity.

Another way to think about ideological contradictions is to view a given institution itself as containing contrasting masculinities within. No single ideology of masculinity is being transmitted, rather a series of ideologies are at play, some in harmony and some in tension with each other. A priest, for instance, does not give a lecture on what masculinity means to the boys of his parish, nor does a teacher to his or her students. So, without a cohesive masculine code articulated anywhere, a schoolboy might experience one construct of masculinity in his gym class, another from his civics teacher, and yet another from the principal. A boy at church might perceive one construct in his minister, another in the Old Testament, another in the figure of Christ, and yet others in the actual men of his congregation. While one might locate certain definitions of masculinity as more predominant in a certain institution or institutional context, those definitions are inevitably challenged within that context which is necessarily composed of a collection of masculinities that are not in harmony with each other. Another way to express this idea is to say that, within the context of one institution or ideology, there is no originary masculinity that dominates seamlessly.

Masculinity, Language, and Discourse

Let us return to the question that I posed at the beginning of this chapter: where does masculinity come from? I have been discussing ways in which masculinity can be thought of as coming from many different places, as coming from everywhere and nowhere at the same time. One response to this question about origin is that it is created linguistically, that language can never be separated from what we think masculinity is. Language is an important aspect of understanding gender because language defines the reality that we experience and because we cannot experience reality without using language. We understand masculinity through the ways in which it is talked about, and, as a result, the ways in which language functions are important to the study of masculinity because they influence how we perceive masculinity. What we imagine when we use the word "masculinity" is strongly influenced by the way we talk about it, including the actual content of what we say, what we do not say about it, and the choice of words in what we say. Because our understanding is entirely or largely mediated by language, masculinity itself is linguistically driven, meaning that to study masculinity we have to examine how it is articulated. The double sense of the term "manhood" (as male identity and as penis) suggests a close relation between the two senses that is already an assumption about masculinity. Cultural norms around language, and resistance to those norms, also dictate what we think masculinity is. It may be culturally normal in the United States to talk about how a car reaffirms a man's masculinity (or deflates it), but in another culture, in which few men own cars, this way of talking about it may not exist. We may be likely to talk about masculinity in relation to the penis or muscularity in our culture, but not talk about it in relation to the prostate. Not talking about masculinity – or the absence of a discourse of masculinity – also relates to the cultural construct of masculinity. It might mean, for example, that masculinity or gender itself is not an important category in that culture, or that men are considered so dominant that there is no need to discuss it.

This link between masculinity and language can exist on the word level as key words can already contain cultural assumptions about what masculinity is, has been, or should be. Etymology can be key: "virtue," for instance, comes from the Latin word *vir*, meaning male (and not female), suggesting in Renaissance Europe that only the man could have the quality. An impotent man, etymologically speaking, is one without power (*impotens* in Latin means "not powerful"), implicitly suggesting that the man who cannot get an erection lacks power, thus that a key characteristic of masculinity cannot be held by the impotent man. Though these linguistic connections might be under the surface, they subtend gender and help construct what we think about masculinity. There is, however, nothing natural about the relation between a word and its actual or perceived root or etymology. Rather, the relation reflects a cultural or arbitrary connection made and then presented as natural or inevitable because it is proven by etymology. So the etymology of "virtue" has been provided as evidence that men were inherently more virtuous, and women less virtuous. Appeals to the etymology of a word, then, can be disguised forms of gender stasis and resist the possibility that ideas about masculinity change over time, and in fact those linguistic connections are themselves arbitrary and invented by culture at a certain linguistic moment.

The approach to gender, in which language constitutes reality, may be objected to by those who think that there are elements of gender that fall outside language. If nearly all men have facial hair or the potential for facial hair, then aren't these non-linguistic elements of masculinity? Doesn't the experience of facial hair create a certain experience that is universal for men in general? The objection to this objection would be that it is impossible to understand facial hair without recourse to language. Facial hair does not have to have any necessary relation to masculinity, but it is through language that we make that connection. Discussions about young boys becoming men because they begin to shave or discussions about the machismo of thick stubble, whatever their source, create this link between facial hair and masculinity, not the actual facial hair. Facial hair on its own, in a certain sense, does not exist if it is not talked about, and only by studying how facial hair is discussed and represented can its relation to masculinity be understood.

A crucial element of the idea of language as central to definitions of masculinity is one touched on above in my discussion of ideology, namely discourse. While institutions have an important hand in creating and complicating masculinity, discourse does not simply function as a tool created by institutions. It is such an important phenomenon that it comes to take on a life of its own, operating both within and outside the framework of institutions and having effects the official institutions may not have intended. Military discourse might be largely a creation of the institution of the military, but it also operates outside the military context per se in ways the military may or may not sanction (through TV, movies, video games, literature, or pornography). For this reason, I will consider discourse in more detail, both as a tool of institutions and on its own terms outside the control of institutions. We can talk about an institution's discourse of masculinity, or about a discourse of an element of masculinity that cuts across a number of institutional discourses such as a discourse of paternity, which might include medicine, psychoanalysis, politics, and religion.

One of the purposes of discourse is to normalize human beings and to make them conform to the power that institutions want to exert over people. Masculinity plays an important role in this exertion of power: because there are certain advantages and privileges accorded to it, masculinity functions as an effective carrot to normalize those within discourse. If you allow power to make you into what it wants, you will receive the benefits of masculinity in exchange. The military might inherently promise certain rewards for following a normalized masculinity (honor, glory, a better body, women who like men in uniforms, a pension, status, etc.), but one element of that masculinity is that its subjects conform to institutional power. Pedagogical discourse can perform a similar double function, particularly in contexts in which girls are not formally educated. If I allow the educational system to form me and exert its power over me, I will reap the rewards of education (a better job, cultural clout, a network of educated men, etc.).

A key aspect of power's normalizing effect is the constructing of an abnormal other. For in order to create a norm, discourse must create or invent an anti-norm, which implies that the norm is the norm by opposition. The best-known example is the invention of "the homosexual" as a sexual morphology, famously discussed by Michel Foucault in *The History of Sexuality*, volume 1.[1] Although "homosexuality" had not previously been articulated as a category, the "species" of homosexuality becomes a problem and a pathology in nineteenth-century medicine, psychoanalysis, and other types of discourses (p. 43). This type of identity is invented as a new problem, but it is invented as a problem in part to construct a group that is a non-problem, whether the articulation of that group is direct or implied. Thus, the invention of male homosexuality as a problem also creates an assumed or invisible male heterosexuality as the non-problem, even if not articulated as such. Because masculinity can often function as an invisible norm, it might be harder to locate normalized masculinity in a given discourse than to locate same-sex male sexuality or other "problem" masculinities, such as criminal, violent, or sexualized African-American masculinity, and effeminate or "castrated" Jewish or Asian masculinity. Still, discursive constructs of non-hegemonic masculinities should be constantly interrogated as to their unstated assumptions about other, possibly hegemonic, masculinities.

Even though masculinity tends to hold this role as the discursive norm in the construction of non-normal subjectivities, normalized masculinity can nonetheless function as its own other through the creation of a certain kind of problematic masculinity. Discussions around Viagra in medical discourse could be taken as an example of how a brand of masculinity not widely defined as problematic has to be made into a problem. The man with "erectile dysfunction" is discursively created as a way to make the erection an invisible norm (through the assumption of a "functional erection"). Viagra's current popularity in the US, both in daily life and in discourse, can be viewed as an attempt to normalize masculinity and to create non-erect masculinity as problem.

It is important to stress again, however, that discourses are not coherent in themselves, that a discourse cannot simply create a type of masculinity and its others as stable identities. Rather, like the institutions to which they have a close relation, discourses are contradictory, both within themselves or between different discourses. We can talk about the discourse of masculinity, for instance, but that does not mean

---

[1]   See Michel Foucault, *The History of Sexuality*, vol. 1, *An Introduction*, trans. Robert Hurley (New York: Vintage, 1978), 42–3.

that the entire discourse implies the same brand of masculinity. On the one hand, there is a reactionary discourse of masculinity with the aims of defragmenting masculinity and of locating an essential masculinity deep within the male body, often articulated as a series of Jungian archetypes that represent the masculine. One discourse around masculinity that has arisen in recent years depicts masculinity as wounded, as effeminized or effeminate, as victimized, or perhaps even as queered, and consequently expresses the need to masculinize men and recreate a less effeminate form of masculinity. On the other hand, however, there are contemporary discourses of masculinity with quite the opposite approach, discourses that are critical of masculine domination. Domination is articulated as a way in which men are themselves dominated by their own domination and suffer from masculinity. There is a discourse of masculinity, too, that evokes an anti-traditional masculinity, the image of the "new age sensitive man" and repositions masculinity as kindler, softer, and in touch with its feminine side. Given these differences, such discourses have the ultimate effect of constructing contradictory discursive masculinities. Similarly, masculinity may be contradictory within the context of a single discourse. In pedagogical discourse, for instance, the idea of the boy might be thought or talked about in one way by certain teachers, while official written policy might proclaim something else. Teachers might argue in the teacher's lounge about what type of masculinity boys should have as models, how they should behave, what should be done about their homophobic or sexist remarks in class, or what novels boys should read in English class.

A further complexity around this issue is that discursive constructs of masculinity can fall into the category of more than one type of discourse. Viagra's relation to discourse is a good example. The drug is part of a larger discourse of masculinity in which demasculinization is avoided by means of the threat of a non-erect penis and the promise of long, hard erections. But Viagra is part of medical discourse as well as of other discourses such as a discourse of capitalism. The idea of a problematic, flaccid masculinity could be seen as a result of a capitalist need to sell a product first and foremost, and explain why it is largely through advertising that this problem and its solution are constructed. The constructs of masculinity conveyed through Viagra can therefore be viewed through various discursive lenses – as about masculinity, as about medicine, or as about capitalism – and these discourses can be viewed as interacting in various ways. Masculinity might need to be a problem in capitalistic discourse so that products can be sold, but in a discourse around masculinity, the problem might be constructed on its own without reference to advertising at all. These various discourses, thus, overlap in complicated ways that have to be examined on a case-by-case basis.

A final aspect of masculinity and discourse to consider is the possibility of resistance. Discourse may be imposed on human subjects who are transformed by its assertion, but that attempt at imposition is not necessarily successful. "Where there is power, there is resistance," writes Foucault (p. 95), but resistance can come from those considered in power and from those considered outside power. No discursive construct can remain stable once it is articulated, even when an articulation of masculinity is invested with power by virtue of its official status. When masculinity is viewed as an imposed form of power, then the imposition of power necessarily leads to resistance against it, even as that resistance may or may not be outside the original field of power. That resistance can come from marginal subjectivities' attempts to resist masculinity's discursively constructed dominance or invisibility. Women might construct narratives of various types to resist discourses of virility, showing other aspects of male sexuality as more important than intercourse-ready erections, or they might make films that resist the discourse of military masculinity as hegemonic, unreal, and oppressive. Or, gay people might respond and try to remove the construct itself as a problem by creating their own discursive categories that confuse the categories themselves. "The boy dyke," for instance, the lesbian who can be taken as a boy, can purposely resist discursive constructs of the lesbian as problematic (aggressive, militant, separatist, too masculine) by subverting the very category of lesbian needed to delineate the supposed sexual problem. In response to power's construction of the idea of the problematic, masculine lesbian and thus of men as the only truly masculine sex, the boy dyke might purposely play with the sexual ambiguity of the category, in daily life and in artistic contexts such as literature, film, or performance art. Indeed, masculinity can be resisted by actual performances (theatrical, cinematic, musical, artistic) that may have a certain effect on a viewer or a communal effect on a group of like-minded viewers. Such performances often involve the body as a tool. A male singer who changes his pitch in a song may be resisting assumptions that masculinity requires a deep voice. Performances of this type may be more palatable or acceptable to some than the gendered practices of daily life that I have discussed. A TV advertisement for beer in which a heterosexual man mistakes a long-haired man for a woman and brings attention to gender confusion to sell beer, may have a very different response than if that event actually occurred to the viewer of the advertisement.

Resistance to hegemonic discursive masculinities does not have to come purely from groups outside the masculine norm. Discourses that privilege masculinity reject or destabilize the norm, an event that occurs with frequency when elements of masculinity are mocked. A *Saturday Night Live* mock-advertisement, for example, once pitched a pill that increases a man's urinal stream. The fake ad plays off the discourse of Viagra as a cultural commodity that some consider necessary, but it does so by using a similar format and similar language as the discourse of Viagra. The ad thus resists the cultural discourse of male erection by showing another obsession that appears entirely useless, comic, and absurd. But in a larger sense, this comic performance on network TV reveals the very link between masculinity and erections as comic and unnatural.

Discursive constructs of masculinity should not, therefore, be viewed as stable elements of institutions or of culture, since even as they are posited, they are resisted in numerous ways. As a result of this process, they should be viewed as constantly agonistic, or as in a continual relation of struggle between institutional power and other forms of power. From this perspective, it is difficult to talk about male power per se, as a stable or monolithic phenomenon. It should be seen as a diffuse, complicated form of power in constant relation to opposing forms of gendered power. To study the discourse of Viagra from this perspective, for example, would include looking at medical ads, medical studies, and men's and women's positive reactions to the drug and its effects, but it would also entail looking at negative responses to Viagra, failures and parodies of the drug, and men who refuse to use it. These two types of discourses – one positive, one negative – could be placed in dialogue with each other to determine what kind of overall response to Viagra is suggested.

Masculinity as Sign

The issue of language can be extended beyond discourse to the sign itself. Not only do we understand masculinity through discourse, but masculinity is influenced, or even constrained, by the ways in which language itself functions. Consequently, the ways in which language functions turn into the ways in which masculinity functions. If we were to poll people on the street and ask them what masculinity is, they might tell us it is something that men have and that it is the opposite of femininity. Underlying this particular use of language is an assumption of binary opposition, an assumption that masculinity and femininity function together as a set of opposed terms and can only be conceived of in that way. This assumption about gender is related to our tendency to think of language in general as oppositional: "thick" means the opposite of "thin," "black" the opposite of "white," "birth" the opposite of "death," etc. A larger supposition underlying this use of language is what Jacques Derrida terms "logocentrism," the idea that language always means what it says, that an easily identifiable meaning is directly present in a given word, and that there is no slippage of meaning in terms of what the word refers to. We think that we can look up a word in the dictionary and find its meaning. In this gendered linguistic scenario, "masculinity" would refer to something that would be obvious to anyone hearing the word, would have a stable referent, and would stand in direct opposition to "femininity." Further, it might be assumed that the word denotes an ontology, a core or essence of masculinity inherent in language. In order for masculinity to remain stable and to be considered to have a core of meaning, language has to be assumed to function in this way, as assumptions about linguistic stability and masculinity operate together to stabilize masculinity and to avoid thinking about signs as stable and fluid. An ontology of masculinity is dependent on an assumed stability of other words linked to that essence as well, including perhaps "man," "power," "virility," or "penis." In this way, masculinity can be accorded a linguistic stability that also implies a stability of the thing represented.

But within the realm of language, "masculinity" is unable to remain a stable sign if we think more deeply about the linguistic oppositions that we tend to take for granted. If we polled 50 people on the street and asked them to explain what the word "masculinity" means, there may be some coherence to the responses, but there would not be universal agreement. Second, the idea that the sign "masculinity" refers only to men cannot hold up: we all know women who we consider to have a certain amount of masculinity and men who we do not. In addition, the opposites that define and attempt to solidify masculinity are in fact unstable: they cannot hold up to close scrutiny since men and women are not opposite sexes, nor are masculine and feminine opposite genders. There are traditionally feminine aspects in many brands of masculinity. The sensitive man, for instance, is one brand of masculinity dependent not on a rejection of femininity but on its necessary incorporation into what a man is or should be. Masculinity and femininity are not opposites because having more of one gender does not decrease the amount of the other. Any person can be taken to have a large amount of masculinity and femininity, or very little masculinity and very little femininity, or some other combination of the two. Acting more masculine in a certain situation does not mean that one is necessarily acting less feminine (and vice versa).

Instead of considering the two genders as opposites, one might think in Derrida's terms of femininity as "supplementary" to masculinity, meaning that masculinity can exist only by virtue of its dependence on femininity. While masculinity might be defined in language as inherently different from femininity, the very fact that it is the opposite of femininity suggests that its definition requires femininity. The need to talk in these opposing terms in the first place suggests that masculinity must be created through its assumed opposite. In other words, it is linguistically dependent on the exact thing against which it is defined. It is as though masculine men want to have their cake and eat it too: I know that I am masculine because I am not a woman, but I need a woman to know that I am a man. This gesture – articulating that masculinity is unlike femininity while at the same time needing that other – paradoxically becomes one of the defining aspects of masculinity.

Masculinity's dependence on its supposed other does not end with a dependence on women, however. For it is dependent on other signs for its definition. What happens if masculinity is not only dependent on femininity as its opposite, but on male homosexuality as other? I know I am masculine because I desire women and not other men. What about race? I know I am masculine because I am white (or black, or Latino), and not Asian or Native American. What about class? I know I am masculine because I am working class and use my body at work and because I am not a noble who lives a life of effeminate leisure. The list of potential others in any definition of masculinity is endless and can never be completed. In linguistic terms, I might say that the sign "masculinity" depends on an infinite number of other signs in order to have meaning. Masculinity is dependent on an endless list of other signs that themselves can never be nailed down. If I define my masculinity as not woman, what happens when a professional female bodybuilder holds the position of woman? What happens when the gay man that I imagine as other turns out to be more macho than me? The impossibility of establishing stable meaning, or the inherent undecidability of the sign, means that masculinity will always need more others in order to define itself. The independence of masculinity can never be achieved, then, since it is dependent on an unlimited chain of others. For this reason, the meaning of the sign "masculinity" cannot ultimately be pinned down in any simple way since it is always in flux.

Another issue here is that, in the same way that masculinity might be opposed to the feminine but in fact require it for its definition, masculinity might include aspects of homosexuality or another other in its definition. For instance, the earring used to serve as a symbol of male homosexuality but then entered heterosexual masculine culture and became a sign of a certain brand of cool heterosexual masculinity. While heterosexual masculinity might be defined as not gay, in fact that proclamation of difference is not composed of pure difference. For this reason, it might be the very proclamation of difference, the act of articulating (whether implicitly or explicitly) that my masculinity is heterosexual and not homosexual that is the only definition of my masculinity. Masculinity is not the actual difference between heterosexuality and homosexuality, but the linguistic act of attempting to separate them. I might try to construct masculinity in pure opposition to other signs, to carve out a discrete meaning for masculinity, to imagine clear-cut categories of gender, but those attempts are in the end doomed to failure. In any binary opposition, the separation is not an impervious dividing line, but a permeable or porous membrane through which elements inevitably pass. In my example, the gay earring passes from being a sign of male homosexuality to being a sign related to heterosexual masculinity. This is, of course, one of the paradoxes of masculinity: on the one hand, men are often perceived as – or perceive themselves as – independent and as able to function perfectly well on their own but, on the other hand, masculinity cannot ever really be differentiated from other forms of subjectivity.

This notion of binary opposition cannot be disassociated from the issue of power. The binary opposition of male/female or of masculinity/femininity maps onto a binary notion of power since binary oppositions often arise because one element of the hierarchy needs opposition to impose (or to continue to impose) its hegemony on the other. The commonly held opposition in the US between blackness and whiteness, for instance, is one way in which white culture maintains its hold over blackness. If blackness remains in direct opposition to whiteness, both racial definitions can also more easily remain discrete and blackness in an inferior position in the hierarchical structure. So when masculinity is part of a binarism of any type, it may be so that it can be positioned on top of the binary and as the half of the opposition that has or should have power. This does not necessarily mean, however, that non-masculinity does not contribute to gender binarism or to a hierarchy of power. A woman might need the split so that a man can be erotic for her, a boy might want a man to be a man so he can imagine what he will become, or a gay man might want a discrete sex to desire. These various subjectivities may also accord power to men or to masculinity for various reasons: a boy may want the man on top of the hierarchy so as to imagine what he can or will become, or a gay man may associate power with eroticism. Like power itself, this recurring gender–power link is not static: since power implies resistance, this power binary can be flipped or destabilized in ways akin to those in which discourses of power are resisted (see pp. 34–5).

Approaching masculinity in this way has implications for what is commonly called gender fluidity. On the one hand, this kind of approach to the sign means that all masculinity is somehow always fluid or unstable, that masculinity always bleeds or risks bleeding over into its definitional others, despite efforts to the contrary. To talk about the fluidity of masculinity, then, is simply to assert a character-istic that it always has and not to say anything novel about it. It might be the case that masculinity *appears* more fluid at some points rather than at others, but that fluidity is always present in some way and might be covered up more convincingly at some points than at others. But, on the other hand, calling gender fluid can, paradoxically, argue against the very possibility of fluidity. The idea of fluidity is based on the assumption that there is some stable notion of gender that is sub-sequently destabilized in some way. I might talk about how masculin-ity is fluid when a macho man unexpectedly acts in a nurturing or maternal way. By considering masculinity in this way, I am in fact assuming that masculinity is a stable thing in the first place and, in this case, that there is some stable notion of masculinity based on the idea that masculinity is not nurturing. I am assuming that masculinity is ontological in its non-nurturingness, and that the absence of this non-nurturingness makes masculinity move away from its ontology and become fluid. Why can masculinity not in fact be predicated, at least in certain contexts, on nurturingness? The images of the loving father, the stay-at-home dad, or the male nurse might serve as key representations of this brand of masculinity.

The implications of thinking about masculinity as always unstable and ultimately indefinable are enormous for the study of gender. It suggests that masculinity cannot be considered alone or on its own terms, but rather has to be taken as in relation to other types of subjectivity. This means that it is not possible to consider masculinity without taking into account the oppositions that are employed to attempt to define it. As a result, most scholars of gender would say that any study of masculinity has constantly to take femininity, homosexuality, and other common forms of alterity into account in order to articulate definitions of masculinity fully. This approach also suggests that one should be on the lookout for gender's permeable membrane, for specific ways in which masculinity is seemingly differentiated from other subjectivities which in the end are incorporated into masculinity. Masculinity might be defined as "not sexed female," for instance, but then in fact play with the fantasy of giving birth (as in films like *Rabbit Test* (1978) or *Junior* (1994), or in texts in which men physically or metaphorically get pregnant or give birth). In this linguistically driven approach, masculinity as sign is in a constant process of definition, and as a result, the inability to define masculinity fully and the attempt to stabilize it can be studied as part of what masculinity is or what it is imagined to be. Texts or cultural contexts might highlight this instability in specific ways, using specific images or terms. Consequently, attempts to define masculinity in a stable way can be interpreted as responses to instability, as a kind of anxiety about undefined masculinity, and the articulation of stability might be indirectly proportional to cultural anxieties about instability. From this point of view, articulations of masculine stability should not be taken for granted, but should be closely examined for the reasons why they refuse to admit instability.

Masculinity in Dialogue

Masculinity can be revealed as unstable by considering its relation to binary opposition, or its position in an endless series of oppositions. A related but distinct lens by which to understand masculinity is the notion of gendered "dialogue." Extending theoretical approaches to language articulated by the Russian theorist Mikhail Bakhtin, this approach assumes that masculinity as sign and as subjectivity cannot be separated from all other signs and subjectivities against which it is defined. Though masculinity might seem to function alone and on its own terms, it inevitably functions in implicit or explicit relation to a series of others. In fact, it is defined by that very dialogue.

This approach implies not so much opposition as the key element, but more a response, a series of responses, or even a kind of conversation with a number of others. It also suggests that masculinity replies to its others, and that these replies constitute part of what it is. A man does not simply say something about women, but in responding to a woman, he defines his masculinity relationally. A man who goes to a female bodybuilding show has a reaction to that show, and that relation between him and the show defines his masculinity. I do not speak or write in a vacuum: everything I say or write is in dialogue with something else, so every aspect of my masculinity dialogues with something else. The dialogue implies not a single definition of the other as not me, but a continual process of not me's. There is no simple opposition between male and female, for instance (as in the previous approach), but a series of oppositions that never end and that are each slightly different from each other. Thus, the opposition of masculine and feminine might be frequent, but the separation of the genders is a constant process, and has to be repeatedly established rather than taken as a given.

To be in dialogue means not only that masculinity is not static, but that it changes by virtue of interactions in space and time. Masculinity might at one point be defined through spatially defined dialogue. If a heterosexual white man shows up at a gay male nightclub and dances, his masculinity would be defined in a certain way as he moves across the dance floor and blends in (or does not blend in) with the mostly gay crowd. That dialogue might be based on difference ("I am here but I have a different sexuality from everyone around me"), or it might be based on similarity ("Though I have a different sexuality from those around me, I am similar because we all like to dance"). But as he travels through rural China, he might experience his masculinity in a very different way (again, as similarity or as difference). He might identify with certain masculinities that he perceives, or he might perceive himself as more masculine than a man he encounters. That dialogue is conversational in the sense that it takes place over time and suggests numerous back-and-forth responses over time. Masculinity does not have any single meaning, even for a given individual, but its definition changes through relations to various external factors that arise. It might be the case, however, that certain elements of a dialogic masculinity recur throughout a number of these circumstances. I might respond similarly to a gay man in situation X as I do to another gay man in situation Y, or I might respond similarly to a certain gay man in two different situations. But the specific way in which I respond necessarily changes throughout my various dialogues. As a black man, I might repeatedly define my masculinity in opposition to Asian masculinity, but I might do it one way on my trip to China and another way when I go to Chinatown in my home city in the United States, and in yet another way when I watch a Jackie Chan movie.

It is not pure opposition that defines masculinity here, but the relation between masculinity and something else perceived as another body or another sign. As Bakhtin might put it if he were discussing gender, there is no "being" to masculinity, but only "co-being."[2] This means that the position or situation of masculinity is central to how it is understood. Masculinity has no meaning in itself, but only in the way it is put in dialogue with an other and in the way in which it is perceived by someone else at a given moment in a given space. Consequently, the same masculinity can potentially mean many different things, depending on how it is perceived. Jean-Claude Van Damme's masculinity is defined in a certain way when a 9-year-old boy interested in fighting sees him, but differently when a 60-year-old pacifist does. Dialogic masculinity is not strictly binary, but because relation defines it, it incorporates both masculinity and the perceiver of masculinity. From this perspective, I might also say that masculinity itself is composed of the relation between the perceiver and perceived. A gay man might perceive the same masculinity in a way unlike the way a lesbian perceives it, meaning that the sense attached to a given masculinity inevitably varies widely. In other words, masculinity is not inside a body, but exists as a relation between the perceiver and a body or a sign. So masculinity, as in my example above, is the actual relation between a 9-year-old boy and Van Damme in a given scene of a film. A dialogic approach might mean that a man is responding to some form of non-masculinity

---

[2]   The concept is coined by Michael Holquist in *Dialogism: Bakhtin and his World* (London: Routledge, 2002), 25.

in some explicit or obvious way: a heterosexual man might position himself in opposition to homosexual masculinity, making homophobic remarks or refusing to establish intimacy with another male for fear of being perceived as homosexual. Or that dialogue might be less explicit: a heterosexual man might not respond at all, or he might only respond to himself internally. But in any case, a dialogue is taking place.

Since dialogue is a kind of conversation, masculinity can be considered a dialogue over a period of time between perceiver and perceived. A CEO might have a relation over a ten-year period with her male board that defines masculinity relationally. While that relation necessarily changes from minute to minute and from situation to situation, there may be similarities in the dialogues that recur over time. This notion of the dialogic is often applied to the novel: a male writer might construct a continual conversation over the course of a novel with another form of masculinity, in his textual responses to cultural constructs, to his own life, or to other works of fiction. That idea of conversation might remain rather static, or it might change radically over the course of the novel. This conversation can also mean that masculinity exists in response to the perception of the other, or that perceptions of perceptions can be part of the dialogue. A man might respond to women's critiques of machismo or excessive masculinity by trying to moderate himself, or he might respond to critiques of softness by trying to harden himself. But in either case, there is a response to the other that becomes part of the dialogic process.

Gendered dialogue does not necessarily have to imply antagonism between masculinity and the non-masculine. White masculinity could be in dialogue with black masculinity in certain circumstances, for example, by virtue of a white man's desire to imitate a black man's relation to rap music or the way he moves his body. What tends to be the case in this approach, however, is that masculinity is not fully incorporated or does not fully become the form of subjectivity with which it is in dialogue, but rather remains as its other. Or, I could say that there is no synthesis between masculinity and those with whom it is in dialogue. The white man who is influenced by rap music does not become ethnically black, but may remain aware of racial difference and want to incorporate only certain aspects of black masculinity into his subjectivity. This kind of dialogue could be contrasted with another synthetic approach in which the other is contained within the definitional idea of masculinity. Thus, if a man's feminine side becomes one aspect of the masculine self to the point that it is no longer perceived as feminine but as a part of masculinity, then this notion of dialogue no longer pertains. The Californian man may have a feminine aspect to him: no longer does he necessarily position himself in relation to or in dialogue with the feminine. Rather, he has incorporated it into himself in a seemingly stable way and that form of masculinity may subsequently be in dialogue with other forms.

In a dialogic approach, masculinity cannot be considered as a simple and harmonious cultural construct since it would have to be perceived in the same way by everyone. Masculinity can be a shared phenomenon only if it is perceived in a given situation in the same way by all people. So we cannot really talk about twenty-first-century American paternity, only about how someone in a given time and space views paternity. This does not mean that an individual perception is free from cultural influence, however, for perception is already inflected or clouded by numerous cultural and personal factors. How any perception is defined is already coded in part by previous perceptions.

This approach to gender raises the possibility of its opposite, the monologic, in which masculinity appears outside relation and exists in response to no one or no thing. Does the cowboy alone on the range not embody masculinity with no inherent dialogue? After all, one might say that there may be no one to perceive him and give him meaning. In fact, the cowboy is in a kind of dialogue because the cowboy is necessarily responding to something. It may be, for instance, a domesticated form of paternal masculinity that he rejects, it may be effeminacy, or it may be his former life as a Wall Street businessman. But there is necessarily an indirect dialogue with something, and that implicit dialogue, which one may have to look closely to locate, defines the cowboy's masculinity and gives it meaning.

As this example suggests, there may be an internal dialogue, as the individual can perceive an element of his or her own masculinity and give it meaning on its own in some situation. This kind of internal dialogue can take place between parts of the self. In this sense, self and other are contained in the same subject because masculinity is fragmented: I can have a moment of distance from my masculinity and perceive my masculinity on my own. I might at some moment perceive some macho act of mine as excessive because I take some temporal distance from that act of mine. An internal dialogic relation might also exist between a perceived ontological notion of masculinity on the one hand and a more personalized definition on the other. Thus, as an individual, if sexual virility provides one ontologically seeming trait of masculinity, I might experience my masculinity as a relation to that ontological notion. While I might try to live up to that definition on the one hand and to be sexually virile in the way that I define it, on the other hand I see that I will never in fact be able to do that, so I might think about myself in relation to the ideal of sexual virility. My masculinity, then, is defined by my perception of a certain ideal of masculinity that I internalize. But, like dialogue in general, that internal dialogue changes in time and in space. As I am having sex, that dialogue might become more harmonious (I feel virile and forget about that dialogue with virility), or it might become more acute (I cannot perform in bed and I cannot forget that dialogue with virility).

Masculinity as Continual Movement

In a dialogic approach, masculinity is imagined as momentary and spatially specific and defined by a series of individual perceptions, but those perceptions might conceivably recur. The dialogic is thus not necessarily constantly changing: young boys in a number of spaces and over a period of time might have the same or nearly the same perception, effectively stabilizing a given type of masculinity. Consequently, Van Damme's masculinity might look more or less the same because of repeated perceptions (which in turn influence other perceptions), and the dialogic would effectively end up creating certain recurring masculinities. How, then, can masculinity be imagined as in a constant process of movement?

It is sometimes thought, for instance, that gender is a continuum, with masculinity at one end and femininity at the other and that human beings (men and women) oscillate from moment to moment between the two gender poles on that continuum. Masculinity is not static: I might have a certain amount of masculinity while I am playing baseball, but less in the evening when I am at home cooking dinner for the kids, that amount being culturally or individually defined and itself open to change. Measured on a continuum, the idea of having a gender – or of having a quantity of gender – could be taken to suggest a possession that is temporary or subject to constant losses and gains. Or, if the continuum denotes how masculine one is, the extent to which one is gendered could be seen as in constant movement (very masculine at one point, not very masculine at another). The idea of a gender continuum, movement-based as it may be, can nonetheless be considered problematic because it assumes that masculinity and femininity are opposites as it positions the two genders at each end of the continuum. To be more masculine is to be less feminine. What if the gender continuum were not conceived of in this way, but if each human was considered to have a certain amount of masculinity and a certain amount of femininity, regardless of sex? At any given moment in time, I might be considered to be more or less masculine, and more or less feminine, since perhaps I am performing certain acts or displaying certain traits that my culture codes in a certain gendered way. Moves across those two continua might also be defined by my own experiences with my gender. I may feel very masculine for certain reasons at one point and very feminine at another point, but those gendered feelings would not be opposites. Or, I might experience some of each gender while doing something. When taking care of my 3-year-old boy, I might have the experience of masculinity (as a father playing with his son) and I might experience femininity (by nurturing him and encouraging him positively). The amount or extent of gender that I experience might change over time too (I feel very masculine and very feminine taking care of my son tonight, but I felt less masculine and more feminine while doing it yesterday).

Whether gender is considered a single or a double continuum, the fact remains that, in a certain sense, these approaches both constrain masculinity to preexistent notions of gender. I am measured in my relation to how gender is already perceived or to how I already perceive it, which is necessarily already inflected with culture. In addition, while possibly more indicative of how gender functions than a single continuum, the use of two continua suggests that there are two and only two genders, constraining gender as a bipartite phenomenon. But numerous other continua could be added (a continuum of same-sex love? of transsexuality?), meaning that a double gender continuum system does not allow for gender to become other than the sum of masculinity and femininity.

How, then, could masculinity be conceived of as in movement and as not constrained by preexistent perception? How could masculinity be considered not in reaction to stasis, but as pure becoming? How could masculinity look forward to change and new forms instead of backward to previously articulated definitions created by me and my cultural context? My masculinity might be defined by an anxiety about my ability to make money and to provide for my family at one point, but that very anxiety might lead to my financial productivity later on. It is not that my productivity is in dialogue with my anxiety, but that the anxiety turns into productivity. How could male heterosexual desire not be thought of as simply heterosexual, as a constant desire for women, but as a constant potential for new productive movement that leads to new desires and opens masculinity up to new becomings? By employing a framework influenced by the theoretical work of Gilles Deleuze and Félix Guattari, masculinity would be defined as a series of possibilities, a series of constant becomings: I might perceive my desire for that woman on the street, but that desire might morph into a desire of some other type for her husband, which creates the possibility of a new kind of relation with him, which might lead to another desire not coded as heterosexual or as some other prefabricated tag. Masculinity would then be constituted by a myriad of masculinities, by an endless series of different masculinities that never recur. And the other gender here would not be a problem or something to be feared or defined as other, but a possibility for movement and change, a possible spring-board for pleasure in change. Viagra, for instance, might provide an example of how masculinity can be imagined this way. I might experiment with sex in a new way with Viagra, because I have been given the medical possibility of a new kind of sexuality. I can have a series of new, productive experiences related to my gender as I experiment with the drug and a sexual partner (or partners). On the other hand, the failure of Viagra might also open up new becomings. I might see that without erectile sex, my sexuality is not blocked, but that new sexual possibilities are created. I might experiment with non-erectile sex, focus on oral sex, etc. Or I might deprivatize the anus to explore its erotic possibilities, experiencing new pleasure from the prostate. From this perspective, the goal is not to see what masculinity *is*, what it represents, how it relates to power, how it is not a binary, or how it is perceived, but to focus on what it can and does become and how it continues to become something new.

A certain brand of masculinity might be thought about as constant movement. We can study the figure of James Bond in relation to political discourse or as in dialogue with 1980s feminism, or we could look at how Bond's masculinity repeatedly changes from one Bond film to

another (and from one novel to another and from novel to film), viewing
the complicated and innumerable gendered moves as the ultimate definition of his masculinity. Bond's masculinity is one of a series of becomings, with no progress or linearity. By virtue of an assumption of constant
movement forward instead of a relation to culture, perception, or signification, this way of conceiving of masculinity means that it is necessarily
non-hierarchical. If I truly move on forever, changing and creating new
possibilities, I cannot remain on top or in a position of domination. In a
larger sense, notions of stable gender themselves, once this movement
begins, break down, and gender stasis is no longer possible.

This approach is opposed to stabilized masculinities or systems that
try to depict masculinity as fixed (such as the military), but it is also unlike
approaches that aim to destabilize gender (as in the section "Masculinity
as Sign" above). It might be the case that destabilizing binarism is a
way to begin to enter this movement, but this movement-centered
approach is really a step beyond destabilizing. It calls for a complete
anti-identitarian approach, whereby terms such as "sexual orienta-
tion" or "sex" or "gender" break down and exist perhaps only as
micro-component parts that might factor in to some of the movements but never fully define them. In addition, other structural elements subtending gender get broken down, with the Oedipal
structure's breakdown the most important. Gender would not be
defined through the Oedipal complex, in which men and women have
defined desires based in family structures and repression of desire.
Desire would not be fixed in object choice or identities like "heterosexual," "homosexual," or "bisexual," but in unpredictable flows of
desire. The Oedipal complex, which is assumed to establish a boy's
heterosexuality, is a major example of how culture attempts to create
masculinities that are stable and based in stasis, and that resist being
broken down. Numerous other cultural entities try to stabilize masculinity as well: capitalism, for instance, might try to create a stable masculinity to keep itself in business, to create men who can make, sell,
and consume.

Masculine subjectivity would thus not be a stable, unified event, nor
would it be considered as something simply destabilized as one element of some binary opposition, or as one element of a series of binary
oppositions. Rather, masculinity would be conceived of as something
that is fully outside a binary system, in a constantly changing process
of movement, always mutating. So masculinity might become like a

woman at some point, but that becoming would be only one of its stages, one way in which it moves on to something else that may or may not have to do with the category of woman. In this sense, then, there is no masculine being, but only a series of becomings.

While this might be an unorthodox and abstract way of considering masculinity, there are in fact certain definitions of masculinity that explicitly take constant movement as a basic element. The idea of masculine self-creation, the self-invented or self-made man, or the new man who is always in the process of constructing or creating himself might be morphologies of this kind of man of becoming. The metrosexual handbook, for instance, has as its mantra "Your life is your own creation," and suggests numerous ways in which a man can create the self as movement and ambiguity.[3] It also suggests that the metrosexual take on gay-like or effeminate-like aspects in those acts of self-creation and gendered becoming.

Taken to its full conclusion, this idea of becoming could efface the very possibility of masculinity as an organizing concept. The man who truly becomes might move from a position of masculinity to another position in which his masculinity is not an aspect of who he is or in which gender has nothing to do with masculinity. Subjectivity, then, would be composed of a series of an infinite number of mini-genders and non-gendered subjectivities that move along in unpredictable ways.

The Excesses of Post-Structuralism: Toward a Moderate Approach to Masculinity

One of the common critiques of these kind of theoretical or representational approaches to the study of masculinity is that they have a tendency to ignore what some consider real aspects of masculinity, that masculinity cannot be reduced to simple games of language, and that post-structuralist approaches to gender have tended to efface issues of rights, oppression, and the concrete. The unfortunate practices of masculinity cannot be wiped away by the wave of a representational or linguistic magic wand. Are we not better off looking for chemical

---

[3]   Michael Flocker, *The Metrosexual Guide to Style: A Handbook for the Modern Man* (Cambridge, MA: Da Capo Press, 2003), 169.

or biological ways to alleviate the negative issues that masculinity raises? If masculinity can lead to rape, war, and other violent acts, should we not focus on legal or cultural ways of transforming masculinity rather than on unstable binary oppositions, discursive constructs, or productive becomings? Could we focus on masculinity as representational and fluid at some moments, and then regard it otherwise in the political realm? Another issue raised in this regard is the actual experience of masculinity. While a man might think that there is no such thing as a masculine essence and while it may in fact be true that there is no gendered essence, many men nonetheless *experience* masculine subjectivity as essence. If a number of men on the street were polled, at least some of them would say that they experience masculinity as an immutable thing within them that defines them. A number of women might say that they perceive it this way as well. How, then, can one offer a model of thinking about masculinity to bridge the divide between post-structuralist ways of thinking on the one hand, and the experience of essentialism on the other? For if so much of masculinity is perception-based, does it not make sense to include the experience of masculinity in how we theorize it? Is a man's perception of essence not part of masculinity?

One way to approach this question would be to take a middle approach to masculinity, to find a compromise between the two positions, and to locate the experience of masculinity somewhere between essentialism and non-essentialism. While walking down the street, an average man might experience his masculinity as both essential ("I am a man and I am like that man over there and like all men") and non-essential ("But I am not like your typical man" or "I am different from most men in this way ..." or "I am not acting at this moment like a typical man"). But one does not have the continual sense of essentialism over a period of time, and then move to a sense of non-essentialism for a period of time ("I am a man on Monday, but I destabilize manhood on Tuesday"). Rather, a man experiences a nearly constant move or an oscillation between these two poles. So as I walk down the street, I might move back and forth between these two kinds of experiences, one moment seeing my masculinity as essential and one moment seeing it as free-floating. That oscillation can be experienced as a tension: do I go back and forth, thinking that my gender is a diverse thing? Or rather, do I attempt, because of this tension, to cover up one of the two ways of thinking? Do I attempt to stamp out the sense of free play and to consider masculinity as essential? Or, on the contrary, do I choose to ignore the essential aspects, perhaps to highlight the free play and to avoid feeling boxed in by essence?

The essentialism that I experience might also place me in a position in which essentialism is not exactly opposed to free play since essentialism might actually help me to understand that free play better. If I think that my testosterone is a key element of my masculinity, that thought about my gender might help frame and reaffirm my free-play definition. I might experience my biology as definitional of my gender, only then to realize that my gender cannot be fully defined by biology. My assumption of a purely biological definition of gender might make me see that non-biological elements also define my gender. The reverse can also be true: because I focus on my masculinity as free-floating and non-essential, I might have moments in which I feel masculinity as a core. So one of these two approaches to gender might be the very thing that then pushes me, that gives me impetus for another approach to my gender. What I am saying, then, is that these two approaches to masculinity operate in a relation that is not necessarily simple or antithetical, possibly defined in tension or possibly defined with each other as enablers (where one leads to its opposite), but still defined in a relation of movement.

Another way to think about this issue of negotiating essence and free play is a bit different. Instead of thinking about masculinity as a pure social or linguistic construct, it could be considered as an in-between phenomenon. Masculinity is constructed, is built up through ideology, domination, practice, language, and other related elements. Precisely because it is built up, it cannot be simply disbanded but should be taken as in place, rather than as essential. It is the perceived naturalness and the repeated build-up over time and over generations, in such a deep and profound way (on the body, in creation myths, and in other ways that make it appear natural), that mean that it cannot simply be undone, that its construction is in essence natural, or at least natural-appearing. In this case, the key question would be not so much whether masculinity is nature or nurture, but what the actual process of the construction of masculinity is. How does masculinity get built up over time? What are the techniques by which masculinity is constructed? It is not what masculinity *is*, or the end result of a series of constructs of masculinity, that is important. Rather, it is the process of the construct of masculinity that matters, the way in which masculinity is built up and made to appear natural and eternal. The experience of the man walking down the street would make sense in this rubric: he views masculinity as essential because culture has convinced him that it is so. So his experience of a masculinity that moves between essentialism and free play is a result of the move between these constructions built up over time along with the experience of fluidity or of deviation from these constructs.

Bibliography

The approaches to masculinity in this chapter are adapted from the work of various theorists who do not directly articulate ways in which masculinity can be thought about in their frameworks. Below, I have listed for each major theoretical concept in the chapter some key works by the theorists that have influenced my discussion of masculinity here.

The concept of the indistinguishable nature of the original and the copy is often attributed to Jean Baudrillard. See *Symbolic Exchange and Death*, trans. Iain Hamilton Grant (London: Sage, 1993); *Simulacra and Simulation*, trans. Sheila Faria Glaser (Ann Arbor: University of Michigan Press, 1994). See also Baudrillard's essay on metaphorical transsexualism: "We are all Transsexuals Now," in *Screened Out*, trans. Chris Turner (London: Verso, 2002), 9–14. Judith Butler takes this theoretical approach to the original in ch. 3 in *Gender Trouble: Feminism and the Subversion of Identity* (New York: Routledge, 1990).

This issue of copy and original could also be theorized in terms of hybridity, a term made famous by Homi K. Bhabha (but not within the context of gender) in *The Location of Culture* (London: Routledge, 1994). For a hybrid approach to the study of masculinity, see Demetriou Z. Demetrakis, "Connell's Concept of Hegemonic Masculinity: A Critique," *Theory and Society* 30, no. 3 (2001): 337–61.

On gender as ideology, see Teresa de Lauretis, *Technologies of Gender: Essays on Theory, Film, and Fiction* (Bloomington: Indiana University Press, 1987). On relations between capitalism and masculinity, see Max Weber, *The Protestant Ethic and the Spirit of Capitalism*, trans. Talcott Parsons (New York: Scribner, 1958). On Weber, see Roslyn Wallach Bologh, *Love or Greatness: Max Weber and Masculine Thinking – A Feminist Inquiry* (London: Unwin Hyman, 1990). On ideology as a concept, see especially Louis Althusser, "Ideology and Ideological State Apparatuses," in *Lenin and Philosophy, and Other Essays*, trans. Ben Brewster (New York: Monthly Review Press, 1971), 127–86. For a good overview of ideology, see Terry Eagleton, *Ideology: An Introduction* (London: Verso, 1991). For the seminal work on mythology in the sense of cultural images that come to appear natural, see Roland Barthes, *Mythologies*, ed. and trans. Annette Lavers (New York: Hill and Wang, 1972).

Michel Foucault famously articulates the concept of discourse and its relation to power. See especially *The History of Sexuality*, vol. 1, *Discipline and Punish: The Birth of the Prison*, trans. Alan Sheridan (New York: Vintage, 1995). For secondary work on Foucault, see Margaret A. McLaren, *Feminism, Foucault, and Embodied Subjectivity* (Albany: State University of New York Press, 2002); Lois McNay, *Foucault and Feminism* (Boston: Northeastern University Press, 1992); Ladelle McWhorter, *Bodies and Pleasures: Foucault and the Politics of Sexual Normalization* (Bloomington: Indiana University Press, 1999); Robert M. Strozier, *Foucault, Subjectivity, and Identity* (Detroit: Wayne State University Press, 2002); *Feminist Interpretations of Michel Foucault*, ed. Susan J. Hekman (University Park: Pennsylvania State University Press, 1996); Naomi Schor, "Dreaming Dissymmetry: Barthes, Foucault, and Sexual Difference," in *Men in Feminism*, ed. Alice Jardine and Paul Smith (New York: Methuen, 1987), 98–110; *Feminism and the Final Foucault*, ed. Dianna Taylor and Karen Vintges (Urbana: University of Illinois Press, 2004).

On the issue of practice, see Pierre Bourdieu, *The Logic of Practice*, trans. Richard Nice (Stanford: Stanford University Press, 1990); *Masculine Domination*, trans. Richard Nice (Stanford: Stanford University Press, 2001).

On the crisis model, see Elisabeth Badinter, *XY, on Masculine Identity*, trans. Lydia Davis (New York: Columbia University Press, 1995); Judith Kegan Gardiner, "Introduction," in *Masculinity Studies and Feminist Theory*, ed. Judith Kegan Gardiner (New York: Columbia University Press, 2002), 1–29; Bryce Traister, "Academic Viagra: The Rise of American Masculinity Studies," *American Quarterly* 52, no. 2 (2000): 274–304.

The concept of masculinity as sign is very widespread in the Humanities, though the approach is often attributed to the influence of Jacques Derrida. While Derrida does not directly approach the question of masculinity as such, questions of gender are central to his corpus. An excellent place to start is the extracts in part 4 in *A Derrida Reader: Between the Blinds*, ed. Peggy Kamuf (New York: Columbia University Press, 1991). A key text is *Spurs: Nietzsche's Styles/Éperons: Les Styles de Nietzsche*, trans. Barbara Harlow (Chicago: University of Chicago Press, 1978). See also Todd W. Reeser and Lewis Seifert, "Marking Masculinity," in *"Entre hommes": French and Francophone Masculinities in Culture and Theory* (Newark: University of Delaware Press, 2008), 25–7; the essays in *Derrida and Feminism: Recasting the Question of Woman*, ed. Ellen K. Feder, Mary C. Rawlinson, and Emily Zakin (New York: Routledge, 1997). For an excellent general introduction to Derrida, see Jonathan Culler, *On Deconstruction: Theory and Criticism after Structuralism* (Ithaca: Cornell University Press, 1982). On etymology, see ch. 4 in

Todd W. Reeser, *Moderating Masculinity in Early Modern Culture* (Chapel Hill: University of North Carolina Press, 2006).

On the notion of the dialogic, generally linked to the Russian theorist Mikhail Bakhtin, see especially *The Dialogic Imagination*, trans. Caryl Emerson and Michael Holquist (Austin: University of Texas Press, 1981); *Speech Genres and Other Late Essays*, trans. Vern McGee (Austin: University of Texas Press, 1982); *Problems of Dostoevsky's Poetics*, trans. Caryl Emerson (Minneapolis: University of Minnesota Press, 1984). On dialogism, see Michael Holquist, *Dialogism: Bakhtin and his World*. On gender and dialogue, see Anne Herrmann, *The Dialogic and Difference: An/other Woman in Virginia Woolf and Christa Wolf* (New York: Columbia University Press, 1989).

On gender as a double continuum, see Eve Kosofsky Sedgwick, "'Gosh, Boy George, You must be Awfully Secure in your Masculinity!'," in *Constructing Masculinity*, ed. Maurice Berger, Brian Wallis, and Simon Watson (New York: Routledge, 1995), 12–20.

My discussion of the topic of masculinity as pure movement is indebted to Gilles Deleuze and Félix Guattari who articulate a notion of becoming in *A Thousand Plateaus: Capitalism and Schizophrenia*, trans. Brian Massumi (Minneapolis: University of Minnesota Press, 1987); *Anti-Oedipus: Capitalism and Schizophrenia*, trans. Robert Hurley, Mark Seem, and Helen R. Lane (New York: Viking, 1977). See also Félix Guattari, "Becoming-Woman," *Semiotext(e)* 4, no. 1 (1981): 86–8. For an interesting use of their theoretical apparatus within the realm of Viagra, see Annie Potts, "Deleuze on Viagra (or, What can a 'Viagra-Body' do?)," *Body and Society* 10, no. 1 (2004): 17–36. See also Annie Potts, *The Science/Fiction of Sex: Feminist Deconstruction and the Vocabularies of Heterosex* (London: Routledge, 2000), 240–55. On the figure of James Bond as defined by constant movement, see Toby Miller, "James Bond's Penis," in *Masculinity: Bodies, Movies, Culture*, ed. Peter Lehman (New York: Routledge, 2001), 243–56.

On masculinity as neither free play nor essential, see Judith Butler, *Undoing Gender* (New York: Routledge, 2004). The work of Pierre Bourdieu could be taken in this middle category as well: see *Masculine Domination*. On Bourdieu and gender, see ch. 3 in Toril Moi, *What is a Woman? and Other Essays* (Oxford: Oxford University Press, 1999); Todd W. Reeser and Lewis Seifert, "Oscillating Masculinity in Bourdieu's *La Domination masculine*," *Esprit créateur* 43 (2003): 85–95.

2

Social Masculinity and Triangulation

From Twoness to Threeness

Much of my discussion of models of masculinity in chapter 1 takes for granted the principle of binary opposition as definitional for masculinity. Masculinity might be in unstable opposition to femininity, for instance, but that instability still begins from the idea that one element is in relation to a second. My discussion in this chapter will treat the question of masculinity when it is defined not in relation to or in dialogue with a single other or with a series of others, but when masculinity functions as part of a tripartite model of gender and sexuality. The basic elements of this model have been famously articulated by Eve Sedgwick in her important book *Between Men* (1985), often considered the text that launched masculinity as an object of inquiry in a literary/cultural context. Of prime consideration here will be relations between masculinity and what is commonly called the love triangle. Why does the image of the love triangle recur so frequently, and what does it suggest about masculinity? How does the love triangle operate as an imagined relationship? I will focus on the triangle composed of two men and one woman and on the hidden relations implicit in this kind of triangle, particularly relations of desire. This kind of tripartite model functions in certain predictable ways, meaning that explanations can be found for how the gendered relations work. Consequently, those predictable types of interactions can be studied and thought about in their relation to masculinity.

At the same time, however, despite its repetition throughout culture, this model of gender cannot be considered as universal, and, as a result, permutations of the model can be considered alongside the model as its own implicit critique. In other words, the ways in which the model does not function are as important as the ways in which it does function and are as revelatory of constructs of masculinity as the model itself. For this reason, the failures or breakdowns of the model – and the reasons why it fails – are central to thinking about masculinity. The sexed triangle is my focus in the first part of the chapter, while the second part of the chapter discusses some key permutations of this kind of gendered triangulation.

Masculine Rivalry and the Anxiety of Homosexuality

To consider this triangular definition of masculinity, I begin by thinking about how two heterosexual men relate to each other and what their way of relating suggests about masculinity. One way to imagine their relation is as based on pure competition and violence through sport, business, politics, or even warfare. Another approach is to consider male–male relations as a peaceful lack of rivalry or as a non-problematic male bonding, in which an imagined masculine sameness permits masculinity to be viewed as harmonious. Men sometimes comment, for instance, that their relationships with other men are easier or less of a problem than their relationships with women because women are so different from men. Men may also imagine mutual protection with other men or an absence of rivalry. On the other hand, men sometimes remark that their relations with other men contain a built-in rivalry, but that rivalry or competition is explicit and far from hostile or vicious, perhaps even one of the ways in which male–male affection or friendship is expressed. Playing together on sports teams or working together on business deals might be viewed as a kind of relationship defined by both rivalry and mutual protection. Male bonding might be viewed as harmonious, either because it is perceived as without rivalry or as a harmless competition that replaces violent or high-stakes rivalry.

But the situation may not be so simplistic: this way of thinking about male bonding may be an oversimplification that permits men to avoid thinking about male–male relationships as problematic and to create or recreate the so-called war of the sexes (or some equivalent) and male–female relationships as more difficult than male–male ones.

Relations between two men can be defined by a hidden or less explicit competition or rivalry in which one man views another as his rival. This kind of masculine rivalry, however, is not simply based on a desire to defeat or to vanquish the rival or to kill him off, but also implies a desire to emulate, to identify with, or to be like him. The rival is a rival precisely because he displays certain traits that his rival wants to imitate, perhaps even serving as a kind of imagined superhuman figure. Part of the problem is that with the hold that rivalry has over masculinity, the man is unable to express his desire to imitate or to be like the other man. He does not or cannot tell that man that he wants to become like him, that he likes what he does, or that he would like to learn from him how to do what he does well.

This inability to express emulation results from a fear of losing in the rivalry, but it is also based on a perceived homophobia since expressing adulation might be seen as expressing a form of homoerotic desire. One of the reasons that identification with another man can be problematic is that it risks becoming or being viewed as desire for the rival. The idea that man X emulates man Y can never be fully separated from the threat that man X desires man Y. The issue here can be articulated as the threat of the inability to separate "identification" and "desire" from each other. A man identifies with another as someone whom he wants to emulate, but is ultimately unable to express his desire for emulation in any overt way.

The jump between the concepts of identification and desire might seem odd and far-fetched in this context, but one way to think about the instability between them is to think about the gender development of the boy. In most cultures and in most time periods, the boy is meant to identify with grown men (male role models), but to desire those of the "opposite" sex. The implied and encouraged gender opposition between men and women, which the boy is supposed to internalize, is not as stable as heterosexual norms might want it to be. If gender itself is unstable, how can the sex reserved for identification and the sex reserved for desire remain separate? What is there, for instance, to keep the boy from identifying with the gender subjectivity of his mother or of women, and thus from desiring his father or men (in the same way that she does)? If the boy's mother desires men and if the boy identifies with her, why can't he also desire men? And what is there to keep the boy from desiring his father, a male member of his household, or a male celebrity? During this time when sexed and sexual norms have not taken a firm hold, the boy maintains an unclear separation between whom he should imitate and whom he should desire.

This childhood instability between desire and identification recurs within the context of the relationships grown men have with other grown men. With his male rivals around him, the grown man might want to identify with them, much as he did with adult male figures while a boy, but that rivalry, too, constantly risks falling into desire. This is not a way of saying that all grown men are in fact homosexual; clearly, this is not the case. But it does suggest a continual threat that a grown man feel, experience, or think he will experience desire for another man in his interactions with other men that he values. This is another way of saying that there is a constant threat of a kind of desire that he himself might perceive or experience as homoerotic or homosexual and, in homophobic cultures, that he fears having tendencies that his culture codes as negative or problematic. It is easy to locate examples of two heterosexual boys or men displaying a fear of homosexual desire in interactions that the two of them have alone together. They may sit with a seat between them at the movies, avoid urinating in urinals right next to each other, or not shower together at the gym. In a larger sense, men's fear or avoidance of physical and emotional closeness with other men (e.g., shaking hands and not hugging, not talking about how they feel) could be taken as indicative of this homoerotic threat. One aspect of this anxiety is that, in certain circumstances, the borders of heterosexuality will actually be crossed and a same-sex act will take place, perhaps even accidentally. It is sometimes imagined, for instance, that a group of heterosexual men could drink too much, slip, and have sex with each other while under the influence of alcohol. Such anxieties about homoeroticism and homosexuality (desire and act) are so fundamental and so widespread that they are often taken as a major definitional element of masculinity.

In addition to the constant homophobic threat, another result of the fluidity between identification and desire is that masculinity is always located in some ultimately indefinable place on a continuum of desire for other men. Such a continuum of desire might be considered to have on one end what Sedgwick calls "homosocial" desire – in which desire for another man is not experienced as erotic even as it might begin to gesture in that direction (since desire itself is fluid) – and on the other end "homosexual" desire, in which one man has clearly erotic and sexual feelings for another man. Female–female desire is more often considered as fluid and difficult to categorize in neat boxes, but male–male desire can also be viewed as always unstable. The main point of thinking about male desire as a continuum is not that desire can be given a mathematical location on a line (to say something like "his desire for his buddy is a four, but his is a six" is impossible). Rather, the point would be that desire cannot be located as discrete in this model: to say for sure that he and his friend are heterosexual friends would not be possible, but to say that he and his friend are homosocial friends would be, since homosociality constitutes a fuller spectrum of male–male desire. The fluidity of male–male desire between the homosexual and the heterosexual are what define their desire, not their precise location on a continuum. In the same way that masculinity is an unstable phenomenon dependent on precise situations and contexts, homosocial desire is not stable and can oscillate depending on the situation or other variables. This approach can be seen as an extension of the destabilization of gendered binary oppositions discussed in chapter 1: while the desire of a man for his friend might not qualify him as gay or homosexual, it does not fully qualify his desire as strictly heterosexual either, since heterosexual/homosexual is just another unstable binary opposition and the line separating homosexuality and heterosexuality is porous. This is not really a way to say that all men are bisexual either since that term implies another defined category (between and in opposition to heterosexual and homosexual) instead of a more undefined, fluid approach to sexuality.

It is important to note that this approach does not assume that all relationships between men are in fact in the same exact grey homosocial area, since each relationship would have to be examined on its own for evidence of its relation to homosociality and might provide certain indicators of its own specific relation to the continuum. Different male–male relationships express a homophobic threat differently: in one relation might be expressed a classic fear of homosexuality (calling certain men faggots, gay bashing), but in another relation, it might be expressed as an attraction to the possibility. Men's jokes about male homosexuality with other men might be an expression of homophobia and a way to dispel the threat by making a joke, or they might be a way to mock the very idea of homoerotic anxiety in the first place, depending on the specifics of the joke. In the latter case, two men might be purposely subverting or resisting the homophobic injunction by playing with it and making it seem ridiculous, or they may be expressing their implicit agreement with the idea that there is a homosocial continuum and that they do have some kind of ambiguous attraction to other men.

The complexity of the way in which desire functions should not be forgotten as male desire for another male that actually qualifies as homosexual might also be hard to locate on the homosocial continuum. A sexual act between two men may or may not imply homosexuality, and even the relation between two gay men might be ambiguously positioned on the continuum or contain an element of homophobia, something that would have to be determined on a case-by-case basis. Two gay men might have sex in a way that contains homophobic elements, such as a fear of too much emotional intimacy or a refusal of penetration and kissing. A sodomitical act between two heterosexual men in prison or an uploaded web video with two best friends kissing could be as expressive of a homosexual anxiety as a complete avoidance of closeness or intimacy. So in the same way that homosociality does not rule out homosexuality, homosexuality does not rule out homophobia.

Masculinity and the Exchange of Women

With these issues in mind, let us return now to the dilemma of the man who has a rival that he risks desiring. What kind of way out of the dilemma is available within the constraints of an emulating, competitive, and homophobic masculinity? How can he get out of his double bind? How can he express his desire to imitate his rival while still remaining in a seemingly non-subordinate position with respect to him? The homosocial response to this problem is to take the detour of heterosexual desire: for man X to desire the same women as man Y already desires. By desiring her, by falling in love with her, by making love with her, by thinking he wants to make love to her (or some variation thereof), he in effect is able to imitate his rival/idol freely (he has the same object of desire), while, at the same time, he rivals his rival through this same desire (he threatens to take the love object away from his rival). This kind of erotic desire, which results from imitating another person, is often referred to as mimetic desire, since we often desire what we see someone else that we admire desiring. The birth of this kind of desire means that the love triangle is not a preexisting condition, does not arise out of the blue, but is in fact created out of the relation between two men. By loving a woman, man X defuses the threat of homoerotic desire by displacing the entire question of desire onto his and his rival's relationship with a woman. It does not come into being in this model because two men happen to love the same woman: it comes into being because of an anxiety about the unstable relationship between the men. From this perspective, homophobia is an important enabling condition of this kind of heterosexual desire, and the relation between the two men is more determinative than the one between the men and the woman that they both desire.

One of the basic assumptions behind Sedgwick's model is that the shared female love object is a passive recipient of male desire, unable to function as a subject in this male-centered and male-dominated triangle. Along with the injunction against desiring or having sex with another man in this model is the underlying principle of women as objects of exchange between men. People and things that serve as objects of exchange function as signs that mediate a relationship between men requiring an intermediary. The object might represent in a non-threatening way the desire for intimacy that cannot be expressed unless it is mediated by external objects. Physical objects such as literature, gifts, or beer can serve as signs of male–male intimacy or of a connection, but in this model, it is women who serve as the ultimate mediators. In a certain sense, then, this chapter is about how the objects that get passed back and forth between men construct the relation between those men and how they construct masculine subjectivity at the same time.

This model of gender exchange is based on a social or anthropological notion of the exchange of women. Under the influence of the work of Claude Lévi-Strauss, anthropologists have treated the question of exogamy, in which tribes felt the need to exchange their women so as to avoid interbreeding. Women would be sent to other tribes as a way of avoiding tribal incest, as a way of putting into practice a kind of cultural incest taboo. But another reason for sending women to other tribes is that sending women elsewhere served to provide a gift from one tribe to another and to maintain a peaceful relationship with that tribe. To give the gift of a woman to another tribe would also mean to receive gifts (other women or actual objects) in return. This idea is far from limited to tribal cultures, however, as the concept influences non-tribal cultures. Royal European women, for instance, were sent to other nations or other kingdoms as a way of cementing national bonds and ties. There are modern versions of this notion of exchange in women too: a man who buys a prostitute for another man for his birthday might be one example.

Clearly, this approach to exchange is based on a very misogynistic view of women, in which women are not considered to be subjects and beings capable of making independent decisions about their own fate, but serve for some other reason that pertains to men. This approach does not assume that women always equal objects of exchange, rather that at certain points and in certain ways, women are imagined to function as objects. It also keeps men from serving as objects of exchange, leaving them only in the role of exchangers. As a result of this exchange, women are transformed from human beings into signs of something else, and their actuality has to be effaced so that they can become non-physical signs of something else that they themselves do not determine. Women do not always function this way, of course, but here they are created as objects of exchange or as signs of objects of exchange for masculinity's own purposes. The exchange of women could also be conceived of not in social but in Oedipal terms: the boy struggles for power with his father through the medium of his mother who functions as a kind of object of exchange between son and father as each tries to maintain his hold over her. Men treating women as objects of exchange may on some level be recreating this childhood relationship in later life, substituting other women for their mother.

In the love triangle, the goal of triangulation is not for two men to desire the same woman, but rather to cement the problematic relations between men. Two men who desire the same woman, then, are in effect bonding by virtue of their desire or love for the same woman, whether consciously or unconsciously. The love triangle, in the end, serves a number of ends for masculinity: it avoids the homoerotic threat and it keeps male domination in place by treating the female love object as object. Sexism and homophobia function in tandem in this model as men are able to maintain their subject status while avoiding the homophobic threat. For the model begins as a struggle for two men to create harmony as it excludes homosexuality and women from the harmony it imagines. These relations of desire are not simply about desire: the object of analysis in this way of thinking about masculinity might be less gender or sexuality per se, and more the way in which power functions through the medium of gender and desire. Male desire may be a displaced desire to share women and to communally reaffirm male power over women. This model, then, is predicated on thinking about masculinity's relation to both sexism and male–male sexuality, or in academic terms, to both feminism and gay studies.

Once this perspective is articulated, it is not difficult to produce examples of love triangles and to think about how they conform (or do not conform) to this model. A well-known example might be the famous love triangle at Camelot, involving Arthur, Guinevere, and Lancelot. In this approach, one would consider not so much how or why Guinevere loves Lancelot, or why she loves two men, or why she commits adultery. Rather, the focus would be more on the way in which the relation between Lancelot and Guinevere mediates the relationship between the two men in the trio. Guinevere would be considered the mediator of homosocial desire between the two knights, a sign of the exchange between the two men who are in a sense rivals who admire each other. Arthur might admire Lancelot's ability as a knight, and Lancelot Arthur's talents as king. From this perspective, it is the relation between the men's rivalry/desire and the heterosexual love triangle that would serve as the focus in analyzing masculinity. The interactions between the men and between the men and the woman might be studied to determine specifically how homosociality functions. There are, of course, innumerable examples of stories and texts of triangulation that could be considered in their relation to this model, such as ancient texts dealing with the war over Helen of Troy, Shakespeare's *Othello* (1622), Shelley's *Frankenstein* (1818), Truffaut's film about a love triangle *Jules and Jim* (1962), or Cuarón's film about two adolescent boys *Y tu mamá tam bién* (2001). The specifics of such relationships in texts can themselves be studied, by asking critical questions such as: What does homosociality mean in this text? How does an exchange of women take place? In what ways are rivalry and desire in opposition (or not in opposition) to each other? How do the men reveal an anxiety of or attraction to homoerotics/homosexuality? What other elements factor into the question?

Triangulation Transformed

Even if homosociality and homosocial triangles are ubiquitous in texts and in culture, these kind of triangles do not always function in a neat or stable way and rarely do the examples simply confirm the model. In thinking about various examples, one may quickly realize that something often goes wrong with the model, that it does not function as is, or that it is transformed in some way. One or more members of the triangle might leave the triangle or even be killed off, or relationships between the various members of the triangle might become strained or impossible to maintain. A principal reason for this instability is that the triangle is based on masculine anxieties and other problems that ultimately make static relationships impossible. The homosociality between the two male characters in Cuarón's film *Υ tu mamá tam bién*, for example, is developed but then destroyed in a scene near the end of the film in which the two male characters end up having sex with each other one night after too much alcohol. Soon after, the mutual female object of desire dies. From the perspective of this model, these two events should be seen as taking place hand in hand: the disappearance of the mediator and the potential homoerotics are clearly connected and depend on each other. The end of the film, then, is about the breakdown of homosocial triangulation: the homoerotic threat turns into actual homosexuality at the same time as the woman disappears because homosociality and a female mediator are both necessary conditions for the existence of the triangle.

Numerous examples of the breakdown of this model could be cited, and reasons for the end or complication of the model could be theorized. Consequently, it might make sense to say that it is not the model's existence in itself that is so important in thinking about constructs of masculinity and the ways in which masculinity functions through detours of desire. Rather, the very transformation or permutation of the model reveals as much about gender, sexuality, masculinity, and power as the model on its own static terms. This triangle is often transformed from a static relationship, and comes to define a relationship moment or change whose meaning is in its relation to the original model. In other words, the inability of the model to function says as much about masculinity as the model's seamless functioning. The possible permutations and complications of the model, which might be more the rule than the exception, are infinite, and the variables themselves are far from stable. What happens if the woman does not function as simple object of exchange? What happens if homosociality actually slips into homosexuality (as in the above example)? What happens if women control the configuration of the triangle and co-opt it for feminist ends? What happens in all-male situations or spaces in which women as mediators are essentially absent (prison, war, sports)? What happens when important non-gender variables such as race, ethnicity, age, and class are factored into the equation? For even as this model is founded on the instability between desire and identification, this approach to gender is structural, founded on the idea that certain stable characteristics are found in men and women in Western culture. One of the issues with structurally based models is that they are based on an assumed internal stability. In this case, one of those stabilities is the presumed stability of sex: that the men have to be men, both in terms of sex and in terms of gender (he is a man and he acts like a man). The mediator, likewise, has to be a woman, again in terms of sex and gender (she is a woman and she acts like a woman). So even if this structure does pervade culture, there are numerous variations on the structure that must be taken into account. Indeed, one of the reasons this model is so helpful in thinking about masculinity is that it can serve as a basis or starting point for thinking about variations on the model, whereby different subjectivities play the role of the various parts of the triangle. What happens to this model when the fluidity of identification and desire is not so fluid after all, when one of the men in the standard triangle is gay and actively desires the other man? Can a transsexual, a cross-dressed man or woman, or someone of indeterminate sex hold a position in the triangle?

Another caveat with using the model to understand masculinity is the question of socio-historical context. Taken alone, the model might seem to assume a transhistorical notion of gender. While this model may in fact recur widely over time and across cultures, it is a mistake to assume that any model of gender functions in the same way atemporally and cross-culturally. Various cultural and historical factors need to be taken into account when thinking about the model in a given context. Thus, for instance, what happens to the model if the strict homophobic injunction is lifted, or if it is lifted in part? Can we talk about this model in classical Athenian society, in which male–male love was often idealized? As I will discuss in chapter 9, race and the nation can reconfigure the triangulation. Class, too, can be a key issue: a peasant and a nobleman might be in a different kind of homosocial relationship than two men of the middle class or of the nobility in a given context. Class may also affect two men's relation to a female object of desire. The model should be constantly placed in dialogue with various other factors so that it does not become a stabilized structure beyond reconsideration that has the effect of normalizing masculinity and gender relations.

So what are some common ways in which the model can be challenged? What other types of triangles could be taken into account? If the model is ultimately predicated on a combination of misogyny and homophobia, what happens when these two variables are mutated? Perhaps the most common way to challenge the model is to consider what happens when the woman in the triangle does not function as the object of exchange but becomes or attempts to become a subject with the potential or the ability to enter into the homosocial bond. This type of resistant triangulation is represented by Truffaut's New Wave film *Jules and Jim*, one of the classic films about the love triangle between two men (the title characters) and one woman (Catherine). The movie begins with a story of a classic homosocial triangle in which two heterosexual men in a kind of playful rivalry desire the same woman, who is constructed from the beginning as a literal object that the two men consciously seek out together. But as the movie continues, the woman, who should function as the passive object of triangulation, becomes an increasingly active subject, attempting to take control of the homosocial relationship and to assert power over the men as their simultaneous desire for her becomes her main tool to have them act as she wants them to. Whereas the men rely on the female object to be a passive co-conspirator in the process of triangulation, Catherine refuses to conspire with them and conspires on her own, in the end killing herself and Jim. Because there is no pure homosociality or objectification of women in the love triangle, the triangle literally cannot survive, and in the final scene Jules goes to say adieu to Jim at the cemetery, an adieu that also signals an end of homosociality. So while the classic triangle is invoked, it is as a kind of structure against which to play off, and the film can be read as about the failure of the homosocial triangle and the reasons for that failure.

Another question about the model relates to the possibility of doubling women and placing them at the base of the triangle and one man at the apex. Is it possible that women function not as objects of exchange (whether resistant or not), but as the actual subjects, and that a man function as the object of exchange between two women? Is there a such thing as female homosociality? One potential issue here is the difficulty of locating the homophobic injunction in the relation between women. While female–female homophobia undoubtedly functions in many ways, it is often thought to be less present between females than between males. That lack of injunction might render the necessity for mediation unlikely between two women. What might happen, for instance, is that because the primary bond is not the relation between women – as it may be assumed to be between the men – the vectors of desire toward the male apex of the triangle are not as weak as with the male–male model, but in fact risk becoming vectors of desire that take over the female–female relationship. One might consider constructs of women who want something from the male mediator beyond cementing female homosociality, or who see that there is a particular advantage to those vectors of desire that are more beneficial than female homosociality. There are examples, for instance, in which jealousy might set in between the two women, meaning that the object of desire does not or cannot remain the mediator. In Metastasio's Italian opera, *Didone abbandonata* (1724), a new character named Selene is created, the sister of Dido (the main character of the opera who exists in the original story on which the opera is based). As if to create the possibility of a female homosociality, Selene falls in love with the same man as her sister (the Trojan hero Aeneas), but in the end Dido commits suicide in part because she and her sister are in love with the same man. When thinking about women's difficult relationship to homosociality, it would be important to think about how masculinity may in fact also be constructing a kind of imagined relation between women or a female homosociality – with the potential for women to function as subjects instead of objects – but then destroying that possibility so that female homosociality cannot be a possible model of exchange and so that men cannot function as objects of exchange in a new scenario that could potentially weaken patriarchy.

Could the subjectivities of the three members of the triangle be mixed up based on other organizing principles besides sex? Balasko's film *French Twist* (1995), for instance, tells the story of a triangular relationship among a heterosexual woman, a heterosexual man (her husband), and a butch lesbian. The latter two characters both desire the heterosexual woman, though there is also a relationship of rivalry between them. In thinking about the triangle in this film, one might question how homosociality functions, whether a butch lesbian character can hold the traditional place of the man, and how the homophobic injunction might play itself out in this case.

What happens when a monkey wrench is thrown into the homophobia aspect of the model? What happens when the two men in a homosocial relationship do not consider themselves heterosexual, or when one of those men is in fact homosexual? While the gay man's desire for the straight man might not be defined by homophobia, his inability to fulfill his desire with the heterosexual man may define their relationship to a female. By desiring her on some level (since desire is fluid for gay men too), the gay man may be able to come the closest he possibly can to fulfilling his desire for the heterosexual man. There may also be situations in which a gay man and a straight woman hold the position of bases to the triangle and are in a competitive relationship for a mediator of desire who is a heterosexual man. In this case, it might not be the injunction of homophobia that defines the relation between members of the base of the triangle: mutual desire for the mediator may stabilize an imagined heterosexuality on the part of the gay man. While these kind of models are not necessarily widespread and may not be models that recur with great frequency, they suggest how the model can be rethought in other sexed contexts.

Although the triangle tends to have the effect of hiding male desire for other men, it might instead permit the possibility of heterosexual expression of male–male intimacy or even of homoeroticism since masculinity can safely desire another man with the safeguard of a mutual female object of desire, whether real or imagined. In Shakespeare's Sonnet 20 (1609), for example, the narrator addresses a man and describes him as beautiful (he "steals men's eyes and women's souls amazeth") and in terms that suggest the possibility of homoerotic desire (the "master mistress of my passion"). The poet can proclaim in his last line "Mine be thy love" but only because he also focuses in the sonnet on his "love's" sexual relations with women ("[Nature] pricked thee out for women's pleasure"). The safety value of triangulation might allow the repressed aspects of male–male relationships to come out of the closet from time to time. This expression may be seen to be permitting heterosexual masculinity to express a fantasy of homoerotics within the heterosexual realm of the homosocial. Even if the model is based on a homophobic injunction, it can still flirt with the idea of same-sex desire or act. If a heterosexual man says something like "I was only one beer from having sex with a guy," his remark might be not proof that he is bisexual, but an indicator of an attraction to the abstract idea of male homosexuality. This desire or curiosity could imply masculinity's desire to understand what it is like to be gay or to have a gay experience, thus an attraction to the idea of masculinity as a becoming (see pp. 45–9).

A further question about the model might be: what happens when the two male members of the model are in fact gay men, when the use of homophobia as one force field in the model is not central to the functioning of the relations amongst its members? On one level, it might simply be the case that gay men completely subvert the triangle because they automatically resist homophobia in their relations and are not interested in objectifying women. On another level, the sexuality of the three members might in fact be irrelevant to the functioning, if the two gay men have internalized cultural homophobia and misogyny and continue to mediate their relations through an exchange of women. The cultural model may be so pervasive that it is internalized even when the actors involved do not perfectly correspond to the standard actors of the model. Though two gay men's desire for a mutual female object of desire might not be explicitly erotic or might have an element of eroticism, gay men can still share a common relation with a woman, such as the diva or the superstar (e.g., Cher, Madonna, opera divas). Gay men's desire for these kind of figures might in fact be not so much about their desire for these women, but rather a way to cement bonds among gay men without the issues that can be involved in direct erotic desire of another gay man. Taken to an extreme, this idea suggests as well that gay men's desire for a given woman cements relations amongst them. In the same way that the standard model of homosociality contributes to creating patriarchal community, this kind of relationship may contribute to constructing a gay community. The extent to which homophobia and misogyny function in these kinds of cases would be a question to consider. When gay men build bonds through women, is the woman being objectified?

A variation on this gay model might include a relation in which two gay men mediate their own desire for each other – or perhaps their own fear of intimate relations – through a third figure, which might include another man. Thus, the recurring image of the gay sexual threesome, the *ménage à trois* in the sexual sense, could function in this way: the inclusion of a third party in a preexisting relation between two gay men might in fact be a way to mediate desire, to have and to not have desire between two gay men. The mediator might thus stabilize and restrain desire between the two men, function as a kind of downplayer of gay male intimacy, and even be a kind of manifestation of homophobia. By virtue of two gay men desiring a third object of desire, they can have their cake and eat it too: have a similar object of desire while at the same time avoiding any possibility of too much desire and going too far in some way. In this sense, it might not be classic homophobia that breaks the bond (though that might be present as well), but perhaps more an anxiety of excessive intimacy which could be a mutated form of homophobia. The third object might also function as a created object or a personal sign meant to create desire between the gay men. Gay men in a long-term relationship gone stale or in a relationship that does not function well or intimately might fall into this category. The inclusion of this object of desire (who must remain a pure object of desire) could be an attempt to create vectors of desire toward the object, which could then be transformed into vectors of desire between the two male subjects of the triangle.

While I have laid out some possible permutations of the model, I could continue to consider numerous permutations and combinations of this kind of thinking about gender and masculinity, as well as the limits of each permutation. The issue can be even more complicated than changing who the actors in the triangle are. What happens when there are more than one triangle at play? How can two triangular relationships relate to each other? What happens when a person factors into two overlapping triangles? Can a character change his or her position in a triangle over the course of time? Can an animal or inanimate object take on the role of mediator? As this series of questions implies, this model opens up innumerable avenues of analysis. I will return to homosocial triangulation in chapters 8 and 9 when I consider how the model is affected by national and racial contexts.

Bibliography

Eve Sedgwick, *Between Men: English Literature and Male Homosocial Desire* (New York: Columbia University Press, 1985). As mentioned, this book has had a major influence on the study of masculinity. Sedgwick essentially brings together academic feminism and the study of male homosexuality to think critically about how men relate to one another. The first two chapters are seminal to the theory as outlined here, but Sedgwick's readings of her texts are excellent insights into specific case studies. The book leans on a number of previous theorists, and going back to these texts in light of Sedgwick's reading of homosociality can retroactively yield new results.

See also René Girard, *Deceit, Desire, and the Novel: Self and Other in Literary Structure*, trans. Yvonne Freccero (Baltimore: Johns Hopkins University Press, 1965). Girard articulates an idea of mimetic desire that has been influential not only for Sedgwick but for other theories of gender as sexuality as well.

The classic source on the notion of the incest taboo and exogamy is Claude Lévi-Strauss, *Elementary Structures of Kinship* (Boston: Beacon Press, 1969); Gayle Rubin's essay is seminal too: "The Traffic in Women: Notes on the 'Political Economy' of Sex," in *Toward an Anthropology of Women*, ed. Rayna R. Reiter (New York: Monthly Review Press, 1975), 157–210.

The idea of a sexuality continuum comes out of a feminist tradition of women's sexuality as a continuum. Most famously, see Adrienne Rich, "Compulsory Heterosexuality and Lesbian Existence," in *Blood, Bread, and Poetry* (New York: Norton, 1994).

For sample secondary work on the homosocial model, see John Troyer and Chani Marchiselli, "Slack, Slacker, Slackest: Homosocial Bonding Practices in Contemporary Dude Cinema," in *Where the Boys Are: Cinemas of Masculinity and Youth*, ed. Murray Pomerance and Frances Gateward (Detroit: Wayne State University Press, 2005), 264–76; Stephen Guy-Bray, *Homoerotic Space: The Poetics of Loss in Renaissance Literature* (Toronto: University of Toronto Press, 2002); A. A. Markley, "Tainted Wethers of the Flock: Homosexuality and Homosocial Desire in Mary Shelley's Novels," *Keats–Shelley Review* 13 (1999): 115–33; Robert McKee Irwin, *Mexican Masculinities* (Minneapolis: University of Minnesota Press, 2003).

For work on the homosocial model in gay male permutations, see Stephen Maddison, *Fags, Hags, and Queer Sisters: Gender Dissent and Heterosocial Bonds in Gay Culture* (New York: St. Martin's Press, 2000).

3

Sexing Masculinity

Masculinity and Maleness

In the last two chapters, I looked at various instabilities and complexities of gender, the characteristics assigned to the sexed body. But in the discussion, while gender and desire were considered unstable and unable to be easily pinned down, sex (maleness and femaleness) was taken for granted as a stable characteristic. Although male desire and masculinity are ultimately unstable and a product of signification, they were still taken to be housed in a man whose biological maleness was assumed. In this chapter, I would like to move a step further in the discussion of masculinity and imagine what would happen if maleness itself, the biological definition of a man, were taken to be a more complicated or problematic concept than is generally assumed.

Even when we think about how complicated or fluid masculinity is, we tend to assume a stable sex underneath. We take maleness, man, or the male sex as a given. We might imagine a man defined as a body with a penis, facial hair, body hair, muscle, and testosterone. Furthermore, we tend to assume that sex is accorded by nature, and that there is a direct link between the male body and masculinity. If an element of gender seems natural but is not, it is often taken as part of masculinity or of the socially defined aspects of being a man. Masculinity might be open to change, but maleness remains fixed. A man can change his relation to violence or homophobia, it may be imagined, but biology cannot change.

The issues of sex and gender are also frequently taken as causal or linear: we imagine that sex is accorded from very early on in a child's life (before birth even) and that gender follows from that. A child may be a boy in the womb, then a baby boy, and his maleness or his boyness emerges from his sex. Because he is a boy, he throws baseballs, or he likes to wrestle. Then, later on, desire follows from there: he notices girls, dates girls, has sex with them, marries one, etc. Desire naturally follows his gender. So one might say that there is an assumed three-part trajectory in which sex leads to gender which in turn leads to desire. This three-part movement is often considered to be given or predetermined developmentally and to subtend the stages of life.

But in fact, this order is not natural, and masculinity does not lead, in any simplistic way, to heterosexual desire. The rejection of homosexuality may serve to create heterosexual desire or masculinity, but as those normative constructions recur again and again and can never be complete or stable, there can be no linear or discrete move from masculinity to male heterosexuality. In addition, we saw in the last chapter how masculinity is closely linked to homosocial desire, which complicates any simple notion of heterosexuality as fully achieved or developed. Relations between heterosexual men cannot easily or fully dispel the specter or the possibility of homosexuality. Although the relation between masculinity and desire is complicated and although masculinity itself is unstable in ways such as these, sex still appears stable underneath the instabilities and maleness does not get complicated.

Linear assumptions about sex and gender might even underlie what we think are complicated approaches to gender. The case in point might be when we talk about gender fluidity. We may know that a man can partially deviate from the sex/gender/desire teleology: he might have a gender that does not follow logically from his sex. If a man acts like a woman (let's say he is nurturing with his 2-year-old son) and if we call this gender fluidity or (using this example) male maternity, in fact we are thinking about this kind of gender fluidity as an exception to an assumed stability of masculinity. His gender is fluid at this moment, but perhaps most of the time it is not (he has only moments of nurturing) or perhaps he is maternal but most other men are not (he is the exception to a gender norm). In either case, his fluidity is presumably in opposition to some kind of non-fluidity or some kind of stable idea of gender. A man who gets in touch with his so-called feminine side likewise: the assumption behind the phrase is that he has a stable masculine side that dominates his subjectivity most of the time. He is a man with a masculine side that defines what he does in general, and even talking about his feminine side might be a way for him to implicitly reaffirm the presence of his masculine side by opposition.

If we are assuming some stable form of masculinity when we talk in this way, we are also assuming a stable notion of sex, or of the male body. We are assuming that there is such a thing as a man and that masculinity is always in relation to that maleness. The question to consider here, however, is: what would happen if the linear assumption of sex leading to gender leading to desire were changed, and not taken for granted? Put otherwise, what would happen to masculinity if sex were not assumed to lead naturally to gender, but if gender led to sex? Or, what if the very ideas that we have about masculinity created what we thought a man is and what the male body is?

I might say that it is our preconceived ideas about what a man is that leads us to imagine what the male sex is. If we have already decided that part of masculinity is a keen interest in sexuality and the ability to perform, then we cannot help but have certain ideas about the penis and its role in masculinity. If sexual penetration is an aspect of masculinity, then the penis has to be a key definitional aspect of the male body. That the word "manhood" can refer both to the penis and to male subjectivity already suggests this crossover between the penis and masculinity. We accord a certain importance to the penis as part of the male body, and certain men (or women) might be obsessed with the penis because they believe that it embodies what a man is. Our ideas about masculinity come to influence what we think the male body and the male sex are. We think a man should be sexually virile, and so we attach great importance to the penis. The male member represents masculinity when in fact it is just a piece of flesh hanging between the legs. Why is so much importance accorded to the penis when there are other parts of the male body that could also come to signify or represent what a man is? Why not the beard or facial hair, for instance? Why does beard not also mean manhood? While facial or chest hair might also be invested with a certain signifying power vis-à-vis masculinity, they tend not to hold the same symbolic power because what we think a man is (our notion of gender) does not lead us to that aspect of the male body in the same way that it leads us to the penis.

Another way to think about this idea is to say that maleness is invented and given precedence over social aspects of masculinity. We invent the male sex and imagine that maleness or that sex to reside outside the realm of the social or the linguistic. We imagine that maleness is a result of chromosomes, hormones, testosterone, muscularity, size of the male body (men are larger than women), etc. But, in fact, it is our ideas about masculinity that already influence what a man is. We have already decided that strength defines masculinity, so therefore we see the male body's relative larger size as a definitional element of a man. Our gendered perceptions create a certain idea of sex. The arbitrary nature of sex becomes clearer by considering other historical periods in which the construct of sex was radically different from our own. In Renaissance Europe, it was often thought that maleness was partially defined by heat, that the male body was by definition warmer than the female body, that man's heat explained other aspects of his sex such as semen, and that woman's colder nature explained why she lactated and menstruated.

From this perspective, language plays a major role in the issue of sexual definition. We cannot understand the male sex outside the realm of language, and the specific aspects of language have an influence on the way we understand maleness. To return to my earlier example: the penis has little meaning in itself as a piece of flesh. It is rather by virtue of our talking about the penis, by virtue of our assigning a certain meaning to the penis, that this aspect of sex takes on meaning. If we talk about the "cock" for instance, there are already various assumptions behind that word that influence what we think the referent of the word is (it wakes up and crows in the morning, metaphorically speaking). It is also by virtue of the meanings that we do not assign to certain elements of the male sex that certain aspects of the body do not take on meaning. Why does the Adam's apple, for instance, not have much significance in what manhood is? When we talk about masculinity or maleness, we do not give much importance to these aspects of the male body, and thus they take on less importance in terms of how we define the male sex.

The issue of discourse, in the way I discussed it in chapter 1, is also important here. It is not simply that I as an individual go about making meaning of the male body on my own, but various discursive formulations around me also make that meaning for me. On one level, the culture in which I function might be what influences my thinking around the penis, and consequently different cultures assign different meanings to the male body. More specifically, various discourses have a particular influence on that cultural influence, and different cultures' discourses create types of maleness. One example is medical discourse and its relation to the erection-enhancing drug Viagra. The penis and erections are made into a key aspect of masculinity when the drug is presented as able to cure a problem. The discourse around Viagra plays off previously existing cultural discourses of virility which dictate that erections are a key aspect of male subjectivity and that maintaining or enhancing them is a way to create masculinity. But with this discourse, Viagra is made into a desired commodity and sells erections. This aspect of medical and capitalist discourse, in turn, has the effect of making erections seem as if they are *already* a key aspect of masculinity, when in fact discourse is in the process of producing the penis as a central element of masculinity for its own specific ends that are not already in place. This discursive technique makes gender into a natural-seeming offshoot of sex, and presents this sex–gender relationship as a retroactive fait accompli. The discourse around Viagra might suggest that an erection is the most natural aspect of masculinity there is, but it is also participating in that constructing. Similarly, other forms of discourse might have the effect of making sex when in fact gender is doing the making. In advertisements (which might include the Viagra example), certain aspects of maleness are assumed to sell products intended to help create or recreate maleness (Viagra, a full head of hair, ties, underwear) when in fact the ads are participating in the process of the construction of maleness. In these cases, the advertisements can be seen as an extension of gender, which is constructing sex.

In the face of the instability of maleness, there are repeated attempts to stabilize how sex is perceived and to avoid thinking about how gender influences sex. The potential problem is that if sex is constructed by gender, then maleness does not have to be the exclusive domain of men. If the male body is not naturally imbued with sexed meaning, then the definition of maleness can in fact be changed. This poses a risk to male subjects who aim to maintain masculine hegemony. Sex may need to be an original and natural concept, and gender a derivative concept, for masculinity to function. In this way, a biological or natural superiority is accorded to masculinity as the incontrovertible basis of its gender hegemony. Thus, a very butch woman can never be a man, since maleness is not open to other sexes. She might be allowed to possess masculine qualities, to be gendered masculine, or to exemplify gender fluidity, but by virtue of keeping sex outside the realm of gender, men can ultimately maintain their hold over a core of maleness and thus the butch woman is unable fully to have masculinity. Anxieties about the sexually ambiguous transsexual, the hermaphrodite, or the drag king suggest that maleness must be maintained as a clear and discrete sex, and as not available to those who do not already have it. To do so could upset a perceived natural order by which maleness is considered the superior sex.

In her influential book *Bodies that Matter* (1993), Judith Butler articulates how one "assumes" a sex.[1] The double entendre of the word means two things about sex and gender: first, that sex is taken on by a man. The human being is not already male, but he has to become or be transformed into a man. When new parents or a doctor announce "It's a boy!", for instance, they are not revealing a preexistent fact, but are making their child into a male. The announcement is so key to the birthing process that being born is nearly indistinguishable from being proclaimed as male or female. Second, to assume a sex means that sex gets taken for granted once it is articulated: after the human becomes a male, he is henceforth taken to be male. Thus, buying blue clothes or playing with trucks is simply considered a reflection of a previous assumption of maleness. This assumption, however, does not end after the announcement "It's a boy!" Rather, sex is repeatedly assumed as the human has constantly to be made into a male. On one level, we create sex numerous times in a given day when we talk about maleness, when we say "man" or even "he," or when we create or recreate a sex in opposition to the female sex. As I will discuss in chapter 4, we also create the borders of the male body as discrete, assuming that maleness is not in movement and that it is entirely stable.

In addition to people such as the hypothetical new parents in my example above, narratives invent maleness as a sex. Creation narratives might be considered one type of text in which this invention of sex takes place, textual moments in which sex is invented and then taken for granted. By virtue of their foundational status, such narratives hide or assume other narratives and keep the invention of sex from being noticed because they present the beginning as foundational and originary, thus beyond dispute. In this way, various elements of maleness and masculinity can be taken for granted or assumed. In one version of Genesis, for instance, Adam the first man is created from the earth by God, and once that event is over, other events can take place (woman can be created as his "helper," the characteristics of masculinity can be established, sexuality can be discovered, the animals can be named, etc.). The male sex is invented by God at the origin of the world, and

[1] See Judith Butler, *Bodies that Matter* (New York: Routledge, 1993), esp. 1–5, 27–31.

is subsequently complicated. But in fact, in this narrative, gender is the apparatus that produces the male sex in the way that it wants to appear. Preexistent ideas about masculinity led to the creation of a creation narrative in which maleness is made into what masculinity already thought it was. Because Adam was created first, and Eve was created from him, maleness precedes femaleness, masculinity can be taken to be the norm or standard, and the woman can be considered an off-shoot of the man and always part of him (though he is not part of her). So the text can be taken (and has been taken) to mean that man's creation before woman already shows how the male sex should be privileged over woman because man was created first by God. The image of sex proves what gender is.

One aspect of this way of retroactively constructing sex is that maleness is made to appear as prediscursive, made to look as if it exists before language. Butler writes that sex is "retroactively installed at a prelinguistic site to which there is no direct access" (p. 5). When the parents of a newborn announce, "It's a boy!", they are constructing the sex of the child by giving him a sex through language. But there is nothing natural or inherent about that sex: those parents produce the sex of the boy when they make their gendered announcement in language. Those parents do not say "OK, I am announcing it's a boy, and it is this announcement that makes this child into a boy." Rather, they act as if that statement about the boy is simply presenting some truth about the child that existed before that exclamation was made. The boy becomes a boy once the linguistic pronouncement is made, but the pronouncement does not acknowledge that the assignment of sex is discursive and that the announcement creates the sex of the boy. The Adam and Eve creation myth could also be considered from this perspective. The birth of Adam's sex precedes the moment when language is invented, implying that God, and not language, created maleness.

This approach to sex/gender assumes that maleness cannot be understood outside language, thus that the penis or chest hair has meaning only through meaning linguistically accorded to it. The penis embodies maleness, then, not because of anything special about it, but because of how it is understood. The linguistic obsession with the penis – not its ability to be erect or the pleasure it gives – makes the organ into the key element of the male sex. One critique of this approach is that it effaces the possibility of non-linguistic meaning, in particular that it ignores the possible influence of drives. What if there are in fact natural aspects related to masculinity that are outside language? If there are, for instance, drives that lead men to desire women, then couldn't those drives constitute a certain non-linguistic aspect of masculinity? After they come into existence, those drives may in fact be influenced by language: a biological urge can arise, and then once that urge enters into consciousness and is acted upon, it may be molded by language and culture. I might have drives that create my attraction to women, but how that attraction gets talked about and what I make of that urge is an entirely different question. Perhaps it would make sense, then, to consider a hybrid approach to this question, by which drives or even other biological elements of maleness function in tandem, or perhaps in tension, with the discursively defined aspects of masculinity. Perhaps my masculinity is located in both of those places, somewhere between my drives and the language that I use to make sense of that biological substratum. In the end, my experience of my sex might be based on an oscillation between these two definitional poles, meaning that it is extremely difficult for me to know when language is creating my maleness and when something else is.

A logical question to ask at this point is: why do most cultures tend to assume the idea of sex, to assume two sexes, and to assume them as opposite? One response to this question is that the heteronormative imperative (the injunction to be and appear heterosexual) requires two opposite sexes in order to maintain its hold over reproductive sexuality and to represent reproductive sexuality as purely heterosexual. In this way, the possibility of homosexuality or of other non-standard forms of sexuality (polygamy, *ménages à trois*) can be more effectively invalidated or disbanded. Also, the idea of two opposite sexes implies their complementarity: wholeness equals one man plus one woman, and for these opposites to attract, the man and woman must be clearly defined. But, as mentioned earlier, masculinity may be more linked to this invention of sex than femininity, and the invention of sex may be in part a construct of masculinity as much as of heteronormativity. At the same time, homosexuality should not be assumed to be the opposite of sexual stability either, though gay people may tend to be more open to sexual instability than heterosexuals overall. A gay man can certainly want his men to be men, not be interested in transsexualism, and fear women who pass as men. Whether this desire is already inflected with heteronormativity is a further question that could be posed.

Another way to problematize the issue of sex as original and natural is by reimagining the obligatory order of sex–gender–desire that I discussed earlier, which Judith Butler does in her widely read *Gender Trouble* (1990).[2] I have dealt with the possibility of reorganizing sex→gender→desire by moving gender before sex (since gender creates sex). But what would happen if we changed the order of these three elements in another way by moving desire up to the front? What would the order desire→sex→gender look like? First, maleness would be perceived as a result of a male heterosexual desire (also a category of gender). If that desire exists first, then it may need to create maleness in a certain way in order for heterosexuality to exist. So the stable category of the man has to exist in order for man to be able to desire a woman. On the other hand, improper desire and unstable sexing can go hand in hand: when heterosexuality does not function normally, non-binarized sexual objects can be desired. It is when male heterosexuality somehow becomes blurred or malfunctions that this kind of sexing apparatus is put into question and fissures are created. These gender trouble spots may occur when heterosexual men fall in love with transsexuals or with men who look like women. In David Cronenberg's film *M. Butterfly* (1993), based on David Hwang's play, a married heterosexual man (Gallimard) falls in love with a transgendered woman, who has a penis. The film suggests that his heterosexual desire (which he imagines and which is also racially coded), in this case, literally creates the sex of the other (and his own by implication), despite numerous sexual acts. As a result of perception gone awry, Gallimard kills himself in shame in the final scene of the film. In Neil Jordan's *The Crying Game* (1992), a heterosexual man learns during a moment of sexual intimacy that the person he thought was a biological woman is in fact a transgendered woman with a penis. Despite his initial repulsion, over the course of the film he gets over his initial shock and horror, in a sense recreating sex for himself as he allows himself to love a transgendered woman.

These two examples suggest that if sex is invented through heteronormativity and gender, then sex can also be reinvented by them. In the case of Jordan's film, sex is recreated in a way that resists dominant sexual constructs, while Cronenberg's film shows how a heterosexual man cannot recreate his ideas of sex even when he already loves that sex. In Genesis, a lesser-known form of invented sex is available in the

---

[2]   See Judith Butler, *Gender Trouble: Feminism and the Subversion of Identity* (London: Routledge, 1990), esp. ch. 1.

text, one in which the man and woman are created at the same time and presumably equally ("Male and female He created them"). A kind of gender that resists the male sex as the originary sex is thus already inscribed in the Bible as a kind of counternarrative to the invention of manhood as originary. Because Genesis provides two options in terms of how sex is created, the idea of sex can be invented depending on which narrative is selected.

Performing Masculinity

So we now know that gender is not a natural result of sex, and that the traditional move from sex to gender can work in the other direction as well. If there is no natural sex/gender underneath and there is no sex per se, then what is gender besides that which invents sex? Is there such a thing as gender at all? If there is no core of gender, then how can gender be talked about? One way to think about masculinity from this perspective is to think about masculinity as "performative," an adjective frequently applied to gender under the influence of Butler's *Gender Trouble*. It is not that a football player is doing something natural when he runs around on the field tackling other men. Instead, he is "performing" his masculinity; he is not expressing some kind of core of being. There is no essence, no biology that makes him do what he does on the playing field. He performs masculinity, but that does not mean that there is some underlying gender superimposed on what he is doing. A man performs his masculinity, but he is not working from some kind of originary or cultural script. Rather, his gender performance implicitly refers back to other people's previous actions which give his own actions authority and grounding. The masculinity of his performance on the field is buttressed by a whole series of associations between gender and football that have been made elsewhere. Those previous acts come from numerous cultural sites that are difficult to isolate – *Monday Night Football* on TV, previous football games at the school, discussions about football after class, films about football, etc. There is no original masculinity for our player since there is no original masculinity to refer to directly (see pp. 17–19), but rather there is a conglomeration of practices related to football that he necessarily echoes. For this reason, Butler writes in *Bodies that Matter* that performativity "cannot be taken as the fabrication of the performer's 'will' or 'choice'" (p. 234).

Through the series of acts he performs and the echoes of norms implied therein, his masculinity comes into being. If our hypothetical football player is butch, makes touchdowns, bullies other men in his school, gets sloshed on Friday night, and so on, then this series of acts and his style of doing them – along with the reference to those previously established masculine norms – in effect constitutes his masculinity. Consequently, there is no simple coherence to his masculinity: he may not always do the same thing or perform the same acts. His performance might look different from one week to the next, or from one weekend to another, but he might perform certain acts again and again, which gives the impression of coherence. The absence of coherence does not mean that he or other people do not try to ascribe a certain coherence to his masculinity, or attempt to make it look consistent. They may attempt to create a coherent idea of what a jock means, and what his masculinity looks like. Because of some of his actions, he might be stereotyped as a jock, but that stereotyping is a way to stabilize an endless collection of acts and styles of his that are inherently unstable and ultimately inconsistent. But on the other hand, by virtue of the repetition of his masculinity, by virtue of doing more or less the same thing over a period of time, he may take on a masculine identity that looks a certain way and that appears predictable. The concept of repetition is central to this way of understanding gender: masculinity comes to have meaning and to be perceived as coherent because it is repeated in many instances in ways that are perceived as coherent. Once that coherence is imagined, people may get used to focusing on certain recurring elements of masculinity, and thus ignore or not perceive elements that do not fit in the image that they already have and for various reasons want to propagate.

So it is not the case that the repetition of masculinity shows how natural masculinity really is. The fact that the football player goes out on the field every day and tackles other players and then watches football on television every night does not mean that he is biologically programmed to do so. Rather, it is the necessity of repetition that reveals the hollowness of masculinity underneath. On one level, the repetition of masculinity makes no sense. Why does masculinity have to be repeated, performed again and again? Butler's answer would be that a man has no inner core, no essence, no nature underneath his gender, and that he needs to keep repeating gendered acts to show that masculinity does in fact exist in the face of a gender emptiness or a threat of emptiness. By tackling football players every day, our player is trying to convince us and himself that masculinity is natural and essential.

Butler's notion of gender as "*a corporeal style*" in *Gender Trouble* (p. 139, her emphasis) is a helpful way to think about gendered performance for a number of reasons. When we talk about a style, we may talk about something that characterizes a writer's work (he or she might have a flowery style or a laconic style). The use of the word "style," often employed in a literary sense, is not accidental: a style of masculinity is also closely connected to language. In the same way that gender is constructed via language and discourse, masculinity is also performed in part linguistically. It is what I say that is a good part of my performance. I might employ a certain vocabulary, or I might repeat certain topics (e.g., "bonding" with other "guys" or "dudes"). In addition, it is through language that we understand someone's performance of masculinity, that we give it meaning. The performer of masculinity does not have full control over how his masculinity is defined by others. Further, a given style of language recurs frequently in a writer's prose, it characterizes much of a gendered oeuvre, but it does not mean that it is entirely deterministic. A literary style does not include everything written: a writer may change styles over the course of time or might break out of a style in a certain work, for instance. Similarly, style is a way to think about masculinity as approximate. Because the jock acts in a certain way over the course of time, he might be perceived as having a collection of masculine traits that come to be defined as his masculinity, like the writer who has a collection of texts seen as having a certain style. He might excel on the football field, not do so well academically, dress in sports garb, etc., and this collection of repeated acts might be viewed under the label of jock. But to imagine or to talk of his masculinity in this way is to simplify gender and not to take into account all his other acts that do not fit coherently into this rubric. What happens when this jock loses on the sports field? Or when he scores straight As in his courses? His overall style might remain in place, but he necessarily has moments when he does not follow this style.

Another reason to think about masculinity as a kind of style is that it implies something open to change. Like a style of clothing (we talk about what is "in style" or "out of style"), a gendered style might be in at a given time period, but it will not be in forever. So a collection of masculine acts might seem to define masculinity in a given time or in a given place, but that style will change as well. The knight might have been a kind of masculine style in the middle ages, but it has since passed away as a major style. Knighthood is a series of masculine performances, composed of acts and styles (saving ladies in distress, taking on other knights, wearing armor, fighting with a lance, and so on). So while certain aspects of that style might recur in modern forms of masculinity, knighthood itself is a style that has more or less disappeared as a discrete category. However, the idea of the knight as definitional of masculinity did not disappear at the end of the middle ages, but remains as one aspect of modern masculinity (even if some would say it is a rarity). Thus, another reason to think about gender as a style is that while a style goes out of fashion, it does not completely disappear. Someone might take on the style of the 1950s or 1960s as a personal style, or we might have a sixties party in which everyone dresses in the garb of that period. In the same way that older styles of clothing still circulate in culture, older styles of masculinity can also be appropriated. So while men do not go around acting like Sir Lancelot all the time, elements of a knightly definition of masculinity might still be a part of how one's masculinity operates. A man might be gallant with women, or a woman might describe a man she likes as her knight in shining armor. This idea of masculinity as a style permits a complicated view of masculinity beyond stereotypes as it takes into account how stereotypes function.

If a man performs his masculinity, where does he get that performance or that style? Does he invent it himself? Clearly, some men perform similar masculinities as other men, which means that they are performing something that is culturally fabricated and not invented by an individual man himself. Traveling throughout different cultures makes it very obvious how diverse styles of masculinity can be, and even intraculturally diverse styles of masculinity can be located. On the other hand, there is no simple gender script that a given man follows to the letter. It might be the case that a man follows a gender script when he plays football: he tries to follow certain rules and certain norms and might carry his body in a certain way, and his performances refer to other performances. But there is inevitably also individual variation in how he plays the sport. His own style might be an individual one: he has his own way of punting, or kicking, etc. Those individualized aspects of his masculinity can still be considered masculine, just that they are outside some kind of gendered norm. So to perform masculinity might best be conceived of as a combination or a hybrid of culturally defined performances on the one hand and individualized ones on the other hand. That combination is so complex, however, that finding the line between cultural and individual performance is nearly impossible.

At the same time, certain styles of masculinity are more codified than others, and less open to individual variation than others. There are medieval texts on how the knight should act, nineteenth-century texts on what it means to be a dandy, and a handbook purporting to represent what a metrosexual is supposed to be (*The Metrosexual Guide to Style* (2003)), with rules on behavior and the like. Much of what defines the metrosexual is a series of acts, while the definition also includes a literal corporal style that should be undertaken (grooming, clothing) to follow this gender presentation.

Despite these codes (in this case, written codes), a metrosexual may very well perform his masculinity in a partially codified manner, as he might have a hybrid style or as he might perform certain aspects in another way. There is always room for maneuver in any kind of code: no spelled-out code can provide ways to act in all circumstances. Another way in which the code of masculinity can be seen as not strict is that men who do not consider themselves metrosexuals per se might appropriate certain aspects of the metrosexual model, meaning that the established code itself is not followed except in small parts, even as aspects of it are disseminated in culture. For these reasons, then, the idea of a code cannot encompass all aspects of a given type of masculinity, and thus it makes more sense to talk about performance than about codes or scripts. These terms and the ideas behind them do not allow for individual variation, and they suggest that there is underlying gender. My culture might create masculinity scripts that I follow, but I never follow those scripts to the letter. Further, those scripts are not words engraved on a page: those definitions are changing even as the scripts are written and rewritten over time and across cultures. Further, because masculinity is so complicated, it is simply not possible to provide all the codes necessary. Situations necessarily arise in which any imagined code cannot explain a priori how to conduct oneself. There may be certain guidelines to masculinity, but those guidelines necessarily contain cracks and fissures.

The performance of masculinity does not just pertain to the gendered or social aspects of masculinity. We have seen how sex and gender can never be disassociated in the end, and that inextricable link applies here as well. A man might perform aspects of his gender when he performs a jocky masculinity, but he may also perform his maleness. In other words, his sex might be thought of as performed along with his gender. He might, for example, ascribe a certain importance to his penis, talk about or perform an act to make his penis seem central to his subjectivity, or show off his chest hair as a key element of his maleness. These performances are ways to construct a certain idea of sex that springs from an idea of gender, which might be viewed as more convincing acts of masculinity because they are seemingly grounded in nature.

A further reason for thinking about masculinity as a style is that the actual relation between style and clothing is important. On one level, the kind of clothing that a man wears is central to the construction of masculinity: clothing is quite simply a key aspect of masculinity. But clothing is also central to gendered performance of masculinity. When I put on a tie and three-piece suit, I might become aware of how I am performing masculinity, by participating in a certain style of masculinity that may or may not feel natural to me. There is nothing natural about what clothing I wear, as there is nothing natural about my gender. Wearing a coat and tie is one way for me to perform my gender, to put one aspect of gender on or to become conscious of donning part of my gender. My avoidance of certain kinds of clothing might also be important: by avoiding overly stylish clothes and wearing a T-shirt, jeans, and baseball cap, I might be performing a certain kind of unmarked masculinity. By avoiding clothes perceived as feminine, I might perform my masculinity. Or, in rare circumstances, I might dress in women's clothes as a paradoxical way to perform masculinity. When I put on a dress and my chest hair sticks out where my cleavage should be, I can perform my masculinity by contrast even as my style of masculinity is an infrequent (but not unheard of) form. As masculinity is not something that can simply be donned, clothing does not provide me with my gender. Rather, the relation between the clothing and my experience of the clothing (or other people's experience of it) constitute the performance. If I feel that donning women's clothes masculinizes, then that gender performance will be very different from one in which I feel that the clothing feminizes or neuters me.

The counter-intuitive cross-dressing example above suggests that masculine performance can include performing the other in order to perform masculinity. I might put on a dress to perform a gender that is not mine, but in essence I am showing that my being like a woman is not possible (if I really wanted to look like a woman, I would shave my chest and do other things to pass better). I am showing that I cannot perform a brand of femininity, that when I try to perform femininity, something breaks down and my performance of femininity is marked as fake. So my performance of masculinity includes evoking and rendering other types of performances impossible. This kind of reverse-performance does not have to pertain to dress. A recurring example from popular culture is late-night talk-show hosts who make homoerotic jokes with members of their band or with male guests. From the perspective here, the point of doing this would be to show that the performance of male homosexuality is not possible, that it can only be revealed as comic (whether a man actually wants to imagine what it would be like to be homosexual is another question), and that queer performance is just that – pure performance with no underlying essence or reality. What this might do is attempt to affirm heterosexuality as non-performative and thus stable, in opposition to performative homosexuality.

While a man might follow a cultural style or create his own style, his performance is far from coherent all the time, and his performance necessarily breaks down at certain moments and is revealed as incoherent. For Butler, drag can allegorize the breakdown of performance.[3] When a woman passes as a man as a drag king, s/he can in fact be revealing that gender is something that is performed as well, that masculinity operates much as the actual show does. S/he is performing performance, revealing how there is no originary masculinity underneath gender. A drag king who does not pass as a man might also show how masculinity is performance since s/he destabilizes the coherent presentation of masculinity. This kind of performance does not mean that gender has something underneath: a woman who cross-dresses as a man does not have a gender underneath that she is transforming when she dresses as a man. Rather, what she seems to be is what her gender is. Drag is far from the only way in which masculinity can be revealed to be an imitative performance, but it functions as one of many possible representations of how gender can be shown as performative. It is important to state, however, that not all drag performs this function, as drag can also be normative and attempt to contain gender instability. Examples of drag should thus be taken on a case-by-case basis to determine their relation to performativity.

As already discussed, the very repetition of gender suggests its inessential nature, but artistic constructs can also perform a similar function. The daily examples of normative "performativity" that

---

[3] See Butler, *Gender Trouble*, 134–41.

I have used in this chapter can be distinguished from "performances." While the former resemble ideologically based practices, the latter refer more to actual stagings of gender which are often contained or intentional (theater, film, music, performance art, etc.).[4] Like gender performance as discussed here, a "performance" in the common sense of the term can show that there is nothing stable behind gender and that there is no original form. Masculine performativity might function in a seemingly coherent way as it is what Butler calls a "reiteration of a norm or set of norms" that "conceals or dissimulates the conventions of which it is a repetition" (p. 12). While a performative act reiterates gender norms, a performance in this sense resists them. Texts with images related to theatricality or clothing might be revelatory of how gender is a performed, and theatrical or clothing metaphors might serve as symbols of gender performativity. Likewise, acting itself might be taken as a metaphor for performativity, or an avenue whereby gender can be revealed as arbitrary. Because a man is literally playing another man (other than himself), he can be seen as performing that role and by extension performing his own role. Or a man may play two roles in a play, each with a different brand of masculinity. The arbitrary nature of masculinity may be revealed by the fact that he changes masculinities, that he performs two (or more) masculinities. An actual actor whose masculinity is well known and whose gender has to be transformed for a given role might also have a similar effect. By virtue of performing as another kind of man, he may be showing that masculinity is literally performative or, alternately, his ability to perform in different ways may be part of his overall performance and give the sense that his ability to adapt is part of his gender subjectivity.

Parody is another important aspect of the breakdown of male gender performance, in the special as well as the common sense of the word. People parody masculinity at numerous points in day-to-day life, of course, but they may also parody what Butler calls "the very idea of an original."[5] The muscular jock who dons an apron and makes a turkey dinner for his mother may be showing not that he is feminized, but that there is no original masculinity in the first place. He is revealing that masculinity has no rules or scripts behind it. Certain texts can

---

4   For this distinction, see Butler, *Bodies that Matter*, 234.
5   Butler, *Gender Trouble*, 138.

reveal the mechanism of parody as well. A TV sitcom in which a man is often shown as not meeting expectations about his masculinity may be parodying masculinity's performance of an idea by showing how a specific masculine man cannot perform the ideal (e.g., *Big Love*, *Home Improvement*, *Coach*).

Gender can also be shown as performative when mechanisms of masculinity appear as overdetermined. If a man acts excessively masculine or performs too much or too well, it can become clear to the viewer or to himself that he is performing his gender. For in order to hide masculinity's performativity, a man may have to limit his performance and contain it as non-excessive. I might say the same about the over-repetition of masculinity: a man who acts too often in a way perceived as hyper-masculine calls attention to his masculinity as something performed. If masculinity is too present, it may end up appearing as comic. McKay's film *Talladega Nights* (2006) could be taken as one example of a cinematic performance of the parody of masculinity through overdetermination. On the other hand, the parody of masculine performance can evoke the difficulty and anxiety of performing an ideal masculinity and then restabilize that difficulty as a new type of masculinity that makes it appear as a new, coherent brand of masculinity. If the gap between an ideal and a non-ideal performance turns into a new type of coherent-seeming performance, then there is an attempt to take control over performativity, to position a new type of man as another naturalized form of masculinity. So the parody itself can turn into its own performance, eclipsing the original object of parody.

With these various parodic possibilities, how can we know when masculinity is parodic? Because masculinity can be called a parody only by someone, the relation between a performance and those who view it and between a performance and those who perform it determines whether it is coded as performance. Whether a performance is considered normative or not is also dependent on context. While some performances might be widely agreed upon as parody, others might be seen as ambiguous. James Bond films might fall in this category: some might read them as hyper-masculine parodies of the performance of masculinity, while others as a classic performance of gender that tries to posit a coherent masculine norm (and in turn influences other performances). Still others might see Bond's masculinity as both, as an oscillation between parody and performance. Perceptions of whether he is parodying masculinity or just performing it might change over the course of the film or from scene to scene. In fact, masculinity itself could be viewed as always moving between parody and performance. While drag can be pure parody and while many would agree that certain representations of masculinity are entirely parodic, other representations can be one or the other at different moments, and that movement can itself define masculinity. As I go about a typical day, I alternate between performing masculinity and parodying that very performance. So the inability ever to fully know whether Bond's masculinity is parody or not might be a way of thinking about or even defining his masculinity.

Bibliography

This chapter relies largely on the work of Judith Butler, and in particular on her ground-breaking *Gender Trouble : Feminism and the Subversion of Identity* (London: Routledge, 1990). The concepts of sex, gender, and desire are Butler's focus, not masculinity per se. *Bodies that Matter* (New York: Routledge, 1993) extends the questions treated in *Gender Trouble* to the issue of materiality. On performance versus performativity, see her "Critically Queer," *Gay and Lesbian Quarterly* 1 (1993): 17–32. On Butler and performance studies, see Jon McKenzie, "Genre Trouble: (The) Butler Did It," in *The Ends of Performance*, ed. Peggy Phelan and Jill Lane (New York: New York University Press, 1998), 217–35.

On the idea of masculinity and parody, see, for example, Robert Hanke, "The 'Mock-Macho' Situation Comedy: Hegemonic Masculinity and its Reiteration," *Western Journal of Communication* 62, no. 1 (Winter 1998): 74–93.

Other work in which masculinity is read from a Butlerian perspective includes: Erik Gunderson, *Staging Masculinity: The Rhetoric of Performance in the Roman World* (Ann Arbor: University of Michigan Press, 2000); Andrew Perchuk and Helaine Posner, eds., *The Masculine Masquerade: Masculinity and Representation* (Cambridge, MA: MIT Press, 1995) (see especially Steven Cohan, "The Spy in the Gray Flannel Suit: Gender Performance and the Representation of Masculinity in *North by Northwest*"); Thomas Strychacz, *Hemingway's Theaters of Masculinity* (Baton Rouge: Louisiana State University Press, 2003).

For a historically grounded book that makes very concrete the idea that gender creates sex, see Thomas Laqueur, *Making Sex: Body and Gender from the Greeks to Freud* (Cambridge, MA: Harvard University Press, 1990).

For a scientific approach to the issues of the chapter, see the work of Anne Fausto-Sterling, especially *Sexing the Body: Gender Politics and the Construction of Sexuality* (New York: Basic Books, 2000).

4

Theorizing the Male Body

Masculinities in Theory aims to question the naturalness of masculinity and to critically examine attempts to produce it as natural. It would be impossible to consider this aspect of gender without dealing with what might be the most central aspect of masculinity, namely the male body. For the male body might appear to be the most natural element of masculinity: after all, almost all men have a penis, testicles, facial hair, an Adam's apple, a prostate, and the Y chromosome. So, how can we talk about these biological aspects of masculinity as unstable, as fluid, or as in movement? Is there really anything unstable about the male body?

Whereas the body might be a physical entity, it is difficult to say that the male body can be objectively defined and that it exists on its own without cultural influence. The male body has a particularly close connection to culture and to discourse and is one of the main avenues through which culture attempts to construct masculinity. As key elements of culture that construct masculinity for various reasons and for various ends, capitalism, the military, and the nation all depend heavily on corporality in order to function efficiently. And in turn, those constructed bodies are disseminated outside the original discourse, becoming copies of that discourse that in turn influence other areas of culture. The male body functions as a kind of tabula rasa or inscriptive surface for masculinity and for culture, and discourse is inscribed on that matter, asserting its power through inscription and reinscription.

My approach to the male body is also predicated on the idea that individual perception of masculinity determines what it is, and that we can never move outside the constraints of gendered perception. Certainly every man has a body, but the meaning accorded to that body is far from objective. In chapter 1, I discussed how masculinity exists as dialogic, as "co-being." The male body, too, can be approached as dialogic: the meaning given to a body differs according to the relation between that body and the perceiver of that body. So even if most every male body has a penis, there is no natural or ontological meaning contained in that organ. It is the meaning of the penis (and of the male body in a larger sense) that is constructed and not natural. Since we experience reality through meanings ascribed to given objects, the male body cannot be avoided as a topic in this kind of book on masculinity.

I might think about this question of perception within the framework established in chapter 3: if gender constructs sex, if masculinity determines what we think the physicality of a man is, then gender is determinative of the male body. For the body is the prime conduit of sex. How do we understand the idea that the male body is determined by how we imagine masculinity? We might retroactively project back onto the male body an idea that masculinity is something hard, imagining the male body as hard even if it is not actually that way very often (or ever). We might also imagine the male and female bodies as very distinct when in fact they are not so distinct because we have a gendered idea in our heads that men and women are opposite or discrete sexes. What we think the male body is can only be influenced by what we already think masculinity is, and we ignore certain aspects of the male body because they do not have much relation to our perceptions. How often, for example, do we imagine someone's masculinity as dependent on how visible their Adam's apple is or what they do with their prostate? In the following pages, I would like to consider the male body from the two perspectives outlined here: first, I will discuss what it means for culture to construct or give meaning to the male body, and then I will focus on how an individual gives meaning to the male body.

Culture and the Male Body

The male body has a particular importance for many approaches to masculinity, but it is also a key locus of cultural meaning in a larger sense. Many issues related to masculinity play themselves out corporally. As we will see in chapter 8, for instance, national constructs are often related to the male body, which serves as a locus where ideas about the nation are constructed, worked out, or problematized through a kind of body politic. In this sense, then, to be able to read the male body is also to be able to read other cultural issues or anxieties in miniature as they get projected onto the body.

The male body might be thought about as constructed because various cultural discourses or images create an idea of the male body. This approach might be viewed as one subcategory of the cultural construct of masculinity. Images, myths, discourse, and practices all construct an idea of the male body: sport, advertising, art, medicine, law, religion and the military, for instance, all depict male bodies in a way that inflects what we think the body is or should be. Without a certain kind of male body, war would be more difficult to wage and, consequently, military discourse stipulates the construction of a kind of male body. The prevalence of the Adam and Eve myth sends the message that the male body is the originary body from which the female body is created, so some might believe that the idea of the husband as the norm and of the wife as his extension is already proven by this myth. Under the influence of capitalism, images of muscular, fit male bodies may encourage men to buy gym memberships, health foods, or exercise equipment. In addition to the influence of these cultural discourses, as in chapter 3, two discrete sexes are usually created or assumed through the cultural discourse of heteronormativity, a creation mediated through the body.

One aspect of this cultural inscription is that the male body may be rendered illegible or unreadable, unable to be interpreted as an ambiguous text. By making the body open to less variation and by normalizing it, cultural discourses may better control how it is understood, and signs on the body can be assumed to contain a preexistent meaning to be understood in a given way. Discursive constraints may provide the male body with few choices in hairstyle, clothing, and other variables, and consequently discourse can seem to function seamlessly and imperceptibly through the body. The military male body might be composed of signs that are easily legible to anyone who sees that body, through a certain uniform and a certain haircut, but that legibility also attempts to keep the body from being read in any other way except as military, providing a given and stable meaning to masculinity and helping it to function seamlessly. The uniformed body of the businessman might be another example of this kind of universal inscription.

Cultural practices construct ideas on the male body by transforming actions into physical aspects of the body. Gesturing is an important way in which the male body is constructed through repeated practices as a man or boy is taught to move in a certain way. For instance, a boy might be taught, when he throws a baseball, not to "throw like a girl," and over time his body takes on this dictum as natural-seeming and a given culture takes on this dictum as part of its culture. Another way to think about this question is as one of habit and of habit's inscription on the male body, or as Pierre Bourdieu refers to a related phenomenon in *Masculine Domination*, as the "*habitus.*" By virtue of the repetition of various cultural practices, the male body ends up appearing to be defined naturally, but in fact habit has effectively become corporality and its inscriptive nature hidden. The habit of men cutting their hair short might make short hair on men seem natural, and in fact, in the past, short hair on men has been taken to be biological.

One of the ways in which culture hides the male body's constructedness is by making it appear eternal. If the male body can be shown to have been a certain way in the past and to be that way still, doesn't that mean that such a male body is eternal? The ultimate example may be the classical idea of the white male body. By idealizing the male body as muscular and perfectly proportioned in various historical contexts (the ancient world, the Renaissance, classicism, etc.), cultures are attempting to construct a transhistorical male body that appears outside temporal and cultural change. But that ideal does not exist, in part because the local reality of the male body in any period is different from the ideal. This belief in an eternal body also forgets periods in which the ideal male body is not so classical or muscular (e.g., the middle ages or the Enlightenment), as well as other kinds of bodies that could be idealized but are not (e.g., the muscular female or the black male body). An ideal male body, then, implies a whole series of corporal exclusions that can themselves be studied as part of the social construct of the ideal.

Practice can be complicated, and hard to examine as imposition on the tabula rasa of the body. One reason for this difficulty is that practice might actually change the body itself, with the result that the imagined body becomes a self-fulfilling prophecy. Masculinity is often connected to eating meat: men might like to grill and to eat meat, and a large hamburger might be seen as masculine and a veggie burger as feminine. Because what one ingests is tied to the body ("you are what you eat"), masculinity, too, can be imagined as "meaty." But in turn, that gendered practice doubles back onto the male body and constructs it in a certain way. By virtue of eating more meat over time, for instance, the male body might actually become more meaty, larger and consequently more linked to muscle growth in the mind. That construct of the body can then double back onto the cultural idea of eating meat, reaffirming and validating the cultural practice. Meaty men might buy grills, host barbeques, and consume a lot of meat. Practice and the body thus exist in a circular relation, each beefing up the other over time in an imperceptible way.

The body does not have to be constructed slowly over the course of a long period of time, as it can be transformed by immediate practices. With circumcision, for instance, culture quickly transforms the male body into a kind of body that it may consider masculine (or not masculine, as the case may be). The result of that practice might come to be considered natural as some imagine the circumcised penis as the incarnation of the penis instead of as one possible type of penis, but the practice itself is culturally defined. While an actual circumcision is momentary, the cultural discourse that makes it seem masculine, erotic, or beautiful operates over a long period of time. Another example of immediate change in the body would be the heroic wound. A man can be wounded in battle very quickly, transforming the male body and masculinity along with it. The wounded body can be taken as a sign of military masculinity: it might be decorated or considered manly. Like circumcision, the wound is embedded in cultural discourses that have already constructed ideas about it (film, political discourse, etc.). That change in the body is not a gradual habit, however, but a sudden body-changing experience that is nonetheless coded by culture.

Power, Resistance, and the Male Body

We know that discourse is central to cultural inscription on the body and to the assumption of power on the body to create subjectivities. In the case of meat, advertisements for steak, for grills, for fast food, and for steakhouses contribute to the construct, perhaps implying that the "non-meaty" male is not masculine. Medical discourse might construct erectile dysfunction as a problem, but it does so via the body. The idea that power projects itself onto the body is often understood as an imposition onto a non-hegemonic form of subjectivity. As discussed in chapter 1 through Foucault, power and discourse are inscribed in gender constructs and create various gendered forms of subjectivity, but this process takes place through the medium of the body. One result of such projections might be a hysterical female body, an unlawful gay male body, a docile Asian male body, or a criminal black male body. In this framework, marginal masculinities are constructed through discourse and power. The criminal black male body can be arrested, incarcerated, and feared, leaving the white male body to discipline and control the other's fate. On the other hand, a male body in the power nexus can be constructed as not a problem, falling outside discourse as an invisible body incarnating the norm. If power operates through the body, it fabricates not simply what Foucault calls "docile bodies" but also resistant bodies. The gay male body might be constructed by power as sexually excessive, and that construct might also be a way to construct a different kind of moderate male heterosexual body. By virtue of creating or calling attention to a gay male body, a certain construct is created or reaffirmed, but a response against negative constructs may also become more possible or likely. In this example, ground is provided to prove the moderation of the homosexual or the immoderation of the heterosexual in opposition to stereotypical constructs.

What happens with this resistance model, however, when it is a question of non-marginal masculinities? What happens between power/ discourse and the male body when the body in question is a white, heterosexual body that is not coded as marginal? Can one talk about a docile or a resistant unmarked male body? How does this body, given power over others, function in this model? For if this body remains docile, it may very well be given power precisely because it is docile. The military male body is accorded power by discourse, even if its power means the solider accepts wholeheartedly the military's construct. On the other hand, the male body, by virtue of remaining docile, is caught somewhere between power and lack of power. Capitalistic discourse might construct a suit-and-tie male body as the normal body, and as the body able to succeed in business and to make money, but that body is also subject to the rules of capitalism. Or, political discourse and the state might construct a military male body, but that body, based on strength and other warlike qualities, is twofold: it is billed as hegemonic, able to fight and destroy foreign enemies, but it is also docile because of its subjugation to the interests of the state. Discourse might create an image of a male body of a certain physical type, including certain ways of moving the body, certain gestures, and certain clothing. As these examples suggest, that body is both docile and empowered, and in the end, the male body could be considered as located somewhere between docility and power, never fully one nor the other.

In turn, that body doubles back into culture, influencing its own conception of what the male body might be considered to be in its ideal state. Young boys, even before legal military age, might begin to imagine their bodies in this way: they might wear camouflage clothes, or imagine certain ways of moving the body (e.g., making their body parts into weapons). So while boys might experience this type of imagined male body as empowering them, in fact that male body is not simply defined by power, since it is in fact also imbricated with another kind of power (the military). The male body, then, in this case is also in a complicated position somewhere between docility and empowerment.

Consequently, attempts to alter the male body should be questioned as to the extent to which they reinscribe power, and the extent to which they resist normative cultural constructs. Tattooing, for instance, could be viewed as both normative and resistant. Culture teaches me to have control of my body, and tattooing is a logical extension of that control. I get a tattoo, endure the pain, and in permanently altering my body in the way that I dictate (by selecting the type of tattoo and deciding where it goes), I reaffirm the cultural idea of masculinity as control over the body. Tattooing can also be a way to take interpretive control of the body. I provide literal signs on the body so that my own body does not function so much as a series of ambiguous signs to be read and interpreted by the viewer. I try to stabilize what my body says to those who see it. Tattooing can also be a way to resist cultural normalization of the body and give it another legibility defined by the man himself. Businessmen who want to resist an unmarked male body might get tattoos under their suits to resist the business world's hegemony over the male body. The interpretive difficulty in these cases of bodily manipulation is to determine whether the tattoo implies a normative inscription, a resistance to hegemony, or both normativity and resistance.

My discussion so far has assumed that the male body is culturally defined. But how in fact can one separate the biological from the cultural? For there may be natural aspects to the male body: what do we do with drives? Testosterone? It is what we make of these that is important, especially through the language that we employ, but it is also the difficulty of ultimately separating the biological from the cultural that should be recognized. The penis is probably the ultimate case in point. It is what we make of the body – along with what culture makes of it – that defines it. But there is still a certain unease with thinking purely in these terms: many men would probably say that there is something special about the penis, that the penis provides a pleasure that no other body part does. They might say that penile pleasure is not so different from female genital pleasure, thus that the penis does not create an absolute definition of masculinity as totally unlike femininity. They might also admit that there are other male bodily parts whose eroticism has been repressed in the service of making the penis the prime definitional part of the male body (nipples or the prostate for example). But they might, on the other hand, also say that penile pleasure is so special and intense that it has to be definitionally related to masculinity, that the penis does not have a special role because of the language and cultural constructs that we use to ascribe meaning to it. Rather, the penis has a special place on its own: culture and language might in fact add to what it is, might transform what it is. But the penis has some kind of natural or extra-cultural aspect to it outside these constructs. One might ask, too, if the same could be said for other parts of the male body. Can the basic experience of having facial hair, something men tend to be aware of on a regular basis, define masculinity? On one level, this is a question of chicken and egg: the male body might be constructed by culture and language, but could it not also be the case that culture and language are *already* inscribed with the male body, that the male body has already influenced language and culture before they have a chance to construct masculinity? To return to an earlier example: "manhood" refers to both the penis and gender identity, and this double sense might reveal how we collapse sex and gender into one category. But what if that collapse itself was already influenced by a perceived relation between sex and gender which preexists language? What if the penis was already considered a thing that linked gender and sex? What if language arose under the influence of the very body that it describes and defines? Or what if the distinction between language and non-language was ultimately impossible to discern? Perhaps the best response to these complicated questions, in the end, would be to say or to assume that biological and cultural approaches to the body function dialogically and are both always at play.

Imagining the Male Body

Culture, discourse, and power may construct the male body in various ways, and that body may or may not resist those constructions. But the way in which the body is understood cannot entirely be subsumed under the category of culture, even as it cannot be entirely discarded either. My question in this section, then, is: how does the psyche imagine the male body? To begin to answer this question, it is important to consider the relation between the psyche and the body and, especially, to remember that the psyche can never actually see the full body. As men go about their daily lives, most of the time they see their arms or their hands, for instance, but most of their body remains covered. Even when naked, a man cannot see most of his body. And naked in front of the mirror, he can never see all of his body at once. So his perception of his body is always partial and fragmented, never accurate. In a very concrete way, male perceptions of the body are imagined from a non-objective vantage point. In addition, if perception is taken as the basis of existence (how we see the world is how it is), then what the psyche perceives the male body to be is what it in effect is. Men may have a certain image of their own masculinity and project it onto their body, in much the same way as gender constructs sex. A man might perceive himself as masculine and thus see his body as muscular or his penis as large. Whether he actually is muscular or whether his penis is large is beside the point (and how can "large" be defined anyway?). His psyche projects itself onto his body, meaning that his body is more about his psyche than some objective reality in flesh and blood. Though the psyche constructs the body, the way in which it functions is not devoid of previous corporal influence. Like language, the psyche may already be affected by bodily sensations that in turn influence how it comes to perceive corporality. Because of penile pleasure, for instance, the psyche may see that body part in a different way from the thumb or the big toe.

The psyche can also imagine the body in which it is housed somewhere else, displacing it onto other objects that allow the psyche to represent the body in ways in which it wants it to appear. Some might project the male body onto the body of a car, taking great care of it, washing it frequently, making sure it has no dents, and so on. With this kind of projection, the perceived characteristics of that object can reaffirm or create an image of the body that the psyche wants it to have. In the car example, projecting the male body onto the body of the car can affirm an idea or an image of the male body as hard, as fast, or as powerful. Or, taken as an imagined approximation of the male form, armor might permit a man to view his body as impenetrable or resistant to attack.

In this approach, the body is the true subject of experience since one can only experience the world through the body and, consequently, masculinity can only be experienced corporally. There is no possibility of a disembodied masculinity defined solely outside or without the body. The body's mediation of the experience of masculinity can be internal or external: I experience masculinity in relation to my own body, and I experience masculinity in relation to other bodies. The dialogic nature of gender applies to the body as it applies to masculinity itself. If the dialogue between me and my body defines an element of my masculinity, so does the dialogue between my body and other bodies. That dialogue can be created by two discrete bodies – my imagined body and another one that I perceive. I see a body naked at the gym, and the relation between his body and mine defines masculinity for me or for him, a dialogue that is different for each of us. Such a definition through corporal dialogue can take place when two bodies perceived as different are in dialogue, as for example, when a man has sex with a woman. He might experience the dialogue of the body as difference, as similarity, or as a movement between sameness and difference. An African-American man might be in corporal dialogue with the body of a white man and define his masculinity through this dialogue (again, as difference, similarity, or movement between similarity and difference).

This perception-driven approach does not mean that the body cannot be reimagined or perceived differently. As the body changes, the psyche can change too. The aging process as displayed on the body might redefine how a man understands masculinity. A balding man may come to see his baldness as virile or erotic whereas he used to see only a full head of hair in those terms. On the other hand, a fixed perception can lead one to change the body to conform to an idea. A male subject might attempt to revamp his body in order to reinvent sex in the service of gender, through steroids, pec implants, or penile enhancement, for example. Once a man has pec implants, it becomes difficult to say whether that aspect of the body is defined as sex or gender: those implants are a direct result of his gender (his idea of what the male body should be), but, once in place, they also become part of his sex. This kind of transformation can also take place through objects that are not actually part of the sexed body but change its physical shape or form. In the Renaissance, for instance, noble men wore codpieces as extensions of their penises. While codpieces are articles of clothing, they also alter how the body gets imagined and at the time they were often perceived as essential elements of the body, inseparable from the penis.

While I have discussed cultural constructs and then perception-based ones in order to lay out two separate ways of thinking about the body, it is in fact often difficult to keep them separate. How can we really know when culture writes through the male body, and when the self imagines the male body in a certain way? The man who gets pec implants might reimagine his body with larger pecs, but he is already influenced by various cultural discourses and images in which large pecs denote masculinity. And, in turn, all those psyches that perceive pecs as masculine produce discourses or images that subsequently propagate the construct.

Although perception and culture may function together to construct an idea of the male body, there is no reason that cultural constructs and individual ones have to be harmonious. Cultures may attempt to construct their norms on the male body, but the body cannot necessarily support those norms. A culture might project an image or discourse of muscularity, but an individual man may not imagine his body as muscular. In addition, culture does not present a harmonious image or discourse of the body either, and the psyche does not imagine a harmonious vision of the body itself. In such a case, there is tension between what culture wants the male body to be and what the body is or wants to become. An adolescent boy might be caught between his own image of what he thinks his body should be, and what he perceives his body to be in actuality. And if the desire for muscularity is perceived as an ascent, a move upward in terms of his acquired masculinity (the more muscle I have, the more of a man I am), then that boy would be caught somewhere on a muscularity continuum, and would possibly always be dealing with an anxiety of never being able to simply achieve a state of ideal muscularity.

If this kind of culture–psyche tension arises, the male psyche may also learn to assuage – or may attempt to assuage – the anxiety. One way in which this can happen is through an imagined self-deprivation of the body, by trying to move outside the realm of corporality itself. Ignoring their body, men might consider it manly to conquer pain or illness not by treating it medically but by pretending that it does not exist. The influential Cartesian tradition established in the seventeenth century considered the mind and the body as separate, with the man linked to reason and the mind and the woman linked to the body, and with the mind defined as masculine and the body as feminine. In this way, the very concept of, or focus on, the body is coded as feminine, and to have a body is to be like a woman. Thus, masculinity might be projected onto abstract bodies linked with power (like the nation, as we will see in chapter 8), while the female body is projected onto actual physical objects (Coke bottles, mountains or other geographies). This uneven projection of bodies has the effect of linking the female body with the physical realm and the male body with the non-physical. Projecting masculinity onto the body of a car might not be about the physicality of the male body, then, but about the power or speed of the car and, by extension, the power and speed of masculinity. Consequently, the car would be not a physical projection of masculinity and a second body, but an affirmation of a man's intangible phallus or of male power as displayed on the body. A man's large, speedy sports car does not mean that he has another body, but that he has the perceived abstract qualities of that car in his own masculinity.

Another way in which male subjects may try to assuage their anxiety of corporality is by speaking the anxiety of the male body, as a way to release it and to separate masculinity from its construct as always self-assured. Anxiety about the body, then, would be not an aberration from masculinity, but part of what defines it. A less narrow and more expressive discourse of the male body could be envisioned, through narratives about castration anxiety, disability, body image, illness, or impotence which position or embrace male subjectivity outside an ideal state. In so doing, male subjects may be less likely to project the concept of corporality itself onto the female body since they would be admitting an experience of corporality that does not affirm dominance or power.

If masculinity can be defined through opposition with its others (especially women and gay men), it can also be articulated through another opposition – the split or tension between the male body and masculinity – by which the male body is viewed as a possible form of alterity for male subjectivity. In this case, the male body does not simply fall outside muscularity since it does not conform to its imagined self. Rather, the opposition between the male body and masculinity might be the very thing that defines masculinity: the attempt to transform the male body into something that it is not might be a struggle of masculinity that actually comes to define it. From this movement-centered perspective, it is not the case that the bodybuilder simply embodies or represents masculinity: rather, masculinity would be defined by the bodybuilder's constant striving to make the body correspond to some image that the psyche has of it, and to make and then keep that other body. Or, it may be the gap between that muscular image and the male psyche that defines masculinity. A man who walks around shirtless strutting his big pecs does not simply incarnate masculinity: his masculinity can be defined instead by the dialogic relation between that man and the discourse or image of the male body in his mind.

The dialogue between the discourse of virility and the impotent man would be a way to consider masculinity in these terms. It is not so much that the impotent man is not a man: that would be too simplistic to say, since no single thing on its own defines masculinity. He might feel demasculinized at certain moments, but he might feel masculinized at others. His impotence might mean that at other moments he remasculinizes himself in other ways. In fact, he might try to remasculinize the self in sex, looking for other ways to give pleasure to another person and transforming how masculinity is defined. But, on another level, his impotence might be something from which he suffers as he imagines himself as unmanly under the influence of his cultural context. In this case, it is the movement or the tension between the culturally defined male body (what the body should be) and the imagined body (what the body is or is not) that defines his masculinity.

This kind of tension or anxiety can be highly stressful for masculinity and suggests an important way in which men are "dominated by their domination," or in which masculinity functions as other to the male body (and vice versa). The rigidity of certain male bodies, or the focus on the penis and the erection as sexual constructs, might make it difficult or impossible for men to experience pleasure or intimacy. If masculinity does not allow for a focus on the male body, men may suffer in the end, for example because they avoid medical treatment or avoid treating certain medical problems. This anxiety-based approach to the male body can be taken together with the idea that the male body tends to be empowered and privileged. One could consider how one approach relates to the other, how the male body's own anxiety about itself creates the desire or need to dominate other bodies, or how the need to dominate other bodies evokes anxiety about the male body.

This kind of tension between culture and perception can be considered through the disabled male body. Disability can be experienced as a demasculinization, and a missing arm or leg represented as a symbolic castration. Disability might prompt the man to reformulate his image of masculinity to incorporate his new body into his idea of masculinity and to reconstruct the psyche. Or, he might try to make his body into a hyper-virile masculinity to assuage an anxiety of demasculinization. Rubin and Shapiro's documentary about male quadriplegics *Murderball* (2005) might be read as one such example, as some of the men in the film appear to focus on remasculinizing the male body in the face of their disability.

But able masculinity can also employ the disabled male body for its own gendered purposes. The corporal dialogue between the able male body and the disabled one could be a way to transform the able body into a more masculine one by comparison, if the disabled body is viewed as unmasculine. In this sense, the disabled body serves as a form of alterity to the able body. The relation between able and disabled masculinity can be more complicated when disabled masculinity functions as both self and other. Able masculinity could experience disabled masculinity's self-remasculinization as a projected sign of its own imagined anxieties of castration. The man who is de-abled, but then re-abled in terms of gender could parallel masculinity's imagined fear of castration and its recuperation or assuagement, much as the woman can signify projected castration anxiety if she is shown to be symbolically uncastrated (see p. 123). This might explain why some men are very taken by disabled men who perform in ways that they view as masculine (disabled bodybuilders or athletes for instance). The disabled male body can provide a form of alterity by which an able man functions as loving care-giver while avoiding the anxiety of perceived homoeroticism in male–male interactions. Cultural assumptions about, or representations of, the asexual disabled body (e.g., the paralyzed man does not have intercourse or even sex) might provide a way for a man to interact with another man without the anxiety of homoeroticism. So in the same way that a female mediator of desire can play the role of dispelling a homoerotic threat between men (as in chapter 2), the disabled male body can assure others that sex will not take place between two men. In this sense, disability might play a role like the female object of exchange, in part perhaps because a disabled man might be perceived as feminine or demasculinized.

Let us return to the question of anxiety and the male body. One way to assuage the anxiety is to avoid dealing with it in the first place, to render it invisible or to repress it. Hiding the male body, in theory, keeps people from seeing that the sex that is supposed to be powerful and strong is not in fact what they imagine, that the male body does not correspond to a certain construct of hegemonic masculinity. The male body very rarely looks like what it is often imagined to be in its ideal state, often hard and muscular with a large penis. The penis is particularly important here: if masculinity's hegemony requires the all-powerful phallus, the flesh-and-blood penis cannot by definition live up to the imagined phallus. The reality of the body part can only disappoint when it is supposed to signify as an image of male power. As a result, the penis must be hidden to avoid exposing the male body as not corresponding to an imagined phallic idea. The male body can be constructed in such a way that it effaces the penis and certain other elements of the body, to the point that the effacement of parts of the male body becomes one of the defining aspects of masculinity. Masculinity is projected onto the male body and made into something that it can never really be, and at the same time elements of the male body that are not convenient for its hegemonic representation are repressed. Potentially sexual aspects of the male body, for example, can be repressed because they do not correspond to a certain vision of what the male body is or should be. Anal eroticism might be coded as queer or homosexual, and a heterosexual man might not want to receive pleasure (or he might not give himself pleasure) through the anus.

The attempt to create a phallic definition of masculinity means creating a stable definition of the male body. A dynamic approach to the male body whereby pleasure can be located in various places may be impossible, and what pleasure means may be codified as a way of creating a certain type of masculinity that can be seen as hegemonic (centered, or imagined as centered, on the penis). Part of this attempt to stabilize the male body is to project onto the female body. A man may think, "I know I am a man because I am not bound by my body, and I know I am a man because women are bound to their bodies." The female body may be considered excessively linked to corporality, in part because women menstruate, give birth, and lactate. This binary coding of the sexes does not necessarily mean that masculinity operates outside the realm of the body however: various male anxieties about the body might be displaced or projected onto the female body. The stereotypes of the female hysteric or nymphomaniac might be techniques to dispel masculine worries about the male body as potentially hysterical or as sexually excessive, or even as corporally driven in a larger sense. By projecting those anxieties onto the other, men do not have to deal with the possibility of their own unstable or non-phallic body, or even the idea of their own body in the first place. This psychic-driven projection can take place individually or culturally, as projections occur when one man projects or when culture projects through discourse in a larger sense.

Given these corporal anxieties, the male body may be spoken only in specific forums, notably sports and warfare. Men might experience a corporal masculinity, but only when talking about certain bodies such as that of the football player, bodybuilder, or soldier (whether wounded or not). Bodily masculinity may not arise except in certain contexts that privilege certain elements of the male body. To show and to talk about the male body in a football context, for instance, might be a way to reveal the male body as strength, as speed, or as agility, and might provide a link between the male body and competition or violence. This careful choice of when to represent male bodies also pertains to visual media, a topic to be discussed in the last section of this chapter.

The Fluid Male Body

In all these cases, the body has been considered as a discrete entity whose perception or whose comparison with another body is entity to entity. But what would happen if the body were not imagined as a discrete entity? We have seen in chapter 1 how fluidity and unstable boundaries can redefine how we think about masculinity and how masculinity is experienced. But what if the idea of unstable boundaries were taken not in a definitional or abstract sense (as about masculinity), but in a more physical sense? What would it mean about masculinity if the boundaries of the male body were considered to be inherently fluid? If perception defines the body, then our perception of where our body ends does not have to be at the place where it physically ends. We often imagine our own bodies elsewhere or in places where they are not. Or, we imagine having body parts different from those that we have, both in our waking hours and in our dreams. In an era in which the body can be altered by implants, mechanical devices, or plastic surgery, the body is increasingly without stable boundary. Those possible alterations influence how we imagine our bodies as changeable: boys might imagine bionic body parts or webs that shoot out of their wrists. The crossing of the borders of the body can also be imagined in ways that actually take place. Various orifices in the male body can be physically passed through. When a man's wife fingers his prostate during sex, when a man has anal sex with another man or with a woman who straps on a dildo, or even when a man puts his penis into a vagina or an anus, the boundaries of the male body cannot be considered to be firm.

Even if (or because) the male body has unclear borders, masculinity may often fear those boundaries and attempt to establish and reestablish them. First, the male body is not a priori male: as discussed in chapter 3, sex has to be invented and materialized again and again. Since sex is invented through the body, the male body has to be constantly invented, and a key aspect of that invention is the creation of corporal borders. The male body may be more invested in bodily borders than the female body. To use the examples above, masculinity may resist sexual acts considered to break corporal borders, such as penetration of the anus by a woman, since such acts allow entry of a foreign body into one of the bodily orifices. This idea of masculinity as bordered might also explain the repulsion of some men to male–male anal intercourse, and thus explain one element of homophobia. It might also be extended to explain masculine fears of closeness, intimacy, hugging or even touching another body, or to explain the desire for hardness and muscularity, which are seen to delineate the body more clearly, with fatness and softness considered too fluid. Corporal bodies can also be affirmed by contrast to perceptions of the female body as more fluid in terms of borders, because of perceptions about menstruation, oral sex with a man, and intercourse. The ability to carry another human being inside the body during pregnancy may, however, be perceived as the ultimate border-buster. So maintaining the borders of the male body allows men to separate themselves from the female body's assumed fluid or unbound nature. Consequently, the male body may fear the female body's corrupting influence, or fear that her unbound nature will also incorporate his body into hers, that his body will symbolically return to its womb-like state inside the female body. Symbols of engulfment such as tornados, floods, and whirlpools can be taken to represent threatening unbordered female bodies that threaten to take over or to de-border the male body. Misogynist fears of women taking over the male body are frequently found in cultural and individual representation, as for example in Nazi propaganda. Resistance to those unbordered female bodies, along with the reestablishment of the borders of the male body, has to be performed as a continual process for the male body to retain its assumed delineated status.

In the same way that there is a tension between the imagined male body and the actual male body, there is a tension between the ordered, bordered body and the unruly or unbordered male body. The very desire to border the male body suggests an underlying anxiety about the possibility of the unbounded. Consider, for instance, the example of a father of a young child whose sex is not visible. When someone mistakes the boy for a girl, the father may have an anxious or angry response because the borders of the male and female child are unclear. This kind of anxiety might also explain, in part, the reasons that color coding for the genders is employed so often. In US culture, blue for a boy is a way to create a color border separating the male from the female body, an extension of the body that might be more legible than the actual body itself. Repulsion toward menstruation and anal sex might signify the fluidity of the body feared by the man. These repulsions may be particularly acute because they reveal signs of the inners of the body, in the case of menstruation because of blood and in the case of anal sex because of the possibility of excrement. The male body in orgasm might also be viewed as a problem, as the experience of orgasm is considered to shatter borders and embody the out-of-control.

On the other hand, however, the breaking of the borders of the male body could be a way to resist masculinity. The man who wants his wife to strap a dildo on and penetrate him destabilizes strict borders of the body, as well as of power, as the act can also symbolically place her in a position of power. Other moments might also suggest a curiosity with the idea of breaking corporal borders. A man might wonder what it is like to have anal sex with a man, not because he is a repressed gay man, but because he is curious about what the act would do to his body whose wholeness he is supposed to maintain. Self-mutilation could also imply a symbolic attempt to destabilize the borders of the body since skin holds great symbolic import as the container of the body. A man may thus be caught between the desire for borders and the desire to shatter them, leaving him in a position of ambivalence.

One aspect of the male body that is particularly indicative of this kind of ambivalence is semen. On the one hand, semen might embody masculinity or maleness since it is the matter that provides the male contribution to reproduction. It can also symbolize the culmination of the sexual act for a man, a physical representation of orgasm. Unlike urine, which is waste and thus not a part of the male body, semen has a function and close relation to male sexuality. On the other hand, however, semen could be considered distinctly anti-masculine since it contradicts some of the elements of the male body previously discussed. It is viscous, fluid, without border, a kind of anti-delineation between the male body and the external world and between the male body and the female body (where it may end up). Semen is also part of the male sexual apparatus that is outside the penis and the erection. The idea that semen can now be stored and used by women who may not even know its human origin suggests even more strongly how semen is far from part of the body, even when used for reproduction. In these senses, masculinity can never be fully bordered through the body and is caught in a position of ambivalence between bound and unbound.

This kind of tension around semen can be manifested in the way in which pornography represents, or is imagined to represent, male orgasm. On the one hand, when the man ejaculates, the male body is shown as fluid, as producing something fluid for the camera, threatening to deborder the body and to show him in orgasmic never-never land. But, on the other hand, his ejaculation can cover up the possibility of representing the male orgasm itself. He may not ejaculate into her, suggesting that he has to be seen ejaculating and not orgasming, and that he may fear being seen as losing control of the orgasmic body. When the man ejaculates on a woman, the anxiety of loss of wholeness can be literally displaced onto her, since the semen becomes part of her body and leaves any association with him behind.

Projecting the Male Body on Screen

If men have an investment in hiding the male body or in hiding certain male bodies, it is in part because there is a close relation between looking and masculinity. In a large sense, the ways in which a man looks are very commonly ways to construct masculinity, largely because men create certain types of bodies in the visual field that correspond to their ideas about gender. Often, a heterosexual man can watch another man, as long as that watching is not erotically coded. Two heterosexual men in a locker room might not notice – or might not say that they notice – the other man's body or his penis. This man does not read another man's body, does not enter into the details of the body and examine them. He cannot or will not detail or describe that body or he will not say that another man is attractive, since to notice it would imply homoeroticism and destabilize his status as a member of the sex that looks, instead of the sex that is looked at. On the other hand, a man's act of looking at the female body might entail a whole series of perceptions of corporal details along with articulations of aspects of that body (descriptions of her breasts, legs, etc.), meaning that her perceived corporal fragmentation stands in direct contrast to his unified, stable status as perceiver. She might not live up to his expectations, but to come to this conclusion is still to have evaluated her and to have control over the act of looking. He might imagine, or assume, that his body is not being looked at as an object, or is not being objectified as a body. Heterosexual men may be unaware when they become erotic objects of a gay male gaze because the very concept that their body can be looked at erotically is absent from their thought process. The mechanism of the gaze, though employed, remains invisible to him as he constructs or reifies a strict opposition between the male look and the female looked-at. Man's love of the gaze, his scopophilia, means that he cannot imagine woman as subject of the gaze or man as object of the gaze.

The male gaze is often thought to be a kind of metaphor for – or extension of – the penis. The male eye penetrates the outside world, and especially the erotic female body. Some women experience male objectification of the female body as violent and invasive, suggesting the idea of scopophilia as a metaphoric violent act or even rape. Consequently, male blindness is often taken as a metaphorical castration: to be without the penetrating eye, a vulnerable organ that can be put out, is to be without a symbolic penis. Consequently, to have control over the look is to have the phallus. Part of that control is the day-to-day gaze and the recurring looking at women in an erotically coded way. It is also the avoidance of being seen by a gay male gaze. But also, that control can be expressed through control over media (TV, film, photography, video games) or art (painting, sculpture). The camera serves as an extension of the eyes and to control the way the camera sees is to maintain and recreate the male gaze. A film or TV show can assume a male, heterosexual gaze by virtue of the way it represents both women and men. Because of the prevalence of film, TV, and other media in twenty-first-century culture, the way visual cultures represent masculinity has great influence over the way the gaze is understood or experienced in culture in a larger sense. Visual culture thus produces masculinity for culture, and, conversely, cultural constructs of masculinity that exist before a visual text influence visual culture. So the way in which film represents the male body contributes to how it is understood in culture, and the way in which culture understands the male body contributes to how it is represented in visual culture. These influences can be mimetic (one directly reflects the other), they can be resistant (one reflects another way of seeing), and they can be dialogic (they respond to each other in complex ways).

The naked or partially naked male body, as a body and not as a person, has traditionally been absent from representation on screen, a further aspect of the attempt to present masculinity as non-corporal. One way to think about the issue is to assume that any representation of the revealed male body objectifies it since the viewer is necessarily gazing at his body. The simple revealing of a male body is enough in itself to destabilize the traditional hiding of the male body and to contribute to its marking. A given TV show, for instance, may aim to reveal male bodies for this purpose, to allow for the assumption of a heterosexual female or gay male viewer, or to confront heterosexual men with naked male bodies. Another approach to this issue is to assume that a male body on its own does not denote objectification, but that a representation of the male body has to be explicitly portrayed on screen as an object. Thus, even when a male body is revealed, the extent to which the image is creating or recreating a hard masculinity should be considered. If the male body is a hard or muscular body, the revealing of that body can simply reaffirm masculinity's status as an imagined hardness, thus not as an actual real-life body, but an imagined or projected one. To show a male body is not necessarily to make it into an object of the gaze. The film itself (the characters or the camera angles) have to show, suggest, or acknowledge that body as looked at. Other characters would have to make comments or respond to the body as a body in some way. To show a male body as incidental or as unmarked can in fact be a way to dispel an anxiety about hiding it by not representing it as an object of the look. The male body can be revealed, then, as not revealed. In Donner's *Lethal Weapon* (1987), for instance, Mel Gibson's fit body is shown in one scene, but only to be linked to an actual lethal weapon in another scene. The male body is far from vulnerable as a body in its nudity, but instead its nudity makes it a metaphorical weapon which it becomes over the course of the film. In this case, temporarily revealing the male body serves to link that body symbolically to other signs that construct masculinity by association.

If the borders of the male body can be fluid, the binary opposition between the male gaze and the gazed-upon does not always function in a stable way either. One element subtending this opposition is the clear separation between identification and desire, a binary opposition whose instability I discussed in chapter 2. The male gaze can, of course, look at men, and can identify with them, but it cannot desire them. As noted in chapter 2, the instability between these concepts can cause an anxiety or paranoia about homosexuality. What happens to the look when identification and desire do not operate in such a stable manner? Can the male gaze also identify with the female body, and desire the male body? What happens when a female lead straddles the fence in terms of gender, confusing the categories of identity and desire? In the final scene of Scott's *Alien* (1979), for example, Sigourney Weaver is both erotically coded and masculinized. Can we only talk about male heterosexual desire here then? Or on the other hand, what happens when an attractive or erotic male body is displayed? Can it really be coded as entirely unerotic for a male heterosexual viewer? In Campbell's *Casino Royale* (2006), James Bond's erotic, fit body is put on display for plot reasons (in the film, in order to attract a given woman whom he needs to seduce to get information). If the eye of the camera is considered the implied eye of the viewer, the erotic body which is meant in a very obvious way to be suggested for a heterosexual woman character in the film, threatens to become the erotic desire of the viewer as he or she is necessarily positioned as looker/gazer. In a case such as this one, a male viewer is forced to at least imagine, if not experience, the possibility of eroticism as the viewer's gaze literally becomes the implied female character's. When the camera's eye is explicitly turned into the eye of the other (in this case, of a heterosexual woman), heterosexual masculinity's position is necessarily destabilized. This is not to say that a given film presents a single type of angle over the course of the film: a film can destabilize the very idea of a single type of watcher by embedding a number of gendered looking positions into its eye or by making the very idea of a gendered camera angle suspect.

Even without these kinds of destabilized camera positions, it should not be taken for granted that a male viewer never crosses over to a heterosexual female or homoerotic viewing position. A man who watches Scott's *Thelma and Louise* (1991), for instance, may have moments in which he identifies with the two female main characters, even as he may also cross back into a masculine viewing position at other points. The presence of a male character in a film who seems to identify with female characters would also invite male viewers to identify with his identifying with them. In the case of *Thelma and Louise*, Harvey Keitel's character adamantly and explicitly supports their cause and seems to identify with their plight. The role of fantasy or sympathy in this gender crossing should be taken into consideration: a man might cross into a viewing position in which he wants to understand the viewing other. Through cross-identification and desire, a man might imagine what it would be like to be a gay male spectator gazing on an attractive male body, without fearing becoming or being viewed as a gay man. While there may be some oscillation in the gendered position of the male viewer, it is the female spectator who is traditionally viewed as more likely to cross over in these kinds of identification practices since women are often used to seeing the world from a woman's and a man's perspective.

Another possible complication in stable viewing positions is that a woman on screen does not have to be a sign of a woman, as a female character can operate as a sign of a man. A woman can serve as a sign of a castration–decastration process, by which a woman is symbolically castrated in some way and then triumphs over that imagined castration (see p. 123). The woman in certain horror films, intended for a mainly male viewing audience, mirrors a kind of attempted castration (through the attempt to kill her), but her eventual triumph over a killer positions her as a kind of man in a woman's body who wins over the undefined enemy. So a female character is not necessarily a sign of that character's sex (since sex is a construct of gender anyway), and a simple identification/desire opposition is not possible when a female character stands in for some aspect of masculinity such as castration anxiety. The converse can be true as well: a male character can stand in for aspects of a woman, and a male spectator's identification with that character could suggest an identification with a trope of woman.

This way of thinking about looking should not be considered transhistorical and transcultural. The revealing of the male body, and particularly the eroticized male body, is becoming more of a commonplace in twenty-first-century media and film, and there are an increasing number of male bodies of various types in advertisements and film. This growing presence might largely be a result of the increasing visibility of homosexuality and female heterosexuality in media, and the male body in advertisements might be a way to appeal to female or gay male consumers. This kind of representation should not be viewed as linear, however: the male body has not gradually revealed itself over time, and the specific relation between revealing and context is important. How can we explain all the male bodies of a period far in the past, such as in Italian Renaissance art for instance? In addition, the representation of the body in one context can be in implicit relation to another context and have meaning through that dialogue. For example, the revealed male body might have a relation to a context in which the male body was not so commonly represented (or vice versa). *Casino Royale* might be a good example: James Bond's naked torso might reflect twenty-first-century ideas on the male body, but that body is coming out of a cinematic tradition of Bond films in which the female body is traditionally and aggressively the object of desire. Consequently, the male body's presence as eroticized body takes on an oppositional meaning as the male body has come to take the place of the female body.

Because film is a visual medium, it tends to reflect on visuality and can be a statement on the very process by which the male viewer is watching or the process by which the male viewer is made into an object of desire. Images of watching, looking, and staring and representations of voyeurism and spectatorship can refer to the actual process of representation of bodies. Simon Beaufoy's British film *The Full Monty* (1997), for instance, is about a group of men who decide to put on a strip show for the community. The film deals directly with their various difficulties in revealing their bodies in public, as their bodies are far from ideal. But though the film is about a show they actually put on in the film, that show can also be read as symbolic of the medium of film or of a culture of male scopophilia in a larger sense. From this vantage point, the film shows how and why the male body is not exposed, providing cultural and individual reasons for it remaining hidden, and in this way, works through the problem of hiding the male body.

While scopophilia is often closely linked to masculinity, there is another way of considering looking, in which the gaze of the man is seen as effeminizing. Instead of the metaphor of the gaze as penile and penetrating, it could be seen as metaphorically vaginal, with the outside rays penetrating into the eye. The image of the man at the keyhole can be taken to represent this feminizing of the gazing man, with the keyhole serving as a kind of vaginal representation. In one scene in *The Full Monty*, for example, the male lead stares at a group of women through a hole in a men's bathroom stall. One of the women proceeds to urinate in the urinal while standing up like a man. The female body is far from gazed upon as erotic object and the man far from erotic voyeur. On the contrary, the female object has become a urinating man, and the gazing man transformed into a traditional female in terms of his viewing position. When female characters gaze on male bodies erotically, a similar process may follow: a reverse-gendered scene in which the woman becomes the gazing man and the man the eroticized woman.

While the binary opposition of man as gazer and woman as object permeates culture, like all oppositions, it should nonetheless be thought about as continually reworked into new viewing positions. In this way, the question of fluid looking is closely related to the issue of the fluidity of the body's seemingly fixed boundaries discussed in the first section of this chapter. The body's boundaries cannot necessarily be located, despite attempts to create them as stable. Similarly, the watching man cannot necessarily maintain strict separation between himself and what he sees, as the boundaries of his vision are as in flux as those of his body.

Bibliography

The power/discourse approach to the body is based largely on the influential work of Michel Foucault. While he does not focus on the question of masculinity and the male body per se, work that could be put in dialogue with the topic includes *The History of Sexuality*, vol. 1, trans. Robert Hurley (New York: Pantheon Books, 1978); *Discipline and Punish: The Birth of the Prison*, trans. Alan Sheridan (New York: Vintage, 1995); "Body/Power," in *Power/Knowledge: Selected Interviews and Other Writings 1972–1977*, ed. and trans. Colin Gordon (New York: Pantheon Books, 1980), 55–62. The idea of "docile bodies" is articulated in *Discipline and Punish*. See also the secondary texts in the bibliography in chapter 1, and Jana

Sawicki, *Disciplining Foucault: Feminism, Power, and the Body* (New York: Routledge, 1991); the essays in Janet Price and Margrit Shildrick, eds., *Feminist Theory and the Body: A Reader* (Edinburgh: Edinburgh University Press, 1999).

On reading the body, see Susan Bordo, "Reading the Male Body," *Michigan Quarterly Review* 32, no. 4 (1993): 696–737; Philip Culbertson, "Designing Men: Reading the Male Body as Text," *Journal of Textual Reasoning* 7 (1998), available at http://etext.virginia.edu/journals/tr/archive/volume7/Culbertson1.html (accessed July 7, 2009).

On the issue of habit, practice, and the body, see Pierre Bourdieu, *The Logic of Practice*, trans. Richard Nice (Stanford: Stanford University Press, 1990); Bourdieu, *Masculine Domination*, trans. Richard Nice (Stanford: Stanford University Press, 2001).

The relation between perception and the body is often considered in relation to Maurice Merleau-Ponty. See especially ch. 1 ("The Body") in *Phenomenology of Perception*, trans. Colin Smith (London: Routledge, 1962). For an introduction to Merleau-Ponty and the body, see James B. Steeves, *Imagining Bodies: Merleau-Ponty's Philosophy of Imagination* (Pittsburgh: Duquesne University Press, 2004).

While the relation between Merleau-Ponty and the male body is not often discussed as such, feminist approaches to his work are useful on the topic. See, for example, Dorothea Olkowski and Gail Weiss, eds., *Feminist Interpretations of Maurice Merleau-Ponty* (University Park: Pennsylvania State University Press, 2006); Judith Butler, "Sexual Ideology and Phenomenological Description: A Feminist Critique of Merleau-Ponty's *Phenomenology of Perception*," in *The Thinking Muse: Feminism and Modern French Philosophy*, ed. Jeffner Allen and Iris Marion Young (Bloomington: Indiana University Press, 1989), 85–100; Shannon Sullivan, "Domination and Dialogue in Merleau-Ponty's *Phenomenology of Perception*," *Hypatia* 12, no. 1 (1997): 1–19; Silvia Stoller, "Reflections on Feminist Merleau-Ponty Skepticism," *Hypatia* 15, no. 1 (2000): 175–82. On sexual difference in phenomenology, see Sara Heinämaa, *Toward a Phenomenology of Sexual Difference* (Lanham, MD: Rowman and Littlefield, 2003).

On the use of gendered accessories to (re)construct the body, see Will Fisher, *Materializing Gender in Early Modern English Literature and Culture* (Cambridge: Cambridge University Press, 2006).

On sex, and the mind/body question in Western culture, see Genevieve Lloyd, *The Man of Reason: "Male" and "Female" in Western Philosophy* (Minneapolis: University of Minnesota Press, 1984).

On writing, anxiety and the male body, see Calvin Thomas, *Male Matters: Masculinity, Anxiety, and the Male Body on the Line* (Urbana: University of Illinois Press, 1996).

On the disabled body, see Gill Valentine, "What It Means to be a Man: The Body, Masculinities, Disability," in *Mind and Body Spaces: Geographies of Disability, Illness, and Impairment*, ed. Ruth Butler and Hester Parr (London: Routledge, 1999), 167–80.

On the bodybuilder, see Marcia Ian, "How Do You Wear Your Body? Bodybuilding and the Sublimity of Drag," in *Negotiating Lesbian and Gay Subjects*, ed. Monica Dorenkamp and Richard Henke (New York: Routledge, 1995), 71–90.

On the borders of the body, see Judith Butler, *Bodies that Matter* (London: Routledge, 1993); Butler, *Gender Trouble: Feminism and the Subversion of Identity* (New York: Routledge, 1990); Elizabeth A. Grosz, *Volatile Bodies: Toward a Corporeal Feminism* (Bloomington: Indiana University Press, 1994). For an example of how the male body's inners can be revealed, see Linda Ruth Williams, "The Inside-Out of Masculinity: David Cronenberg's Visceral Pleasures," in *The Body's Perilous Pleasures: Dangerous Desires and Contemporary Culture*, ed. Michelle Aaron (Edinburgh: Edinburgh University Press, 1999), 30–48. For an important case study in representations of the borders of the male body, see Klaus Theweleit, *Male Fantasies*, 2 vols., trans. Stephen Conway (Minneapolis: University of Minnesota Press, 1987).

For a general volume on the male body see Nancy Tuana et al., eds., *Revealing Male Bodies* (Bloomington: Indiana University Press, 2002).

On semen, see Murat Aydemir, *Images of Bliss: Ejaculation, Masculinity, Meaning* (Minneapolis: University of Minnesota Press, 2007).

On scopophilia, film/media, and the male gaze, begin with Laura Mulvey's extremely influential "Visual Pleasure and Narrative Cinema," *Screen* 16, no. 3 (Autumn 1975): 6–18. See also Mulvey's "Afterthoughts on 'Visual Pleasure and Narrative Cinema' Inspired by King Vidor's *Duel in the Sun* (1946)," *Framework* 15–16–17 (1981): 12–15; E. Ann Kaplan, "Is the Gaze Male?" in *Women and Film: Both Sides of the Camera* (New York: Methuen, 1983), 23–35; Steve Neale, "Masculinity as Spectacle," *Screen* 24, no. 6 (1983): 2–16. More recent work that deals with this question includes Carol J. Clover, *Men, Women, and Chainsaws: Gender in the Modern Horror Film* (Princeton: Princeton University Press, 1992) (see ch. 2 for a discussion of how the woman on screen can embody traits of masculinity in the context of the horror film); Steven Cohan, *Masked Men: Masculinity and the Movies in the Fifties* (Bloomington: Indiana University Press, 1997); Peter Lehman, ed., *Masculinity: Bodies, Movies, Culture* (New York: Routledge, 2001) (see especially Lehman's own essay, on the male body and the "melodramatic" penis on screen; see also Toby Miller's essay on James Bond's penis); Peter Lehman, *Running Scared: Masculinity and the Representation of the Male Body* (Philadelphia: Temple University Press, 1993); Kenneth MacKinnon, "After Mulvey: Male Erotic

Objectification," in *The Body's Perilous Pleasures: Dangerous Desires and Contemporary Culture*, ed. Michele Aaron (Edinburgh: Edinburgh University Press, 1999), 13–29; Sean Nixon, "Exhibiting Masculinity," in *Representation: Cultural Representations and Signifying Practices*, ed. Stuart Hall (London: Sage, 1997), 291–336; Nixon, *Hard Looks: Masculinities, Spectatorship and Contemporary Consumption* (New York: St. Martin's Press, 1996); Andrew Perchuk and Helaine Posner, eds., *The Masculine Masquerade: Masculinity and Representation* (Cambridge, MA: MIT Press, 1995); Kaja Silverman, *Male Subjectivity at the Margins* (New York: Routledge, 1992); Zoe Sofia, "Masculine Excess and the Metaphorics of Vision: Some Problems of Feminist Film Theory," *Continuum: The Australian Journal of Media and Culture* 2, no. 2 (1989), available at http://wwwmcc.murdoch.edu.au/ReadingRoom/2.2/Sofia.html (accessed July 16, 2009); Yvonne Tasker, *Spectacular Bodies: Gender, Genre and the Action Cinema* (London: Routledge, 1993).

For a different way of thinking about the watching man as phallic, see "The Scoptophilic Instinct and Identification," in *The Collected Papers of Otto Fenichel*, vol. 1 (New York: Norton, 1953), 373–97.

For a book on the male body for a general audience, see Susan Bordo, *The Male Body: A New Look at Men in Public and Private* (New York: Farrar, Straus, and Giroux, 1999).

5

Masculinity in Disguise

Throughout much of this book, I have thought about ways in which masculinity is defined through opposition, especially with respect to women and male homosexuality. Chapter 2 treated ways in which masculinity and homosociality are set up against potential homoeroticism. In chapters 3 and 4, I considered how distinct and non-fluid sexes are created in part to construct the female body as man's other. In later chapters, I will examine how racial and national masculinities are constructed as unlike forms of masculinity coded as racially or nationally other. While this oppositional approach takes many forms, some of which are complicated and some of which are more straightforward, the need for rejection means that masculinity is not independent or autonomous, even if one motivation behind rejection is to proclaim male self-sufficiency. This way of considering masculinity has become almost axiomatic: it is often thought that femininity is defined by connection and masculinity by rejection, that women build nurturing, intimate bonds while men establish their independence and avoid close bonds.

In this chapter, I would like to discuss a different way in which masculinity is performed. The title of the current chapter is "Masculinity in Disguise" because it focuses on how male subjects construct their gender subjectivity by embracing or appropriating what might seem antithetical to masculinity, especially traits ascribed to women, gay men, or lesbians. These traits include physical ones such as breasts and pregnancy, but also external signs of the other through which a literal or figurative cross-dressing occurs.

Effeminacy and Men as Women

There is no denying that the threat of effeminacy frequently factors into masculine self-definition. Effeminacy often signifies the threat of a man becoming like a woman, but effeminacy is not necessarily the opposite of masculinity. A man's fear of becoming effeminate does not have to mean that he is not masculine, and a man can lack masculinity and still fear effeminacy. A man can be both very masculine and very feminine at the same time. Effeminacy and emasculation, while often taken as synonymous, also point to separate aspects of gender. Being like a woman and being unlike a man are not necessarily equivalent, a corollary of the idea that masculinity and femininity are not opposites. In some cases, effeminacy can actually masculinize a man. A male singer who can sing a large range of gendered voices may be considered more masculine than a man who cannot. Similarly, emasculation can reaffirm masculinity, as evidenced for instance by the castrato, a man who was literally emasculated but whose masculinity was often reinforced by the musical effects of his lack of genitals.

While certain signs of effeminacy recur with some frequency (e.g., a high voice, a certain way of walking or dressing), it is not possible to assign universal traits to effeminacy, which (like masculinity and gender) is always culturally coded. Virility might seem to be the last human trait that could be coded as anti-masculine, but in certain contexts immoderate virility makes a man effeminate. In Renaissance culture, for example, moderation in sexuality was connected to masculinity and immoderation to non-masculinity. Or, while we may tend to associate male homosexuality with the effeminate, other cultures do not or did not. In the ancient Greek world, same-sex sexuality could be a sign of virility if one was the sexual penetrator. In other contexts, a man with qualities that may seem effeminate to us was considered to embody an acceptable type of masculinity, as was often the case with the dandy or the Renaissance courtier.

If effeminacy is as unstable as masculinity, it is also because what looks effeminate does not directly or ultimately denote effeminacy. In fact, effeminacy or other types of non-masculinity may permit a man to better hide masculinity so that he can deploy gender hegemony more effectively. A man's softness or wound may permit him seemingly to lack hegemonic traits so that he can take others off guard and assert greater power over them in a less direct way. As a wolf in sheep's clothing, a man can deploy effeminacy or woman-like traits for ends that are anything but non-hegemonic. In the rest of this chapter, I will focus, in particular, on contexts in which heterosexual men put on feminine clothing and other female accoutrements for reasons seemingly unrelated to gender. I will use the term "cross-dressing" to denote a temporary or isolated act of volition, unlike "transgenderism" or "transvestism," which tend to denote more permanent or habitual states. I will not consider here gay drag or performance, which often include exaggerated traits of femininity and tend to function very differently from the model discussed here.

In one reading, masculinity's desire to don traits of a woman could be taken as indicative of a desire to understand the other, to see what it means to be in her literal, physical position. Cross-dressing or appropriating aspects of the female body might also signify an attempt to become a male feminist, to have the opportunity to take a pro-woman stance without the contradictions of a man doing so. This approach would be a way to explain, for instance, the use of an apparatus that men can wear to simulate pregnancy, complete with a machine that kicks. In Renaissance poetry, certain male poets imagine birthing as a metaphor for writing poetry, the use of which could be construed as a way to equate poetry and birth so as to relate to this element of female subjectivity. A man could also give up his masculinity by dressing down, or purposely rendering himself effeminate so as to have the experience of another gender presentation considered lesser than his own. This desire can never ultimately be fulfilled, since the gender change is necessarily partial and since he can never actually have the experience of another sex, which depends on the perceived permanence of a sexed body.

Another approach to cross-dressing is to view it not as rendering a man effeminate or womanlike, but paradoxically as affirming masculinity by contrast. A man or boy who dresses as female for Halloween may not in fact be considered effeminate or less masculine for his disguise, but quite the opposite. His cross-dressing may ultimately signify that the attempt to incorporate the feminine into or onto the male body is doomed to failure, proving that a man cannot pass as a woman. The laughter that the schoolboy in a dress evokes from his peers on the playground may mean that he can never be a she. Cross-dressing may be a way to perform masculinity's inability to be anything but male and thus to reify sexual binarism. The specific ways in which he does not pass and the techniques by which passing is rendered impossible (by him or by others) could be studied as aspects of gendered subjectivity. A man may dress as an extreme version of a woman, for example, in order to go as far as possible toward another gendered position. The donned signs of extreme or exaggerated femininity (e.g., too much makeup, very large fake breasts) can better make the contrast between the "woman" and the man beneath. Or, a man may cross-dress in ways that very visibly highlight the male body. He may select a low-cut dress, for example, that reveals his chest hair or a sleeveless dress that allows his arm muscles to show.

The idea that a man who fails to become a woman reinforces masculinity can be considered in a model in which masculinity approaches femininity to outdo women. In films such as *Tootsie* (1982) or *Mrs. Doubtfire* (1993), male characters pass as women, but they are far from feminized. In the face of a potential masculinity crisis, they assert their masculinity by becoming better women than the women. Dustin Hoffman's character in *Tootsie* proves herself to be more of a feminist than the other women in the film, suggesting that the most effective woman is a man dressed as a woman. Showalter analyzes these films in this way, positing this model within the cultural context of a backlash against feminism.[1] In cases in which a man takes on a woman's position, the question of whether he is trying to appropriate the other to seize an advantage over her and prove his masculinity should be asked. The situation may, of course, be complex: a man may be pro-woman or sincerely trying to experience another subjectivity while at the same time, or at certain moments, attempting to take over femininity and reassert himself through the other.

In a related model, a heterosexual man cross-dresses not so much to be a better woman than women, but to gain access to an all-female space. The idea behind the early 1980s TV series *Bosom Buddies* is that two male friends (the "buddies") cross-dress in order to gain access to an all-female residence. Not surprisingly, one of them desires one of the women who live there, and cross-dressing is a technique to penetrate to the recesses of the all-female space in part to better seduce women with whom they might not otherwise have a chance. In the film *Sorority Boys* (2002), a group of male students decide to cross-dress and move

---

[1]   Elaine Showalter, "Critical Cross-Dressing: Male Feminists and the Woman of the Year," in *Men in Feminism*, ed. Alice Jardine and Paul Smith (New York: Methuen, 1987), 116–32.

into a sorority when they get kicked out of their fraternity. One of the men becomes interested in one of the sorority women, and despite his (bad) disguise, she ends up attracted to him, suggesting that his essential masculinity can never really be hidden or that the cross-dressed man is so irresistible that women turn lesbian for him. His virility is ultimately affirmed by, and not despite, his female garb. Men might become women to get the girl, to penetrate her space symbolically in order ultimately to penetrate her. By entering her space like a spy, he is supposed to get close to her to gain secret information, which he can use for purposes of seduction. What is really disguised, then, is not so much him as much as his attempts to become more virile with respect to women.

This process corresponds to a psychoanalytic model of gender in which a man overcomes – or attempts to overcome – castration anxiety through the fetish. In the classic Freudian account, a man who fears castration or suffers anxiety about masculinity also wants to release that anxiety. One solution is the fetish, a substitute penis that makes up for his own which he fears losing. As a castrated man in the Freudian schema, a woman takes on a substitute penis when a man fetishizes some penile aspect of her body (like a foot). The fetish symbolizes for men that a woman has overcome her supposed castration. He gives her a penis with his fetish, but in so doing, he also symbolically gives himself a penis, assuaging his own anxiety of losing his. The woman with a symbolic penis is made to signify the recuperation of a man's image of his virile, non-castrated body. The fetish can also be directed to clothing on a man's own body. Heterosexual men who are erotically aroused by putting on women's underwear can be seen to be assuaging castration anxiety via a fetish with a connection to the female body, or more precisely to female genitalia. By donning a woman's underwear, he is metaphorically castrating himself by becoming like her, but that metaphor is literalized as non-castration when his actual penis is brought back into the equation. This castration–decastration process could be taken as a symbolic parallel to the cross-dressing scenarios presented above: by cross-dressing as a woman, the man castrates himself de facto, but then goes through a recuperation process that ultimately remasculinizes him.

The model of masculinity in which the man cross-dresses to recreate his masculinity could be extended from clothing to the realm of the female body, aspects of which he can adopt. As discussed in chapter 4, the body, as an extension of the psyche, is imagined more than it is composed of physical, delineated parts. So, I might talk about cross-sexing, then, in a manner that is not actually transsexual, but gendered, with the male body's becoming female as one aspect of gender change. Because gender constructs sex, representing a man with a female body part says more about masculinity than about maleness or femaleness. Many of the same questions asked about gender change can be posed with respect to cultural production in which masculinity takes on femaleness: when the male body becomes woman-like, is the male subject trying to understand female embodiment or to take it over? Is he aiming to remasculinize?

Men may take on breasts or the ability to breastfeed, or they may become able to give birth, perhaps the most prevalent sex change of all. In the middle ages, Jesus was represented as lactating and maternal to fabricate an image of Christ as human caretaker. In the film *Junior* (1994), Arnold Schwarzenegger plays a character who becomes pregnant in a scientific study that he is conducting, and over the course of the film, he becomes very attached to his unborn child whose sex is unknown. Texts such as this raise the question of how the male body, in this case the body of a former champion bodybuilder, is related to something as seemingly essential to female subjectivity as pregnancy. It may be no accident that in this case a former bodybuilder's body is the one that becomes pregnant. The muscularity of the male body may be a precondition to fall into femaleness, and this imagined contrast between male and female bodies, the source of the comedy, reaffirms sexual binarism instead of destabilizing it. On the other hand, muscular masculinity may be precisely what allows for the desire to experience female pregnancy, and thus a change of masculinity, in a way that might be impossible for a less masculine man who experiences anxieties of actually becoming female.

At the same time as these aspects of the female body temporarily become part of masculinity, it is important to consider which aspects of the female body are not part of these sexed changes. Menstruation and the vagina, for example, are probably not as commonly appropriated by men, suggesting that the choice of the aspect of the female body that a man takes on already implies certain gendered ideas about what sex is and about how a man can resex himself. In short, pregnant men may symbolically function in ways that a man with a vagina cannot.

Queer Heterosexual Masculinity

Male cross-dressing can be understood by relation to women, but it can also be taken as a desire to flirt with homosexuality. The heterosexual man who successfully cross-dresses may end up in situations in which homosexuality becomes a possibility. In one scene in *Mrs. Doubtfire*, for instance, as the title character (played by Robin Williams) takes the bus dressed as a woman, the male driver flirts with him, and noticing his leg hair, comments that he likes a woman with hairy legs. While the bus driver may presumably be open to gender non-normativity, Mrs. Doubtfire refuses to flirt with him and by extension with homosexuality. While the film evokes homosexuality as a possibility, it is for comic effect only, and depends on the stable assumption that the cross-dressed man will never consider the possibility of homoeroticism. In such scenarios, masculinity flirts with the idea of homosexuality, but in order to contain its possibility and to reaffirm heterosexual masculinity through the gesture. Because cross-dressing inevitably suggests or leads to homoerotics, such texts may evoke it in order to expunge the thought and to move on in the narrative, which is presumably about something else. Cross-dressing can thus permit the performance of heterosexuality and of the binarism of sexuality, assuaging men's fear of becoming gay or queer.

Still, in some cases it may be difficult to discern to what extent a man wants to experience femininity and to what extent homoeroticism. Cross-dressing may in fact begin from a man's desire to approach some aspect of homosexuality through the avenue of gender change, which may be perceived as less threatening. The flip side of this situation is the potential homoerotic desire of a heterosexual man for the cross-dressed man. A man's desire for a man passing as a woman may signify his own interest in homosexuality or anti-heteronormativity, or it may be a way to work through homosexual inclination or homophobia. In Neil Jordan's film *The Crying Game* (1992), for example, the presumably heterosexual main character Fergus ends up in an amorous encounter with a female-appearing character named Dil. Though he vomits when he sees her penis for the first time, he learns over time to accept his own queer desire and to take on a new and complicated orientation. In some cases, non-normative gender presentation may be a source of eroticism in itself, with the gender mixture or combination not simply a code for homosexuality but another gender presentation altogether.

If a heterosexual man can cross-dress as a woman to take over femininity, he can appropriate male homosexuality as well for various ends of his own. In contemporary US popular culture, heterosexual men often flirt with the idea of homosexuality – whether through jokes about their being gay, or about the queerness of other straight men. From one perspective, these cross-orientations affirm heterosexuality by contrast, in a sexual version of the cross-dressing model discussed earlier. The very idea that a late-night talk show host is actually gay or queer is dispelled when he makes a joke in which he evokes his own potential homosexuality. An increasing number of straight men play gay men's parts in films, and that sexual cross-over can represent men's flirtation with homosexuality. Or it can serve to increase his range of performance and render him more attractive to women. The equivalent of the cross-dressing films mentioned above is the growing cinematic genre in which heterosexual men pose as gay to gain some advantage, as in *The Closet* (2001), *Strange Bedfellows* (2004), and *I Now Pronounce You Chuck and Larry* (2007). In the last two films, two heterosexual men pose as a gay couple to procure certain domestic partner benefits. They eventually come out as heterosexual, but also as better friends than they were before the sexual disguise. Becoming gay can be a way, then, to create a bond, with homosexuality serving as a trope for a kind of male–male intimacy often viewed as lacking in heterosexual men. In these kinds of representational flirtations, the idea of a male–male relationship is viewed as attractive – and becoming gay (metaphorically or temporarily) can be a way to deconstruct certain traits of masculinity. A man's becoming gay may refer him back to his boyhood before homophobic injunctions and heteronormativity required him to have non-intimate relations with other males. Appropriated male homosexuality can thus serve as a technique to move into a new space of masculinity critical of the gender status quo. Heterosexual queer masculinity, as a specific gender presentation, may have willful, political intentions when queerness is taken on as a tool for gender disruption. For a heterosexual man that sees the possibility of appropriating femininity as difficult or undesirable, queer heterosexual masculinity may provide an outlet to question gender normativity.

But queer masculinity is not always non-normative. In the three movies mentioned above, for instance, the men are trying to get something by posing as gay, meaning that they may fear losing something as straight men. Similar questions should be asked, then, about sexuality as were asked about gender. Is the man acting gay trying to remasculinize himself? Is he trying to obtain something for himself or to defuse a threat that male homosexuality is somehow better than his own sexual or gendered subjectivity? Does he somehow need to queer himself in order to make himself more attractive to women?

Lesbians Make the Man

If heterosexual masculinity is constructed through male homosexuality, it does likewise in relation to lesbianism. Stereotypically, heterosexual masculinity takes special erotic pleasure in thinking about or watching lesbian sexual acts. Pornographic films aimed at heterosexual men often include a sex scene between two women. Men may be aroused by the idea of a woman who describes herself as bisexual, or they may express titillation at the idea of two women having sex or the idea of a *ménage à trois* composed of themselves and two women. Some men are aroused by women who fight (in roller derbies or wrestling matches, for instance) because they imagine or fantasize that the fight will turn into sex, that female aggression is potential sexuality. In addition, a certain strand of cultural production, usually created by heterosexual men, represents male lesbianism. The nineteenth-century French poet Charles Baudelaire, for example, wrote poems about lesbians, as have other poets such as John Donne. It may appear strange to those who do not experience this kind of eroticism that a man writing lesbianism is not considered anti-masculine or queer, but in fact reaffirms masculinity. In this sense, even among men who view gender as very stable and fixed, male sexuality has the potential to be destabilized since heterosexuality is constructed in relation to a certain kind of homosexuality. What does this relationship, in which heterosexual masculinity is seemingly anti-heteronormative, signify?

This kind of desire should not necessarily be taken as a brand of queer desire or a way to queer masculinity or heteronormativity, but rather as a hypermasculinity, as another way in which masculinity is detoured through the other in order to assert itself. In this sense, masculinity disguises its functionings through representations of same-sex female sexuality. Erotic watching (a man watching two women have sex) is in a certain sense the ultimate form of scopophilia because masculinity is completely disengaged from the sexual act. His ability to watch the act is doubly pleasurable because it is purely visual: he is not involved at all in the sexual act and is thus outside of possible anxieties about performance, premature ejaculation, erectile dysfunction, etc. In other words, his sexuality can be entirely defined by looking, affirming the advantages accorded to the gaze. Watching a woman and a man have sex threatens to be homoerotic in nature because the man may be aroused, at least in part, by a naked man having sex. Since identification and desire are fluid, heterosexuality can never be fully maintained in a stable way. With lesbian sexuality, the man can watch a sexual act between two people without this anxiety. A man who makes a titillated remark about the idea of a woman having sex with another woman, then, might be gesturing toward his desire for non-threatening scopophilia. In pornographic scenes, two women may act like men as one of them uses a dildo to have "intercourse" with another woman to mimic a heterosexual couple. In this way, the act might begin as a way to avoid male anxieties about heterosexual sex, but then symbolically return to the male body so as to dispel the threat that the penis might be superfluous. Such kinds of representations rarely take lesbian sexuality on its own terms, but rather construct it for masculinity's own ends which are related to male gender subjectivity.

Lesbian representation of this type may not be prompted by masculine subjectivity per se, but may instead be closely linked to homosociality. Here, it is not a heterosexual woman who functions as the mediator of desire for two men, but rather a lesbian sexual act or relationship. A male poet who writes a lesbian poem might not simply be depicting female same-sex desire or act, but attempting to relate to other men, by using the poem as a tool to bond with other men over a kind of eroticism that they relate to but that excludes male homoeroticism. Two men talking to each other about lesbian sex might be performing a similar function, and lesbian porn scenes could themselves be seen as an exchange of a certain kind of women among men.

The exchange of lesbianism extends the notion of triangulation to incorporate, instead of reject, male homoeroticism. If two men are exchanging women – perhaps because of some kind of rivalry (e.g., two poets trying to prove their poetic talents) – one root cause, as discussed in chapter 2, is homophobia or fear of homosexuality. This kind of exchange is thus a special kind of mediator of desire for male subjects and for social signification. On the one hand, it displaces homophobia through a double woman function. What could be less homoerotic or better prove that two men do not have desire for each other than two women having or potentially having sex? These two women serve the purpose better than one woman, for while one woman might choose one of the men and disrupt the triangle, the men can relate to the imagined lesbian act equally and not worry that the lesbian couple will chose one man. But on the other hand, it is possible to view the lesbian act as allowing men to approach male homosexuality without coming close to it. In this way, imagining lesbianism is a technique whereby men can flirt safely with the idea of homosexuality and can have fantasies of women that are also fantasies of two members of the same sex. This potential displacement might be more at play in representational circumstances in which the women both act like men. A porn scene in which two women take out dildos and have intercourse with each other may evoke the subtext of a gay male sex scene. In this sense, then, the two women function together as signs of male homosexuality. This gender configuration is dependent on representational connections between lesbians and gay men. Lesbianism could be a form of homosexuality that permits discussion about, or a flirtation with, male homosexuality in a context in which it may be more difficult to talk about the latter and in which male and female homosexuality are categorized together under rubrics such as "sexual orientation." Still, this flirtation can ultimately serve to expunge homoerotics or an anxiety about homoerotics. In this sense, then, lesbianism serves as yet another disguise for masculinity to recreate itself in a way that is simultaneously visible and invisible.

Bibliography

On cross-dressing as a tool to remasculinize, see Elaine Showalter, "Critical Cross-Dressing: Male Feminists and the Woman of the Year," in *Men in Feminism*, ed. Alice Jardine and Paul Smith (New York: Methuen, 1987); Tania Modleski, *Feminism without Women: Culture and Criticism in a "Postfeminist" Age* (New York: Routledge, 1991).

For a sample study of how male authors appropriate female voices within a specific context, see Elizabeth D. Harvey, *Ventriloquized Voices: Feminist Theory and English Renaissance Texts* (London: Routledge, 1992).

On the use of birthing metaphors by male writers, see, for instance, Katharine Eisaman Maus, "A Womb of his Own: Male Renaissance Poets in the Female Body," in *Sexuality and Gender in Early Modern Europe: Institutions, Texts, Images*, ed. James Grantham Turner (Cambridge: Cambridge University Press, 1993), 266–88. See also Sherry M. Velasco, *Male Delivery: Reproduction, Effeminacy, and Pregnant Men in Early Modern Spain* (Nashville, TN: Vanderbilt University Press, 2006).

For Sigmund Freud's influential essay on castration and the fetish, see "Fetishism," in *The Standard Edition of the Complete Psychological Works of Sigmund Freud*, vol. 21, trans. James Strachey et al. (London: Hogarth, 1953–74), 152–7.

On the castrato, see Joke Dame, "Unveiled Voices: Sexual Difference and the Castrato," in *Queering the Pitch: The New Gay and Lesbian Musicology*, ed. Philip Brett, Elizabeth Wood, and Gary C. Thomas (New York: Routledge, 1994), 139–54.

For masculinity as not mourning a lost homosexuality, see Judith Butler, "Melancholic Gender/Refused Identification," in *The Psychic Life of Power: Theories in Subjection* (Stanford: Stanford University Press, 1997), 132–50.

For sample work on male lesbianism, see Thaïs E. Morgan, "Male Lesbian Bodies: The Construction of Alternative Masculinities in Courbet, Baudelaire, and Swinburne," *Genders* 15 (1992): 37–57.

6

Non-Male Masculinities

In the previous chapter, I focused on ways in which masculinity is disguised – as female, queer, gay, or lesbian – but in all cases I was operating under the assumption that a stable male body underlies the disguises. A man might appropriate birthing or he might cross-dress, but underneath he is still a man. Disguise may stabilize more than destabilize the male body's link to masculinity as the contrast between non-masculine dress and the male body has the net effect of highlighting the maleness or masculinity underneath. But, as discussed in chapter 4, masculinity has no natural attachment to the male body, even if it is commonly considered a male belonging. Consequently, masculinity should be examined in its recurring relation to other kinds of bodies besides male ones. For, as Eve Sedgwick writes, "sometimes masculinity has got nothing to do with … men."[1] In this chapter, I would like to consider what happens when masculinity is not directly or naturally connected to a body coded as male. In particular, I will focus on masculinity's relation to female and transsexual bodies.

Female Masculinities

When masculinity is taken as a disembodied phenomenon, existing on its own outside the confines of a given type of body, then traits ascribed to masculinity – such as power or virility – can be considered on their own terms, without regard for the sex of the body possessing them.

[1] Eve Kosofsky Sedgwick, " 'Gosh, Boy George, You must be Awfully Secure in your Masculinity!'," in *Constructing Masculinity*, ed. Maurice Berger, Brian Wallis, and Simon Watson (New York: Routledge, 1998), 12.

Thinking about how military prowess functions in and on the male as well as the female body, for instance, provides a more complete picture of military prowess than simply looking at the trait as possessed by men. In this way, gender can be considered more fully, and natural links between supposedly masculine traits and male bodies can continue to be destabilized. Masculinity inscribed on the female body is not simply male masculinity transposed, however, but should be viewed as another type of masculinity that may nonetheless have connections to male masculinity. Military prowess among female soldiers might be constructed very differently than it is for male soldiers, and individual or cultural reactions to female prowess might differ from responses to the same trait in men. In other words, the way in which female masculinity is understood – whether by women who exhibit it or by others, or in cultural discourses – may differ from the reception of its male counterpart simply by virtue of being housed in a female body.

One approach to examining female masculinity is through the ways in which cultural discourses receive or construct women coded as masculine. These women could include key morphologies of female masculinity, such as tomboys, drag kings, amazons, female bodybuilders, or butch lesbians. Or, they might be specific female figures such as Margaret Thatcher, Janet Reno, or Xena the warrior princess. Such women may call attention to female masculinity because of perceptions that masculinity is housed in a body where it should not be, and reactions to those women can be very revealing about cultural ideas on gender in a larger sense. Female masculinity may contribute to a larger cultural anxiety about what a woman is or should be, or it may evoke a threat that men will lose their supposedly natural hold on masculinity if women do not take flak for breaking out of their assigned gender. Negative responses to women who exhibit masculinity help insure men's domination over masculinity, making them its sole purveyor. The idea that female masculinity reveals masculinity's arbitrary connection to the male body is a central premise of the ground-breaking work of Judith Halberstam, who writes in *Female Masculinity* (1998): "far from being an imitation of maleness, female masculinity actually affords us a glimpse of how masculinity is constructed as masculinity."[2] Because these negative responses to women may be necessary to maintaining masculinity as male, female masculinity may be purposely evoked in

---

[2] Judith Halberstam, *Female Masculinity* (Durham, NC: Duke University Press, 1998), 1.

order to invite such responses and to contain gender fluidity. Part of the anxiety created stems from the fact that, like effeminacy, female masculinity destabilizes imagined binary oppositions between male masculinity and female femininity.

Despite the potential of female masculinity to illuminate the study of gender, it is surprising, Halberstam points out, how often female masculinity has not been taken into account in academic work on masculinity, and also how often female masculinity is not articulated as a viable gender presentation on the female body (ch. 1, esp. pp. 13–19). We rarely talk about "her masculinity" in the way we talk about "his masculinity" or "her femininity." Like cultural discourses, academics who study male masculinity only may be contributing to maintaining masculinity as male. One way to incorporate masculinity into gender studies is to pose some of the same questions about male masculinity with respect to female masculinity: Is it homosocial? Is it part of an unstable binary opposition? Is it defined through alterity? Does it attempt to remain stable and avoid instability? Questions of race, nation, and class should also be factored in, as perceptions of female masculinity are commonly mediated by these factors. Cultural anxiety may be linked, for example, to the rise of working women whose manual labor is seen as masculinizing in a given cultural context. With the examples above, one might ask questions such as: How does a given culture construct the tomboy as a gendered category? What cultural anxieties about gender do amazons reflect? How did UK voters receive or respond to Margaret Thatcher's masculinity? And what do these reactions say about gender in a given context?

As power is so closely linked to masculinity that it may appear as inherently masculine, women who have high or visible government positions (like Thatcher) might be particularly linked to female masculinity. But precisely because there is no natural or inherent link between masculinity and power, there is no reason that a woman with or in power must be considered masculine. Some would say, for instance, that Hillary Clinton is not masculine, despite her power and influence in the political realm, and that she has not exhibited masculinity but found a non-masculine way to hold power. On the other hand, some might make connections between Clinton and masculinity, viewing her gender as a type of female masculinity and seeing her as a man in a woman's body, a woman who acts like a man, or more of a man than many men. The same could be said of other traits potentially considered masculine. Like political power, military prowess may not be viewed as masculine when housed in certain female bodies. Some military women may be seen as masculine, while others are not. A strong or powerful woman like Wonder Woman, whose superhuman powers could possibly code her as masculine (like male heroes such as Superman), may or may not be viewed as masculine. Anxieties of female masculinity may mean that techniques are invented to keep potentially masculine women from being viewed as appropriating masculinity. Wonder Woman's feminine outfit, her voluptuous breasts, and her heterosexuality could all be considered ways to offset potential masculinity. The gender of another Wonder Woman – one with an androgynous outfit, small breasts, and short hair, but with exactly the same powers – would most likely be received very differently as a symbol of female power.

Although female masculinity should not be seen as male masculinity simply transposed onto another sex, reactions to female masculinity are nonetheless related to, or prompted by, male masculinity. We have seen that the desire to keep masculinity male is central to this link. But also, in a cultural context in which anxiety about male effeminacy is acute, a negative reaction to female masculinity may be explained by the transfer of the fear of emasculation onto women's supposed gender dissonance. These two anxieties may simply be part of a larger attempt to (re)construct a binary gender system. Male masculinity might influence how female masculinity is perceived, but the converse is also possible since female masculinity could exert an influence on male masculinity. In some contexts, female masculinity opens up a space for male masculinity to question the very naturalness of the link between sex and gender, or between the male body and masculinity. A visible example of female masculinity may have the effect of disassociating masculinity from the male body enough to create a fissure in gender representation, and this splintering may have gender ripple effects that make other sex–gender relations (e.g., male femininity) seem equally possible or acceptable. A man who is taught how to do something considered masculine may be more willing to accept his difficulties in performing that action when the teaching is done by a masculine woman.

Female masculinity can serve to reconstruct gender in other ways as well, especially as a purposeful tool or strategy for gendered ends. National ideologies might in fact need female masculinity to promote the nation's interests. During wartime, when many men are away, a nation may try to construct female masculinity to replace its missing male masculinity, as suggested by the well-known example of Rosie the Riveter from World War II. Or, because of fears of national effeminacy, a nation may want more masculinity for itself and desire female masculinity to help buttress the perceived strength or power of the nation. On a more individual level, female masculinity could be a strategy to empower women to move into realms traditionally occupied by men. If cultures crystallize certain non-physical traits around the male body, then female masculinity can serve as a way to evoke women's desire for those traits. In her *Vindication of the Rights of Woman* (1792), for instance, Mary Wollstonecraft argues that "exclamations against masculine women" mean nothing if "the attainment of those talents and virtues, the exercise of which ennobles the human character, and which raise females in the scale of animal being" is implied by the phrase "masculine women." Making female masculinity part of her pro-woman project, Wollstonecraft wishes that women "may every day grow more and more masculine."[3] Female masculinity in this case is a call to open up new gender presentations for women and to help make them culturally legible.

Like male masculinity, female masculinity should not be taken as monolithic or as defined in any one way. As my various examples suggest, it takes no single form that can be stably or simply defined. Even if lesbianism can be closely connected to female masculinity, there is no universal link between the two, as female masculinity can be heterosexual and as lesbianism can be unmasculine. Because it tends to occur more rarely than male masculinity, as an exception rather than the rule, female masculinity may never be fully accepted as a stable gender presentation in the same manner that masculinity is culturally assumed by men. Its less frequent occurrence means that it is commonly noticed more easily than male masculinity – one precondition for the critique it may provoke.

Still, it should not be thought that female masculinity cannot be assumed by a woman. In Ridley Scott's film *G.I. Jane* (1997), for instance, the main character Jordan (played by Demi Moore) is not accepted as a full member of her military squadron training to become Navy SEALs. At the end of a violent scene in which she proves her masculinity with the squad leader, she screams, "Suck my dick." From

[3]   *The Works of Mary Wollstonecraft*, ed. Janet Todd and Marilyn Butler, vol. 5 (London: William Pickering, 1989), 74.

this moment on, her masculinity is represented as stable and complete and the other SEALs recognize her acquisition of masculinity. In this case, the assumption of female masculinity takes place when G.I. Jane metaphorically takes on a penis, suggesting that the assumption of female masculinity requires a metaphorical sex change. Discursively defined, the penis comes to signify a stable female masculinity, with male masculinity playing a key role in that representation. Here, female masculinity needs to be metaphorically male to function or to complete itself. In other cases in which female masculinity is assumed, the extent to which male masculinity is evoked could be considered.

A key issue in the discussion of female masculinity, at least in its recent US guise, is its overlapping relation with lesbianism. In particular, women considered to be very masculine – whether their sexuality is actually understood or is invented – may be collapsed into the category of the lesbian. Some thought that Margaret Thatcher was a lesbian in part because of her political power. To tag Thatcher in terms of sexuality instead of gender means that she can be contained as a supposedly stable or knowable type of woman, whereas her masculinity might be harder to accept or to comprehend. Her masculinity may not be legible as a gendered morphology, and thus has to be transformed into a sexual one that is more culturally legible ("lesbian"). Another way to think about this transfer is as a crisis in the category of woman. When a powerful or strong woman has traits considered masculine, she cannot remain a woman, implicitly defined as a heterosexual woman, so the perception of a man-like woman falls into the category of the lesbian. Morphologies or examples of female masculinity might be examined to determine how or if the threat of lesbianism subtends the figure. Is there, for example, a cultural anxiety that the tomboy will grow up to become a lesbian? Does she have to be represented as clearly heterosexual (in films or child-rearing manuals, for instance) in order to dispel a fear that she will grow up and become a lesbian? Can the tomboy be a pre-pubescent representation of the adult lesbian? Or someone with a gender that has yet to be determined?

While female masculinity is potentially lesbian in cultural representation, it may also be experientially intertwined with lesbianism. The highly masculine categories butch or stone butch nearly always include lesbianism as one aspect of subjectivity. A person may identify as one over the other – as butch more than lesbian (or vice versa), even if she is seen to fit both categories and if one goes hand in hand with the other, or a person may oscillate between gender and sexual self-identifications. Cultural constructs of the butch or the lesbian may also focus on one aspect over another. She may be considered masculine more than lesbian (or vice versa), or the focus on gender may be a way to avoid talking about her lesbianism. Female masculinity can be a sign, a metonymic stand-in, for lesbianism, in a homophobic context in which lesbianism cannot be articulated as such but can only be approached indirectly. Such situations could include ones in which lesbianism is made visible but unarticulated, thus present but without fear of reprisal.

In premodern periods, before what we now call the lesbian existed as a discursive morphology, representations of women who had sex with other women often had a direct relation to female masculinity or to the sexual act. In early modern Europe, for instance, the tribade, a female figure who was defined largely by the idea that she rubbed other women with an enlarged clitoris (*tribein* in Greek means "to rub"), was considered to resemble a man because she had sex like a man rather than like a woman. While this figure has some cultural connections to what we now refer to as the lesbian, the tribade has more to do with defining a woman who acts like a man in bed than with creating a separate morphology. In many premodern cases, sexuality and female masculinity are so indistinguishable that some kind of an oscillation, whereby a woman is defined through gender (masculinity) at one point, and through sexuality (act or desire) at another, defines the figure.

We know that, on one level, female masculinity is a threat to male masculinity, a challenge to its hegemony, and that attempts to ignore or to suppress it could be viewed as ways to maintain the male body as the sole purveyor of masculinity. But on another level, women's attempts to have or to obtain masculinity may be considered positive by male masculinity, as they imply that there is something very desirable about it. That some women want to possess masculinity affirms its inherent value. One assumption behind this attitude is that the move from femininity to masculinity is upward, unlike the move from masculinity to femininity (often called "effeminacy" and labeled as negative and considered a move down). Sportswomen in traditionally male sports may be viewed positively because they are seen as trying to become like men and to acquire masculinity. A man watching a star female basketball player may be captivated by her move upward, or a man at a female bodybuilding show may be erotically aroused by a masculine woman because he sees her as a woman who aspires to be masculine. Or he might admire a sexually aggressive lesbian's ability to seduce another woman. A butch lesbian might be seen in a positive light by men who value masculinity because she proves to them that women want to be man-like. In such cases and in the *G.I. Jane* example, a butch woman's masculinity may be considered as complete and even superior to a man's. On the other hand, however, men might admire female masculinity in this way precisely because they know that women, according to their own definition of masculinity, can in fact never reach true masculinity. Without what are considered necessary aspects of masculinity (penis, testicles, or other corporal markers), women are unable to have masculinity fully. In what I refer to as an asymptotic view of gender, women are able to approach masculinity through these gendered traits, but in the end are not given the chance to reach it fully. Physical traits like the penis turn into proof, or reassurance, that the woman is unable to profit from masculinity in its fullness or totality. A man may feel amused by a very butch woman whose masculinity flatters his, but then ultimately see her masculinity as less complete than his own. Thus, in cases of a woman's masculinity, it is possible to consider to what extent or at what point her masculinity can be complete from the perspective of others, especially when the other is a heterosexual man invested in a limited notion of masculinity.

In some cases, women can purposely attempt to acquire signs of masculinity temporarily, as for instance by disguising themselves in order to acquire masculine traits. In Barbra Streisand's film *Yentl* (1983), for instance, the female main character decides to pass as a boy in order to study the Talmud, or to acquire what she sees as advantages accorded to Jewish masculinity. The nineteenth-century French female writer George Sand routinely dressed in men's clothing as a way to acquire many of the advantages that men had in the period but that remained unavailable to women. These kinds of female cross-dressing scenarios or situations raise some of the same questions as those in which men don women's clothing in non-queer contexts (see chapter 5). On one level, she may take on traditional signs of masculinity to better understand the experience of masculinity. Or, like the man who cross-dresses in order to be a better woman than any woman and thus to appropriate femininity for his own ends, a woman might be attempting to be a better man than a man can be, one who displays traits coded as non-masculine or non-phallic such as intimacy or intuition. This response to masculinity may be a way to construct or to contribute to a new type of masculinity that a woman wished existed more commonly. In other cases, a woman may cross-dress so as to show herself not passing as a man, or to approach masculine gender presentation by looking more like a boy or a gay man than a hetero-sexual man. Such a move or strategy can serve to reveal stable masculinity as fictional since the net result is not a man but a gender hybrid. This strategy is itself a kind of asymptotic masculinity, unlike the one discussed above, in which a woman purposely approaches masculinity through signs (such as dress), but never reaches masculinity or passes as a man. The goal in this case is not to reach masculinity, however, but to approach and then subvert it from within, to mimic it, in order to show that it is not unapproachable.

Transsexual Masculinities

The idea that masculinity is not the exclusive property of the male body can be taken to yet another level when transsexuality is placed in dialogue with masculinity.[4] Indeed, if both masculinity and a male body can be acquired by a body born or sexed female, then it is extremely difficult to argue or to assume that masculinity ever belongs to men. This is not to say that masculinity is suddenly acquired from scratch by a woman. A woman who transitions to a man already exhibits some masculine attributes, and the transition may be less about gendered traits and more about acquiring the traditionally sexed traits of masculinity (pecs, body hair, muscle, or hormones, for example). But those sexed traits imply masculinity too, since an idea of masculinity in the mind determines the desire or need to reconstruct the body to harmonize with it. That desire to make the body correspond to an interior masculinity does not necessarily mean that sex trumps gender, but makes masculinity into a tool for sex change. Further, the desire by some male-to-female (MTF) transsexuals to want to leave behind the signs of masculinity (e.g., penis, deep voice, body hair, testosterone) and to acquire female or non-male traits suggests that masculinity and maleness are not always valued or privileged. What many consider the

---

[4]   I use the term "transsexual" here, but the term "transgender" is widely used as an umbrella term to incorporate a large range of transsexualities (with and without surgery, pre- and post-op, hormonal and non-hormonal, etc.) as well as gender-variant practices and subjectivities.

ultimate inherent and indisputable characteristics of masculinity – its value – cannot define it in any essential way if this aspect of transsexuality is recognized and taken seriously as part of the gender system.

From one perspective, then, transsexuality is a key sign or indicator that masculinity and men are not naturally linked. A female-to-male (FTM) transsexual who passes as male, but is then found not to be a man, may evoke a negative or hostile reaction precisely because of an anxiety that masculinity can be taken on or assumed by someone who is not a man, and that man and masculinity are not stable referents. Transsexuals or representations of transsexuality can also function as signs of the arbitrary nature of the sign because they automatically destabilize gender. The question whether a FTM transsexual has a penis or not, and the unknowability of the answer for someone who has casual contact with him, means that sex does not subtend gender, that a biologically based definition of man is impossible, that male bodies can be reimagined in various ways, and even that the very idea of male and female must be disbanded in favor of a more complicated gender system. For these reasons, transsexuality has been taken as the ultimate incarnation of a post-structuralist approach to gender in which referent is dissociated from signified. The idea can be taken further if all of us are taken as transsexuals, metaphorically speaking. Once sex and gender are radically dissociated in this way, then the non-transsexual's gender cannot be stable either, and any gender is necessarily in movement. Indeed, new or unstable gendered embodiments are not limited to transsexuals, for all people in various ways imagine transsexuality, or what it would be like to be embodied differently. Men may imagine or dream about having a vagina or breasts, even if only momentarily. Such fantasies suggest that on some level, for all of us, sex and gender are disengaged and their link is at least in part arbitrary.

Sexual undecidability is further foregrounded by the often unstable border between FTM transsexuals and butch lesbians. The distinction may hinge on hormones, or surgery, for example, or in cases where surgery has not or will not take place, this distinction may be largely linguistic. If a FTM transsexual has no penis but considers himself a man, then it may be language and signification that ultimately define his gender and his sex, and not the body. Traditional notions of desire and sexuality, too, can be complicated by the ambiguity, as for instance when a gay man sexually desires a butch lesbian, a straight woman desires a transsexual man, or a FTM's sexual desire does not fit neatly into simple binary categories.

While transsexuality can be taken as an important destabilizer of masculinity, on another level it can be taken as the exact opposite, as a way to stabilize masculinity's close relation to the male body and to reject the arbitrariness of sex and gender. When a transsssexual wants to become a man, and not a woman, to pass as a man, to live life as a man, to create a coherent gender identity where sex and gender correspond in a stable way, to acquire gender advantages traditionally accorded to the male body, then masculinity may appear desirable over femininity, perhaps even hegemonic, and may not be destabilized but in fact (re)affirmed. Some women who have transitioned or are transitioning to become a man may feel that their masculinity is not performative or fluid and that the very notion that gender is performative does not allow for a transsexual subjectivity. Consequently, Butlerian approaches to gender can be in tension with transsexual ones, or the idea that gender is performative can clash with the idea that gender is essential. A transsexual position may find queer approaches to gender, in which one plays with gender to de-normalize it and keep it in motion, naive or exclusionary if such approaches are taken to be universal. On the other hand, if it is not gender per se, but the experience of gender, that is taken as essential, the two theoretical positions are not so antithetical. The woman who wants to become a man may experience a missing masculinity but may not assume that all masculinities are essential.

The transitioned FTM transsexual may be conceived of, by himself or by culture in a larger sense, as having assumed a sex. He might describe himself as fully a man, complete with girlfriend and male body. FTM transsexuals on talk shows might be shown shirtless, lifting weights, with muscles and chest hair so as to demonstrate that she has become a he. The audience might comment that they cannot tell that he used to be a she. One assumption in these kinds of TV segments is that certain signs of masculinity prove the stability of masculinity and dispel doubt about the FTM's masculinity. FTM transsexuals may also state that they are completely or wholly men. If asked about their genitalia, a man with a vagina might explain that the absence of a penis makes no difference since he feels wholly a man. In this way, anxiety about the possibility of a man with no penis is contained. He may not explain that masculinity is a complicated thing or that his masculinity offers another definition of masculinity, or that it is not the penis that makes the man in the first place.

Such a move to full masculinity can be one reason for tension between butch lesbians and FTM transsexuals. A butch lesbian may think that subverting or playing with masculinity as a woman is political, in a way that biologically changing sex is not or never can be, and that it implies gender subversion without buying into the natural link between man and masculinity. On the other hand, a FTM transsexual may respond that an actual change of sex is the ultimate subversion of gender. He may also present himself as a feminist FTM transsexual who subverts sexism and male dominance from within. These tensions and critiques assume an opposition rather than an unstable distinction between the butch lesbian and the FTM. But the unstable border between them and their disagreements about gender suggest that maleness itself is fluid and unable to be pinned down.

Finally, there is an entirely different way of conceiving of masculinity's relation to transsexuality, one in which the transsexual who passes does not reify a stabilized notion of masculinity but reveals very physically that masculinity is a complicated phenomenon. A FTM transsexual, for example, who has taken hormones, has had a mastectomy, but has a vagina could perform gender in a way rarely seen in culture at large. If that man has sex with a woman, the sexual act of a male and a female body with two vaginas can also reconfigure traditional masculinity. Thomas Beatie, a FTM who became pregnant and gave birth in 2008 exemplifies for some that masculinity cannot be antithetical to giving birth. Transsexuality can thus be taken as embodying gender movement itself, as a form of gender presentation in which masculinity is never stable, in which the movement of gender, or of sex, is one definitional element of transsexuality. This way of considering gender means that the goal of transsexuality is not to cross over into masculinity, but to remain in a constant state of crossing or to conceive of gender as a perpetual movement from and to. In this way, then, transsexuality can embody a whole approach to gender in which transsexual representations potentially signify the reconfiguration of the gender system as a whole.

Bibliography

On female masculinity, see Judith Halberstam, *Female Masculinity* (Durham, NC: Duke University Press, 1998), who focuses on lesbian female masculinity to the exclusion of female heterosexuality. See also Jean Bobby Noble, *Masculinities without Men? Female Masculinity in Twentieth-Century Fictions* (Vancouver: University of British Columbia Press, 2004); Eve Kosofsky Sedgwick, "'Gosh, Boy George,

You must be Awfully Secure in your Masculinity!'," in *Constructing Masculinity*, ed. Maurice Berger, Brian Wallis, and Simon Watson (New York: Routledge, 1995), 11–20. An interdisciplinary/theoretical book on heterosexual female masculinity broadly conceived has yet to be written.

On premodern morphologies of female masculinity, see especially "Perverse Presentism: The Androgyne, the Tribade, the Female Husband, and Other Pre-Twentieth-Century Genders," ch. 2 in Halberstam, *Female Masculinity*; Valerie Traub, *The Renaissance of Lesbianism in Early Modern England* (Cambridge: Cambridge University Press, 2002).

For a sample approach to historical female masculinity and its relation to national ideology, see "Nelson's Women: Female Masculinity and Body Politics in the French and Napoleonic Wars," *European History Quarterly* 37 (2007): 562–81. (Wilson provided me with the Wollstonecraft citation).

On the unstable border between butch and FTM transsexuality, see Judith Halberstam, "Transgender Butch: Butch/FTM Border Wars and the Masculine Continuum," *GLQ* 4, no. 2 (1998): 287–310 (see also ch. 5 in Halberstam, *Female Masculinity*); Jean Bobby Noble, "Sons of the Movement: Feminism, Female Masculinity and Female to Male (FTM) Transsexual Men," *Atlantis* 29, no. 1 (2004): 21–8. On drag kings, see "Drag Kings: Masculinity and Performance," ch. 7 in Halberstam, *Female Masculinity*.

On transsexual masculinity, see the appropriate essays in *The Transgender Studies Reader*, ed. Susan Stryker and Stephen Whittle (New York: Routledge, 2006). On transsexual narratives and the stability/instability of gender, see Jay Prosser, *Second Skins: The Body Narratives of Transsexuality* (New York: Columbia University Press, 1998).

On the use of the term "transgender," see David Valentine, "We're 'Not about Gender': The Uses of 'Transgender'," in *Out in Theory: The Emergence of Lesbian and Gay Anthropology*, ed. Ellen Lewin and William L. Leap (Urbana: University of Illinois Press, 2002), 222–45; Valentine, *Imagining Transgender: An Ethnography of a Category* (Durham, NC: Duke University Press, 2007).

For the controversial idea that we are all transsexuals in postmodern culture, see Jean Baudrillard, "We are all Transsexuals Now," in *Screened Out*, trans. Chris Turner (London: Verso, 2002), 9–14.

7

Masculinity and Racialized Subjectivities

Making Racialized Masculinities Visible

Throughout this book, I have discussed theoretical lenses through which to view masculinity, including the destabilization of binary oppositions, triangulation, the assumption of sex, and scopophilia. Once race is factored into the gender equation, however, such approaches have to be reconfigured to take this key aspect of human subjectivity into account. Masculinity may define itself in strict opposition to male homosexuality, for example, but what happens when that specific homosexuality is coded as black while the masculinity against which it is defined is white? Or vice versa? What happens to scopophilia if the man watching is white and the male body viewed is black? Race may not be a simple or discrete add-on in these relations, but require a rethinking of the actual model itself. Consequently, I might be critical of my own discussion of racialized masculinity in a separate chapter of this book, since race should not be a later addition to the study of masculinity either but should in some way be part of any study of gender. Gender and race are so often connected and dependent on each other that it is difficult to talk about one without talking about the other. Theories of masculinity that do not take race into account must be nuanced by considering race, precisely what this and the next two chapters will move toward doing. Masculine anxieties are projected onto gendered others, but race can be a key factor in how those projections get played out. And the idea that gender creates sex has racial implications. Because the construct of the nation, closely linked to but also separate from race, strongly influences the study of masculinity, I will focus on that topic in detail in chapter 8. The theories of triangulation discussed in chapter 2 can be reconfigured depending on the racial makeup of the three members of the triangle, a topic to be taken up along with questions of interracial masculinities more generally in chapter 9.

If masculinity is more visible or more fully understood when seen or studied in and on non-male bodies, as discussed in the previous chapter, it can also be said that masculinity is more visible and more fully understood in and on racially diverse bodies. It might be more noticed when inscribed on racialized male bodies, on which one does not expect to see it in a certain way because of certain preconceived notions of race. An Asian bodybuilder or an effeminate black or Latino male body might make some notice masculinity or its absence in a way that might not happen as easily with a white body not coded as racial. For race and gender are overlapping, closely related subject positions that construct each other. An African-American man may be automatically considered more masculine because of his race, whereas a Native-American man may be placed into the category of the effeminate even before his own individual subjectivity is considered. The person who notices the Asian bodybuilder because he or she is surprised by the possibility of the combination of muscularity with an Asian body suggests a preexistent idea about the relation between race and gender.

In terms of the question of gender visibility, it is crucial to consider how whiteness as a racial construct relates to masculinity. Whiteness may not be perceived as linked to masculinity at all, or masculinity may be inherently defined as white and thus not racialized. If the word "masculinity" is evoked in a given context, one may in fact imagine a white male body, but without attributing a racial coding to it. I have discussed attempts to hide masculinity as umarked so that it can function invisibly without opposition. The racialized equivalent of this phenomenon occurs when white bodies pass as raceless. The very use of the word "white" suggests an attempt to appear colorless, thus raceless, when in fact very few white people are actually white. If a key morphology of masculinity is implicitly defined as white, any hegemony or advantage assigned to that masculinity can be attributed to the category of whiteness, while non-white bodies are made into another masculinity. The figure of the bodybuilder, for instance, may be imagined as white when in fact there are numerous non-white bodybuilders. In this construct, the idea of muscularity, symmetry, and the perfect male body are implicitly linked to whiteness, meaning that non-white bodies do not theoretically reach such perfection or do so exceptionally. But that link between race and perfection remains invisible if the white subject does not admit a racial coding. In this sense, whiteness and masculinity operate in the same manner when they are hidden as relational or constructed subjectivities. So white male subjects may be doubly motivated – for reasons related to gender as well as to race – to efface their contingent subjectivity. As an umarked category, whiteness may help efface masculinity, and, conversely, unmarked masculinity may help whiteness pass unnoticed. It may be unclear whether the coat-and-tie white businessman tries to create and maintain an unmarked subjectivity because of his race, his gender, or perhaps more likely, some fuzzy combination of the two. The fuzziness of these two unmarked categories, the ultimate inability to separate out race and gender in any clear way, should be constantly kept in mind in the study of masculinity, whether white or non-white.

Certain definitions or morphologies of masculinity might be so racialized that the racial assumptions behind them are not even considered. The Southern gentleman, for instance, is assumed to be white to the point that the idea of a black Southern gentleman does not make cognitive sense. The martial artist might be automatically assumed to be of Asian origin, to such an extent that the Asian man cannot take on any other form of masculinity and a non-Asian man has to evoke Asian masculinity to be a martial artist. Other definitions of masculinity might, on the other hand, incorporate the possibility of racial diversity, such that diversity is one of their defining elements. Masculinities defined by sport might allow for a black or a white version, meaning that the double racial possibility is one constitutive element of the figure of the sportsman. But that definition of masculinity might also mean that other racial codings are excluded. In this case, a Latino or Native-American basketball player may be unimagined or unthinkable in the cultural mindset.

Although I am using the terms "race," "racial," and "racialized" here, my discussion also incorporates, or assumes, a broader notion of ethnicity. Sometimes the distinction between race and ethnicity is unclear, of course, while at other times the line of demarcation can be rather firm. What I am discussing here usually applies to race as well as ethnicities and cultural groupings, which can be gendered in various ways. In the same manner that whiteness is hidden as racial construct, unmarked ethnicities are kept from being marked. In the American context, white Anglo-Saxon men might try to hide their race, ethnicity, and gender all at once. Ethnic categories of masculinity may thus be marked or unmarked in terms of gender: the Southerner or the Jew may be labeled effeminate while the Yankee or the Protestant's masculinity remains unmarked but masculinized by opposition with an effeminate other. As I will discuss in chapter 8, national groupings function in ways similar to race: the German may be assumed to be more masculine than his French counterpart, simply by virtue of his nationality. While race, ethnicity, and nationality are all closely interrelated forms of subjectivity – all with connections to gender – many of the techniques of analysis discussed here apply to all three of these aspects of subjectivity, while others apply more easily to just one or two. Because of their overlapping nature, however, it is often difficult to separate them out with respect to gender and, consequently, it is often difficult to talk about them in discrete terms. A further problem is that ethnic, racial, and national constructs are themselves so unstable, and so culturally and temporally determinate, that any attempt to discuss them in theoretical terms necessarily hides their complexity and oversimplifies them. Even the very idea of a category of "race" is a modern invention, and thus culturally and temporally contingent, despite the fact that the concept existed in other ways before its current formulation.

Masculinity, Race, and the Analogical

One way to think about the mutual imbrication of race and masculinity is through the concept of the analogical, by which assumptions of similarity are made because of perceptions of similar physical or non-physical traits. The most common example of this phenomenon is the recurrent association made between certain races and women, the feminine, or effeminacy, which implies that certain racial groups are like women ("feminine"), or are men that have become womanlike ("effeminate"). For some, Asian or Asian-American masculinities, for instance, fall into this category because of perceptions of small size, hairlessness, or timidity, traits regarded by some as female-like. In early modern Europe, some considered the Amerindian to be excessive, and thus like women, who at the time were often viewed as immoderate in a number of ways, under the influence of Aristotle and other cultural texts. In this way, a given race can be imagined by one person or in the cultural imaginary as effeminate when it is advantageous for the person or group doing the imagining, often because it accords them greater power. The effeminate Amerindian prepares the way for white Europeans to come to the New World and do as they please, as they think they can do with women in Europe. Once analogical constructs are made, the ground is prepared for other links to be automatically made, and the racial group may be seen as predisposed to act like women or to be effeminate in new ways or situations. These analogical constructs thus predict or predetermine how racial masculinities are imagined, often by or for people who have little or no actual contact with them. Once these connections are made in the mind, one might be surprised if an Asian man acts in a certain masculine way or breaks the analogical link, when in fact it is the presence of the analogy in the first place that should come as a surprise.

Effeminate codings of race may also denote their corollary – emasculation. The effeminate man and the emasculated man are not identical or synonymous since the former denotes a man who has become more like a woman, the other a man who has fallen from his status as masculine or male. The emasculated man resembles a woman only if woman and man are considered opposites (not a man = woman). Or, he may also be considered like a castrated man, even if he is not really castrated or even if he has no connection with castration. An Asian or Native-American man considered emasculated might resemble a woman, then, but he may also be imagined to resemble a man with no penis or testicles. The association might result from a perceived lack of masculine traits or of a true or full male body, meaning that the mechanism behind the perception of emasculation might be either gender or sex.

One cause or offshoot of this kind of analogical thinking is that it allows another form of masculinity to be defined as more like masculinity by implied or expressed opposition, and to possess characteristics assumed to be held by hegemonic masculinity. In binary thinking, a construct of an effeminate Native-American man on the frontier may suggest a corresponding construct of a non-effeminate white man, which could be applied to the more specific figure of the cowboy for example. Any kind of gendered coding of a non-hegemonic grouping, then, should be analyzed not only for the kind of presuppositions behind it, but also for the kind of presuppositions behind the hegemonic group making or benefiting from the coding. In this way, those constructs or stereotypes can begin to be destabilized when they are revealed as ideological presuppositions that favor someone else. Within the realm of masculinity, the associations with hegemonic forms of masculinity are often with power or the ability to control, dominate, or rule over the other. With these links, it is unclear whether race or masculinity is at the origin of the construct, meaning that it is hard to tell whether masculinity or whiteness accrues more symbolic power from the constructs. While hegemonic white masculinity may commonly be opposed to masculinities of color, there is no reason that oppositions have to be made by white men or even have to involve them. An Asian male subjectivity might be defined in opposition to a white one, or African-American masculinity may be defined vis-à-vis Jewish masculinity. In all cases, the broad question of how and why racial associations with gender are being made – and in particular, possible attempts to create or affirm power or hegemony – should be considered. Often, such associations relate to nations' attempts to rule over other nations or races, a topic to be discussed in more detail in the next chapter.

This form of gendered analogy pertains not only to feminizing or devirilizing racial groups, but also to hypervirilizing them. In the US context, one recurring cultural analogy is the racist construct of the African-American man whose penis is imagined as long and whose masculinity is considered as excessive or as in overdrive. He might be taken to be excessively violent or excessively sexual. Stereotypical images of the macho Latino man (with a hairy chest and gold chains) might also be linked to a quantity of masculinity or be thought of as too much. On one level, the excessive or immoderate man might be taken as ideal, perhaps because of a capitalistic context in which emphasis on earning as much as possible and acquiring as many goods as possible codes excess in a positive light. But, on another level, this representation as excessive or immoderate does not necessarily suggest that the white man is his less masculine or effeminate other who lacks masculinity or has an insufficient quantity of masculinity. Rather, the image of the man in gender overdrive might be a way to suggest that he is out of control. The African-American man is so gendered or so sexualized, or so the racist logic goes, that he is unable to control himself since he wants to have sex, to break into houses, or to rape women. The man of excess, then, can be just as subject to the rule of hegemonic masculinity as the effeminate man, and consequently, the construct of non-excessive or moderate applies to the white man or to another racialized group seen as ideal by contrast. In this case, the implied contrasting man or group of men or people – the moderate one or the one in control – is justified in attempting to control black men, whether by simply watching him closely on the street or by incarcerating him where possible. This kind of thinking about excess can be a way, too, to code a group as lacking and thus not fully legitimate in terms of masculinity. The white man may be disturbed or anxious by the black man's virility or by a perception of gender similarity with himself, and respond to this anxiety by coding his racial other as lacking in some way (without intelligence, culture, self-control, financial success, etc.). In this sense, an excess of masculinity can be transformed into a lack, and lack may be a way to evoke excess in a different guise.

Though two racial groups may in fact be coded as opposites (excessive versus lacking masculinity), their opposition might imply, paradoxically, a similarity as a non-excessive and a non-lacking form of masculinity end up as others that together frame the moderate man in the middle as the dominant form of racially coded masculinity. So if the effeminate Asian man and the hypervirile black man are taken together not as two separate constructs but as part of a larger system of race–gender codings, the white man may be privileged as the man in the middle, neither too masculine nor too unmasculine, or as the man with the right or perfect amount of masculinity. Ending up in the middle is a way for white masculinity to be accorded the privileges of the happy medium and to keep those privileges away from the men coded otherwise. In this sense, a certain quantity of masculinity is implicitly or explicitly assigned to certain groups or to certain individuals because of their racial positioning. The very idea of quantifying gender in this way serves as another tool for assigning a clear and supposedly mathematical hegemony to a given racial–gender group.

These analogies are made with sexual as well as with gender constructs. Certain racial or ethnic groups may be more closely linked with sodomy or homosexuality than others, or be considered more likely to be actually homosexual. Arab men, for instance, may be more closely linked with homosexuality because of certain perceived characteristics that dovetail easily with same-sex sexuality (male-identified, homosocial, visibly affectionate with other men). The stereotype of the gay male "rice queen," a white gay man who desires and pursues younger Asian men, might fit into this category. A gay man might already view Asian men as more gay or as more effeminate than himself, meaning that he can affirm his own masculinity or heterosexuality by taking one as his sexual partner.

Constructs of racialized forms of female masculinity can be taken into account from this perspective as well. In the same way that certain forms of male masculinity might lend themselves more easily to certain racial constructs rather than others, a construct of female masculinity might be more closely connected to a given racialized construct while others are neither imagined nor culturally comprehensible as a possible category. African-American female masculinity, for instance, might be more likely to be imagined as a possible form of female masculinity than Asian-American female masculinity. This kind of presumption might be as much about female masculinity as it is about male masculinity. A certain racialized female masculinity might be imagined as possible because its corresponding male masculinity is considered so masculine that it spills over into women. Or, Asian-American female masculinity might be considered unlikely or unthinkable, in part because Asian culture as a whole is conceived of as effeminate, or because Asian men themselves are considered as non-masculine.

This issue of the analogical means that racial masculinities are linked with gendered traits, but analogy also operates with respect to gendered processes when the development of masculinity is taken to resemble a certain racial development. The most common construct may be the savage (or the primitive) in the developmental model of the Freudian schema. The primitive is considered not to have moved forward in terms of his own cultural development, unlike his Western or European equivalent who moves forward toward a state of increasing civilized perfection. The primitive does not develop or advance culturally, nor does he develop an unconscious or superego which allows him to repress certain elements of his primitive nature. On the other hand, the European is able to repress his libido and his selfish desires in order to live as a civilized person. This imagined civilizing process has been seen to parallel Freudian sexual development. The boy is considered to have a period of same-sex desire, in which he desires his father and identifies with his mother, in the classical Oedipal model, but the "normal" boy then moves on and becomes heterosexual whereas the adult homosexual is unable to leave this period of his life and to avoid identifying with his mother and desiring his father. Similarly, the primitive man is supposedly unable to leave behind an early period of civilization and to move on to a more civilized era. In this way, a structural or developmental analogy between these two groups is perceived. This analogy might be applied to various types of racial groups seen as pre-civilized or as non-European. The Native American might be representationally homosexual because he has supposedly not developed far enough. The black man may be seen as full of libido and pre-civilized because his gender and his racial category are both underdeveloped. In the introduction to his book *Racial Castration* (2001), David Eng develops this thesis, writing with respect to Freud's *Totem and Taboo* and "On Narcissism": "we witness a convergence of homosexuality with racial difference, a coming together of the homosexual and the primitive as pathologized, banished figures within the psychic landscape of the social proper."[1]

As the line between cause and effect is often unclear in analogy, it is hard to determine to what extent race influences gender and to what extent gender influences race in this model. Does the black man evoke libido because his race is seen as undeveloped? Or vice versa? It is more likely that there is a complex interplay between cause and effect by which race and developmental status can be cause or effect and by which each can influence or create the other. This kind of process-based analogy functions, for example, when connections are made between coming-of-age and racial codings. The Asian man may not be linked with coming of age, thus with achieving masculinity, and viewed as boy-like instead of man-like. The perceived lack of a maturation process can mean that other boyish characteristics are ascribed to him: he may be imagined as playful, comic, or androgynous. This construction can also retroactively explain his physicality: his body might be imagined as boy-like or prepubescent because he and his race symbolically never developed to become men.

The various kinds of analogical thinking I have been discussing here, the various ways in which race is combined with masculinity, are widespread throughout time and pertain to innumerable cultures, but they should always be considered within their specific sociohistorical context and not be taken as universal. Even the constructs I have used as examples in this chapter are not universal, but are culturally coded, and would not make sense to people from certain cultures. These specific codings change in complicated ways over time, even as basic

---

[1]   David L. Eng, *Racial Castration: Managing Masculinity in Asian America* (Durham, NC: Duke University Press, 2001), 13.

associations may remain relatively static over a defined period. Certain men may be coded as effeminate because of a cultural need at a certain point to dominate that group for certain specific sociohistorical reasons, and the way that effeminacy is constructed may mutate so as to adapt to new social conditions and to respond to previous analogical constructs. Even if constructs consistently privilege one group, the specificity of that privileging may have to change and adapt in order to maintain its effectiveness.

Racialized Binary Oppositions

The question of the analogical is closely tied to the use of binary oppositions discussed in chapter 1. To link Asian-American masculinity with effeminacy or African-American masculinity with hypervirility is to suggest qualities of another kind of masculinity by opposition. That opposition attempts to delineate two forms of racialized masculinity in a discrete way and to ignore shades of gray in favor of binarism. A form of masculinity may be positioned in opposition to woman at one point, and to another racial masculinity at another point, oscillating between a gendered and a racial other. That definitional oscillation operates, of course, with respect to other forms of alterity as well (the male homosexual, the boy, the nobleman, etc.). Over time and in various situations, then, masculinity's binarized definition changes in terms of the opposing element. That other does not have to be defined by simple racialized opposition (white man/black man) or by an opposition based solely on sex (man/woman), but by a more complicated, two-part opposition (masculinized white man/effeminate Asian man, for instance). Alterity, then, can be thought of not as a single other, but as an analogical link, a racial and gendered other all in one. While race is my focus here, the double analogy can function in other ways as well, for instance with respect to sexuality, class, or (as we will see in the next chapter) nationality. Effeminacy and homosexuality, for instance, might be merged forms of alterity for heterosexual masculinity, or the seemingly effeminate nobleman might function as an other for working class masculinity in terms of both class and gender.

An analogical link might be double, composed of race plus gender, but it could also contain even more analogies housed in the body of a single other. That other might evoke a complicated combination of constructs of race, nationality, gender, sexuality, class, etc. A class–gender analogy might be key at one moment or in one situation while a race–class analogy might be key at another time or in another situation. A noble Indian man perceived as androgynous might be construed as other by virtue of a certain combination of elements of his subjectivity. Those elements taken as other to the perceiver necessarily select out certain parts of subjectivity and ignore others. The Indian man above may also be English-speaking or soccer-obsessed, elements of subjectivity that might be similar to that of a white man who constructs him as other. But ignoring such elements allows for a more discrete, binary opposition and thus a clearer self/other distinction.

These analogy-based binary oppositions operate in the same ways as more standard oppositions. They, too, are inherently unstable, and suggest that when they are evoked, it is because masculinity requires others in order to be defined and not because that racialized masculinity actually is a certain way. Masculinity is dependent on its others for its definition, and it constantly risks falling into the opposed elements established as other. Thus, despite constructs that represent the other as different, the white man repeatedly risks becoming like the effeminate or excessive racial subject that he makes his other. The black man might be considered out of control in terms of sexuality or violence, but how can his supposedly abundant or excessive masculinity not be considered desirable on some level too? Certain cultural constructs often linked to black masculinity (gestures, language, or rap music, for example) can be employed to assuage white men's anxiety of their own lacking masculinity when a white man identifies with a perceived element of another racial masculinity to masculinize himself. The imagined elements of the racial other might thus be curative for the gender anxieties of white men. The black male body, while its erotic potential is sometimes discounted in US culture, can be something to imitate for white male subjects in terms of sexuality or other corporally defined aspects of masculinity such as sports or bodybuilding. A white man may even imagine himself as a black masculine body, as a Michael Jordan or a Denzel Washington for instance, or he may imagine himself as an Asian martial artist. With the possibility of racial incorporation, how can a white man know when he should define himself in opposition to black masculinity and when he should appropriate it? American culture may define black masculinity as white masculinity's ultimate form of alterity, but how, ultimately, can a white man know when a black man is other? While white men might perceive racially coded opposition, they are also ambivalent or even anxious about that opposition as they cannot help but move back and forth across that perceived border of self and other.

On the other hand, identification with another racial masculinity may suggest a desire to subvert white masculinity by including non-white aspects within it. White male subjects may incorporate what they perceive as elements of black masculinity in order to subvert white masculinity and to destabilize its hegemony. White men might take on elements of Asian masculinity when they believe that they can subvert their own gender subjectivity through traits such as a feminine *yin*. Or, an anxious white male subject could be trying to construct a certain racial masculinity in order to forge a new, less hegemonic, masculinity with which he can identify. A heterosexual white man may imagine Asian men as effeminate because he himself feels effeminate and wants a non-white racial masculinity with which he can identify. Another identificatory possibility is that racial perceptions may be a way to live out gendered fantasy fulfilled through that construct. A heterosexual woman, for instance, who does not desire virile men might contribute to a construct of Asian men as effeminate because they are the kind of man that she wants to desire. Or, a heterosexual man may live out homoerotic fantasies through another racial man coded as woman-like, and thus resembling his usual object of desire.

In the same way that the man who cross-dresses may be trying to be a better woman than the woman herself or may be aiming to be a more gender-balanced man (see pp. 120–4), the attempt to incorporate or to appropriate racial masculinities should be examined for potential co-opting on the part of another racial masculinity. White men may try to co-opt black masculinity in order to increase their hold over it and to keep it from possessing advantages that they feel they lack. In the film *Soul Man* (1986), for example, a white man chemically changes race to get a university scholarship earmarked for African-American students. However, his taking on blackness is not prompted by a desire to experience another racial masculinity, but by a desire to take it over and appropriate the perceived advantages accorded to it. With respect to Asian masculinity, other male subjects may attempt to appropriate the masculine aspects of martial arts into itself, as in certain films like *The Karate Kid* (1984). The new masculinity, a white–Asian combination, may be a way to forge an even better one than had previously existed. The issue of the race of T. E. Lawrence in representations such as the popular 1962 film *Lawrence of Arabia* is one such example. The character is a "white Arab" who fights for Arabs and for the British and whose subjectivity is located somewhere between the two groups. Is the film a way for white/European masculinity to co-opt Arab subjectivity for its own ends, or is it a way to destabilize ethnic masculinities? Often, determining whether the appropriation reconstructs or deconstructs hegemony may be difficult, and the ultimate response may be that it does both at the same time.

Constructs of male others may be fabricated as oppositional in various ways, but the construction of alterity can also function through absence when a racial coding is expelled from the possibility of opposition in the first place. In the United States, where black/white functions as the primary racial opposition, other racialized masculinities may not factor in as potential or possible others. Despite the number of Latino men in the US, Latinos may not be on the radar screen in terms of gender subjectivity for some, even as a form of alterity. Similarly, Jewish or Native-American masculinity might not be perceived as in opposition to white or other masculinities, and fall outside the system of binarized constructs. For this reason, a given masculine subjectivity may not be considered to have much of a relation to systems of masculinity at all. Not serving as other can render a brand of masculinity invisible or less binarized than others that commonly play a role in opposition. Gendered binarisms can thus exclude on two levels: by making the non-hegemonic half of the opposition an inferior or less valid form of masculinity, and by keeping a group out of the opposition in the first place. In both cases, however, exclusions serve to maintain one group's hegemony.

While gender clarity is a sine qua non in the fabrication of binarism, the concept of indeterminacy can be attached to a form of masculinity, as a way to keep it outside binary opposition, and the operative opposition might be between a more determinate and a less determinate masculinity. A construct of Native-American masculinity may be predicated on instability because the group is perceived as without a national homeland. Gender may be indeterminate because Native-American masculinity is imagined in a borderless space, perhaps in opposition to white American masculinity whose borders are defined and clear. In the film *Transamerica* (2005), the pre-op transsexual main character Bree, who is in the process of becoming a woman, has a male Native-American love interest named Calvin. The character's gender indeterminacy means that he can function as the love interest of a character in gendered transition, as Calvin, too, is symbolically in between sexes. This construct may also refer implicitly to the figure of the so-called berdache, a gender-indeterminate Native-American morphology of gender that was often an accepted aspect of Native-American culture. In some cases, this construct as outside opposition can be a way to relegate Native-American masculinity to the outside of gender subjectivity, but in other cases it can serve as an identificatory element that masculinities interested in moving outside binary definitions adopt (as in the film cited).

Although the kinds of oppositions that I have been discussing may largely be the product of hegemonic gender constructs, they can nonetheless be internalized as part of non-hegemonic masculinities. An Asian man may buy into effeminate analogies, and respond in various ways to them, by accepting as well as rejecting them. Or, a more complicated form of internalization, referred to by Daniel Boyarin as "double consciousness" in his analysis of Freud and Frantz Fanon, can be operative.[2] In this model, a man of a racially non-dominant masculinity internalizes racialized–gendered forms of alterity while remaining simultaneously conscious of himself as other (because of his race) and as not other (because of his masculinity). Subject to hegemonic constructs, he is both their victim and their enabler as he simultaneously suffers from and deploys them. A Jewish man, for example, may be gender same but racial/ethnic other, disempowered by racial emasculation but benefiting from his masculinity or his maleness. He may transform these oppositions into new ones that allow him to construct others. The black man who suffers from oppressive oppositions between black and white masculinity may respond by transforming a racialized opposition into gendered or sexual alterity in order to deal with or to respond to the oppositions which disempower him. For instance, the black man may define himself in opposition to women, to homosexuality, or to effeminate Jewish men. Conversely, a Jewish male subject may respond to his cultural coding as effeminate by constructing another binary opposition such as white/black (with Judaism considered white)

---

[2] See Daniel Boyarin, "What Does a Jew Want? or, The Political Meaning of the Phallus," in *The Psychoanalysis of Race*, ed. Christopher Lane (New York: Columbia University Press, 1998), 211–40.

or heterosexual/homosexual and by placing himself on top. A gender or racial opposition can be transformed into another type of opposition, but the two constructs are connected since one hinges on the other as disempowerment is transformed into empowerment at the expense of a new type of other. This hinge model can be viewed as a result of the transfer of internalized binary oppositions of hegemonic culture to the non-hegemonic. As Boyarin discusses this principle within the context of Fanon's work, "the colonizer's misogyny and homophobia become internalized in complicated ways, then projected by the colonized against women and gays. It is not I who have these despised characteristics; it is they!" (p. 225). This internalization–projection can be seen as an attempt to reracialize one's own non-hegemonic masculinity to move toward a dominant white or white-like masculinity.

Racialized Gender, Racialized Sex

In chapter 3, I talked about ways in which the repetition of gender constructs over time leads to or creates the idea that they are inherent or natural aspects of the body, even as the very repetition signifies that constructs are unstable because they have to be constantly remade in order to affirm themselves. This way of thinking about gender can be applied to the gendering of race and the racializing of gender. The cultural assumption of the black man's penis as particularly lengthy is a case in point: cultural views of the black man create a discourse of his penis or of his biology, even as those views try to hide their status as arbitrary or constructed, and present his penis as biologically or naturally long. The body of the Asian man may come to be perceived as feminine when in fact it is not some objective idea of sex that is the basis of the perception but rather a racialized version of gender. He is not feminine for some genetic reason but because of cultural perceptions of what a man is or should be. The circumcision of the Jewish man may come to be perceived as a type of castration which in turn proves his inherent effeminacy, his emasculation, or his similarity to the female body whose genitalia have been taken as castrated-like in certain contexts. Or, the Asian man may be assumed to be biologically emasculated because of the perception of his naturally small penis, when he may already be assumed to be effeminate even before his penis is seen or sized up. A perception of a non-masculine male body or of maleness may double back onto gendered perceptions, and affirm or reaffirm them. If one perceives Asian penises as small and thus the Asian body as non-masculine or effeminate, then one may be more likely to see Asian men's personalities as more feminine or non-masculine as well. In this sense, then, racial and gender constructs function in tandem to (re)construct the ways in which male bodies are perceived. A certain kind of racialized male body is being constantly constructed and reconstructed so as to make racialized bodies into discrete categories, much as men and women are made into discrete sexes. Once discrete, a sexed–racialized body can be assumed to act in a certain way that may be taken as natural and coherent, and the analogies discussed above applied to those bodies in a stable way. Hegemonic male bodies may then be assumed to be different and superior by contrast, as power masquerading as biology is asserted over the racialized male body.

The style of gender performativity has a connection to race as well: masculinity may tend to be performed in one way in one racial or ethnic context, and in another way in other contexts. What this suggests is the lack of inherent or natural masculinity for a given racial group. A given racial masculinity might be coded as natural, but any masculinity perceived as unified is only an agreed-upon style linked to that group and to a certain kind of body. The repetition of that style then comes to stand in for that racial masculinity. While a man performs a racialized style of masculinity, he may also perform another style of masculinity than that assigned to his body. In this way, cross-racial performances of masculinity can reveal the arbitrariness of racial masculinities and of racially coded male bodies. When a white actor plays a non-white character in a film, for instance, he reveals the mechanism of performance underlying racial masculinity.

Resisting Analogical Constructs

Discourse is a central element of the racialized gender constructs that I have been discussing. Legal discourse in the old South made the African-American man out to be a criminal or a rapist, justifying his hypermasculinity and thus his lynching. These kinds of constructs should not be seen as stable ones that reflect some reality of race and gender but as oppositions that create responses and resistance, even as, on the other hand, they are reified and internalized, and not always easily disbanded.

The oppositions established in or through discourse may create interdictions that paradoxically have the effect of creating new forms of masculinities. If white men are not supposed to have a relation with black men in some context, then the former may respond to that interdiction not by simply avoiding black masculinity but rather by creating a relation with it that he may not have had in the first place had the interdiction not existed. Cultural constructs of black masculinity as other may, therefore, in fact create the very desire for interracial friendship or love that is theoretically denied or considered impossible.

These kinds of associations are inherently unstable, and thus internally problematic for the reasons discussed, but there are also more explicit or more conscious strategies for resisting them. When gendered–racialized constructs are evoked, they may be immediately juxtaposed with counter-examples to show how the construct does not hold. For some, this might mean that the construct is not true or is a stereotype. Clearly, these constructs can simply be refused by dissociating or destroying the analogies made between race and gender. When someone makes a statement about Latino men as macho, someone else may critique that person by citing examples of Latino men who do not fit the stereotype. On the other hand, resistance to such stereotypes can in turn provoke resistance, as someone may proclaim that they know someone who fits the stereotype or that stereotypes come from somewhere. But the net effect of the articulation of the construct and its critique can be a more complicated phenomenon, a subjectivity in movement between the two positions. Latino masculinity might end up defined not by the stereotype of machismo per se, but by the recurring interaction or tension between the stereotype and its articulated absence. This definition of racialized masculinity corresponds to ways in which masculinity (and gender in a larger sense) is defined by its oscillation between stable and unstable, between essential and fluid (see pp. 49–52).

Supposedly stable constructs of racial masculinity can also be voluntarily resisted through various counter-cultural representations. One strategy to destabilize or to resist them is to overdetermine them, as a way to bring them out into the open. David Cronenberg's film *M. Butterfly* (1993) exemplifies how racialized masculinity is expressed or revealed as overdetermined by perception. In the film, the main character Gallimard, a French diplomat with views of Asian culture as submissive to Western culture, falls in love with an Asian whom he believes to be a woman but who is in fact a transgendered biological woman with a penis. Despite the fact that they perform sexual acts together and have a love affair over a period of time, Gallimard never realizes that M. Butterfly has a penis and a male body underneath his/her clothing. The movie highlights, or calls attention to, the fact that Gallimard has made such strong connections between race and gender, and that he has reconstructed sex through the lens of his own views of Asian culture as submissive. The film can be seen as a critique, or even mockery, of the race–gender nexus itself as it reveals the blinding extremes to which a white European man can take these connections. Because the film is structured by intertextual references to Puccini's opera *Madame Butterfly*, the role of Western cultural discourses in creating such constructs is highlighted as well.

Artists or writers explicitly overdetermine racial–gendered codings to make them visible in other ways. In his photographs, Robert Mapplethorpe takes certain constructs of black masculinity, such as the hypersexualized black man with a large penis, and instead of denying the stereotype per se, makes it a centerpiece of his photos. In one of his famous photos in *Black Book* (1986), for instance, Mapplethorpe shows a naked black man with a very large penis and a paper bag over his head.[3] He seems to be making the point that the black male body is considered by culture as corporal only, that analogical constructs between race and masculinity in this case efface the face, as it were, and focus solely on the biological aspects of the body, particularly the penis. As the more human aspect of the body, the face is radically erased or hidden to show in a very visible way what it is that culture can do or does to the black male body in terms of seeing and being seen. The photograph thus overdetermines – or shows how culture overdetermines – the black male body as corporal and defined by the penis. In *Black Skin, White Masks* (1952), Frantz Fanon discusses how the black man can take a racial stereotype that he is assumed to embody and overperform it by making a scene.[4] If he senses, for instance, that he is being viewed as criminal-like on the street, he might start to act like a

---

[3]   Robert Mapplethorpe, *Black Book* (Boston: Bullfinch Press/Little, Brown, 1986), 68.
[4]   Frantz Fanon, *Black Skin, White Masks*, trans. Charles Lam Markmann (New York: Grove Press, 1967), 114.

hyper-criminal. In a double entendre, Wallace calls the idea "acting out," or "a strategy for the subversion of fetishism and stereotype in which the colonized cause a scene, as not to be trapped, framed, within one."[5] By performing to excess the stereotype that codes him, the black man reveals how it is a constructed stereotype that overdetermines others' attitudes toward black masculinity, hopefully as a step in the process of destabilizing them.

Perhaps a more common approach to this problem is to focus on taking racialized masculinities on their own terms and contextualizing them without imposing cultural norms from another group. Many racialized masculinities are predicated on constructs made by another segment of culture. A close study of what masculinity means within the context of that actual group and not in hegemonic culture or in another cultural group can reveal new ways to consider masculinities and have the ultimate effect of resisting those hegemonic constructs in the first place. African-American masculinity, for instance, is sometimes considered to contain an androgynous aspect, a vestige of gender constructs found in parts of Africa. Consequently, African-American masculinity may not be coded as hypervirile when taken on these terms, but as at least partially androgynous, which may be a more authentic way to imagine it. Thinking in these kind of terms allows for hegemonic analogies to be destabilized, replaced, or even disbanded by reference to non-hegemonic formulations of gender. Or, it may create a third version of racialized masculinity that does not wipe out hegemonic constructs, but oscillates between hegemonic and authentic ones. A hypermasculine coding and an androgyny, for instance, may both be in play and together define the construct of African-American masculinity.

There can be a gap between hegemonic gender constructs and more authentic ones in a more fundamental way when the very category of masculinity is different in the two contexts. Certain cultures do not consider or focus on the concept as much as others, which means that masculine constructs can say more about the culture or race that focuses on them than on other cultures. In some contexts, sexual acts or sexuality might be the closest approximation of what is commonly

---

[5]   Maurice O. Wallace, *Constructing the Black Masculine: Identity and Ideality in African American Men's Literature and Culture, 1775–1995* (Durham, NC: Duke University Press, 2002), 175.

called "gender" in English. One's sexual position (top/bottom) or one's relation to power in sex might be categorizing factors more than masculinity. Consequently, employing the concept of masculinity to code the gender of a group may be culturally off key in the first place, and even the use of the very concept of masculinity may be inappropriate and hegemonic on its own. Languages may not have gender in a grammatical sense, and the concepts of gender and masculinity may not be articulated. Rather, other elements of subjectivity may be more likely to be organizing principles that resemble, but do not equal, masculinity or that dovetail so closely with it that they have to be taken into account. Miescher studies the interaction between age and gender in southern Ghana, arguing that "seniority has been as crucial to the construction of identity as gender."[6] To carefully examine how a culture defines gender on its own terms or in its own way can, therefore, reveal how other cultures impose gender constructs on that group for their own definitional ends.

Racialized Scopophilia and Masculinity

In chapter 4, I discussed the relation between the masculine love of looking (scopophilia) on the one hand, and the male body on the other. To repeatedly look in an erotic way at female bodies creates and affirms an opposition between the viewer and the viewed, and defines viewpoint by taking control of materiality. To be the man who watches implies power. If I see the other in a certain, fixed, way, then the image I have can be more easily made into the supposed knowledge of that person or group, and the way I decide they look can become the way they are. Conversely, my lack of interest, whether intended or not, in controlling a person or category of person can render that group invisible from view. A heterosexual man may not watch or see gay men or Asian-American men, and this perception of invisibility consequently becomes attached to those groups' codings, de facto defining them and presumably stabilizing their identities as somehow hidden or not worthy of note.

---

[6] Stephan F. Miescher, "Becoming an Ɔpanyin: Elders, Gender, and Masculinities in Ghana since the Nineteenth Century," in *Africa after Gender?*, ed. Catherine M. Cole, Takyiwaa Manuh, and Stephan F. Miescher (Bloomington: Indiana University Press, 2007), 254.

While scopophilia is often considered within the context of gender and sexuality (heterosexual man watching the female body while not wanting to be objectified himself, or gay man watching male bodies), race should also be factored into the scopophilia equation. It may be a racialized masculinity, for instance, that is given control of the gaze. Of central importance here is the question of fixing the other or of creating a stable notion of how racialized masculinity looks. A white male gaze may be hidden as object of that gaze, while certain non-white forms of masculinity are displayed very visibly, suggesting that whiteness and masculinity function in tandem as invisible norms. Men may be more than willing to depict or show non-white bodies, as long as they are shown in a given way. White European masculinity may, for instance, want black African masculinity to be shown naked to affirm its own associations with clothing and thus with culture. Or, the black male body might not be allowed to be seen as erotic so that the potential for eroticism can be reserved for whiteness.

When racial masculinities look or are looked at, the question of whether racial fetish is at play should be asked. The non-white man can be overly eroticized as the object of the gaze, a racial fetish that constructs his body as not about his own body or self but about his race. As the object of erotic gazing, the racially tagged man is seen in a certain way – and only in that way – by the one who desires him. The gay white man whose erotic desire is directed at seeing Asian men defines the other as object and his own white racial coding as subject and viewer, without the possibility for fluidity in how the other is seen. The recuperative gesture vis-à-vis castration can be carried out through a racialized form of fetishized masculinity, as is often done through the medium of women, in part because the non-white man is both man and non-man (symbolically), or is both phallic and non-phallic. The racially coded man stands in for the castrated man, at least temporarily, and allows the white man to feel less castrated by opposition. The other may serve as phallus and thus replace the man's lost phallus, whether because he identifies with him or because he desires him (or through some combination of the two). Gay men who have a penchant for men of a certain ethnic group may be trying to use certain racialized masculinities as a substitute phallus to recuperate their own perceived loss of masculinity. Or, the white man's black buddy may serve as a technique for him to have the phallus if the black man *is* the phallus.

Within the realm of scopophilia, racial masculinities may be predicated on a move between being seen and not being seen. Black masculinity in the US can be viewed from the perspective of such a contradiction. On the one hand, the black man is hypervisible: he is present as a fixed image (rapist, criminal, drug dealer, etc.), but on the other hand, he is an invisible man and cannot easily be seen (as object of desire, in positions of power, etc.). That contradiction may be definitional of black subjectivity since cultural scopophilia alternates between allowing and not allowing its representation. The white male body may not simply be hidden, but revealed in certain guises in order to provide the impression that the white male body possesses given characteristics. The fit male bodies revealed in certain cinematic contexts can make male bodies appear virile and strong, but that appearance may be racial as well as gendered. The sport of bodybuilding, and even male muscularity as a concept, may be considered as inherently white under the influence of Greco-Roman and Renaissance representations of the ideal male body. But such assumptions about white muscularity cannot help but render white male subjects anxious as their own visibility threatens to reveal that they are not always muscular and to out the hidden non-muscular white body that would weaken white hegemony. It is the dialogue between the seen and the unseen, then, that can in the end define the white male body.

It is often thought that racialized masculinity is framed, in both senses of the word. The director of a film can frame racialized masculinity in a certain way to his own advantage, as can the photographer, the artist, or the writer. That framing can be extended to those who do not themselves do the actual framing. The viewer of a film may imbibe the representation put before him/her, and that viewer may, in fact, be a member of the racialized group represented. In *Black Skin, White Masks*, Frantz Fanon evokes the image of the black man who comes to the cinema and sits down, knowing that his own fixed image will inevitably be shown: "I cannot go to a film without seeing myself. I wait for me. In the interval, just before the film starts, I wait for me. The people in the theater are watching me, examining me, waiting for me" (p. 140). While Fanon evokes the image of the cinema, his comment could be taken as indicative of a larger phenomenon of cultural scopophilia in which black or non-hegemonic masculinity is predestined to appear in a certain way, even or especially in absentia, and that the man represented can only watch the images unravel, unable to change the images that everyone around him sees.

Fanon is also suggesting the need for a consciousness of how racialized male bodies are framed and for resistance to such images. Images to directly counteract or work against such representations can be posited (e.g., Asian bodybuilders as non-effeminate, black bodies as neither hypermasculine nor fetishized, or white male bodies as just average bodies). But, while important, these types of resistance do not call attention to the larger problem of the process of framing. How can the framing of racial masculinity be revealed as framing? How can the actual mechanisms by which culture frames be exposed? It is important to call attention, in particular, not just to how masculinity is depicted or framed, but to how and why the framer is gazing at the object, for representations of masculinity can be about the looker's own racial anxiety, or a need to project from the outside onto a discrete and specific object.

Moving the emphasis from the racially coded object to the non-racially coded looker can reveal how an image, or images in a larger sense, are products of the hegemonic looker and the act of looking. In one of Mapplethorpe's photos in *Black Book*, a large penis of a black man is photographed hanging out of a business suit, with his head and upper body not part of the photo (p. 69). While on one level, this kind of penile-centered image might be seen as affirming a stereotype of black masculinity, on another level it suggests that when the stereotype of the black male body is taken to an extreme, its stereotypical and fixed nature is brought out into the open, both literally and figuratively. The viewer who may be aware of the stereotype but never have in actuality seen a black male penis – or one that conforms to the stereotype – may be forced to respond to the stereotype. He or she may respond by arguing that not every black penis can be like that, and that the image of the stereotype reveals that it cannot always hold. Because the man's head is not shown, the image suggests a certain kind of racial looking, an imagined viewer who is only looking at or only seeing the man's mid-section or penis, thus framing the man in a certain way instead of seeing him as a businessman or a whole body. Other photos by Mapplethorpe depict black men in order to reframe them in a certain way. In one photo, a black male body is shown on a pedestal, but without showing the face, to suggest that his body may have the potential to be seen as an erotic object of beauty but that his face/head cannot do the viewing or that his body and face/head cannot function together as a full symmetrical body. The image also shows the man sitting, not standing, on a pedestal as if to suggest that his body is not a full or upright object of artistic beauty (pp. 50, 51). Such representations attempt to make the male body into an object of beauty as well as to comment on how black masculinity is not normally placed in positions of eroticism or artistic beauty, which may often be reserved for white masculinity. At the same time as they call attention to the expulsion of black male bodies from traditional positions of beauty, they ask questions about the nature of viewing bodies. In seeing these photos of Mapplethorpe, the viewer might ask why there are not well-known sculptures of black bodies in Western culture and what this absence means about artistic looking. The status of hegemonic watcher is called into question when the viewer asks why the black male body's face is covered but the viewer's own is not. In these kinds of ways, attention can be brought to the representation of racial bodies and their relation to the process of scopophilia in a large sense.

African-American masculinity is sometimes thought to resist clichés of representation through the "cool pose." If dominant culture represents African-American masculinity as (actually or potentially) violent, or as invisible in other circumstances, African-American male subjects can take on a cool pose, acting in a visible or performative way to subvert those constructs. To walk, talk, or act coolly reconstructs the gaze, forcing the dominant culture to revision it in another way that it does not define. In their book on the cool pose, Majors and Billson describe it as "a ritualized form of masculinity that entails behaviors, scripts, physical posturing, impression management, and carefully crafted performances that deliver a single, critical message: pride, strength, and control." They add: "Black males ... manage the impression they communicate to others through the use of an imposing array of masks, acts, and facades."[7] This pose might frame or reframe African-American masculinity in the minds of those who practice it and those who observe it, but it can still risk falling back into an essentialized form of visuality if taken to a extreme and if a new cliché is simply established in place of another one.

---

[7] Richard Majors and Janet Mancini Billson, *Cool Pose: The Dilemmas of Black Manhood in America* (New York: Lexington Books, 1992), 4.

Another technique to make a cliché of racial masculinity not an issue is to call attention to looking itself within a text, to show how people look at male bodies. In the film *The Full Monty*, for instance, a black character appears to audition for a male strip show in front of a group of men who are already planning to participate in it. One character remarks on his name "Horse," suggesting that he has a large penis (that he is "hung like a horse"). The potential for a racial cliché is dissipated, however, when a white character named Guy comes to the audition and strips, revealing that he is extremely well endowed, as the men watch in pleasurable awe. This racial juxtaposition uncovers the difficulty of a priori assigning a certain kind of penis to any single ethnic group and consciously reframes racialized masculinities within the context of questions of watching and homosocial scopophilia. The men watching these two men emblematize masculinity's surprise at racial non-clichés and thus call attention to culture's larger presuppositions about racial male bodies.

The issue of framing and invisibility should also be interrogated to determine why certain types of masculinity are not frequently represented in the realm of gender. Asian or Native-American masculinities may be absent from certain types of hegemonic representation, not framed at all in the first place. Why are Asian men not depicted in certain visual representations, such as the famous Golden Spike photo taken in 1869 at the completion of the transcontinental railroad in northern Utah? Attention could be drawn to the reasons why Asian masculinity was kept out of the picture in the first place, despite the important contribution of Asian men to the railroad construction, and the ways in which visual images themselves can be changed or thought about differently in light of that invisibility. In short, the question of cultural framing, of how and why the racialized male body is or is not photographed or depicted, should be asked alongside examinations of how specific male bodies are represented racially.

Bibliography

A key collection of essays is Harry Stecopoulos and Michael Uebel, eds., *Race and the Subject of Masculinities* (Durham, NC: Duke University Press, 1997).

African-American masculinity has sparked numerous studies. For a particularly sophisticated study, see Maurice O. Wallace, *Constructing the Black Masculine:*

Identity and Ideality in African American Men's Literature and Culture, 1775–1995 (Durham, NC: Duke University Press, 2002).

On the cool pose and scopophilia, see ch. 1 in Wallace, *Constructing the Black Masculine*; Richard Majors and Janet Mancini Billson, *Cool Pose: The Dilemmas of Black Manhood in America* (New York: Lexington Books, 1992); Herman Beavers, " 'The Cool Pose': Intersectionality, Masculinity, and Quiescence in the Comedy and Films of Richard Pryor and Eddie Murphy," in *Race and the Subject of Masculinities*, ed. Stecopoulos and Uebel; Kobena Mercer, "Black Masculinity and the Sexual Politics of Race" and "Reading Racial Fetishism: The Photographs of Robert Mapplethorpe," in *Welcome to the Jungle* (New York: Routledge, 1994).

For African-American masculinity's relation to both the Euro-American model and the African model, see George Roberts, "Brother to Brother: African American Modes of Relating among Men," *Journal of Black Studies* 24, no. 4 (1994): 379–90.

For the recurring relation between blackness and queerness, see Kathryn Bond Stockton, *Beautiful Bottom, Beautiful Shame: Where "Black" Meets "Queer"* (Durham, NC: Duke University Press, 2006).

For sample work on how cultures may not have a Western notion of masculinity, see Emmanuel Akyeampong and Pashington Obeng, "Spirituality, Gender, and Power in Asante History," *International Journal of African Historical Studies* 28, no. 3 (1995): 481–508; Stephan F. Miescher, "Becoming an Ɔpanyin: Elders, Gender, and Masculinities in Ghana since the Nineteenth Century," in *Africa after Gender?*, ed. Catherine M. Cole, Takyiwaa Manuh, and Stephan F. Miescher (Bloomington: Indiana University Press, 2007), 253–69.

For a sample study of cross-racial identification, see Leerom Medovoi, "Reading the Blackboard: Youth, Masculinity, and Racial Cross-Identification," in *Race and the Subject of Masculinities*, ed. Stecopoulos and Uebel.

On the white male body as incarnating the buff body, see Richard Dyer, "The White Man's Muscles," in Stecopoulos and Uebel; also ch. 4 in his important book *White* (London: Routledge, 1997). See also Thomas DiPiero, *White Men Aren't* (Durham, NC: Duke University Press, 2002).

On the effeminate Jew, see Matthew Biberman, *Masculinity, Anti-Semitism and Early Modern English Literature* (Burlington, VT: Ashgate, 2004); Daniel Boyarin, *Unheroic Conduct: The Rise of Heterosexuality and the Invention of the Jewish Man* (Berkeley: University of California Press, 1997). On the male Jewish body as effeminate and diseased, see ch. 2 in Sander L. Gilman, *Freud, Race, and Gender* (Princeton: Princeton University Press, 1993).

On Asian and Asian-American masculinity, see David L. Eng, *Racial Castration: Managing Masculinity in Asian America* (Durham, NC: Duke University Press,

2001); King-Kok ChXeung, "Of Men and Men: Reconstructing Chinese American Masculinity," in *Other Sisterhoods: Literary Theory and U.S. Women of Color* (Urbana: University of Illinois Press, 1998), 173–99; Jinqi Ling, "Identity Crisis and Gender Politics: Reappropriating Asian American Masculinity," in *An Interethnic Companion to Asian American Literature*, ed. King-Kok Cheung (New York: Cambridge University Press, 1997), 312–37; Joon Oluchi Lee, "The Joy of the Castrated Boy," *Social Text* 23, nos. 3–4 (2005): 35–56. On the Golden Spike photo, see Eng, "I've Been (Re)Working on the Railroad: Photography and National History in *China Men* and *Donald Duck*," in *Racial Castration*, 35–103.

8

Masculinity and the Nation

The Nation and the Analogical

It would be impossible to consider race and ethnicity without a discussion of the closely related question of the nation. Nations have a tendency to define themselves partly in relation to the racial and ethnic constructs that they also put forward. It might be a single ethnic group that incarnates the nation (e.g., the traditional view of the German nation as defined by blood), but the mixture of races and ethnicities might also define the idea of the nation (e.g., a melting pot for the US or a mosaic for Canada). That relation might be complicated by national definitions as outside race. The Gallic model, for instance, defines a French person as a citizen first and a member of a racial or ethnic group second, but that theory of citizenship does not mean that racial constructs are actually absent from national definitions or discourses.

In the same way that analogies are made between race and gender, connections are often made between the nation and gender as human traits are ascribed to the nation to put forth a certain image of what it is or should be. Consequently, the gender of a nation is an important aspect of gender studies since those cultural codings affect everyone in a nationally based context. Links between woman and the nation might be more immediately obvious than those between man and nation. The Statue of Liberty or Mother India could be examined as gendered embodiments of the United States and India, as could the ideologies subtending the tropes. Likewise, reasons why some cultures talk about a "motherland" and attribute maternal features to the nation could be considered. The recurring figure of Marianne, a voluptuous woman who embodies France and whose breasts are important to her representation, suggests numerous cultural connections between the French nation on the one hand, and certain supposed traits of woman and the female body on the other.

While the question of the relation between the representation of nation and woman cannot be ignored and is far from irrelevant to this chapter, my focus here will be on the endless number of cultural associations made between masculinity and the nation. Some cultures refer to a "fatherland" rather than a "motherland." If France is traditionally represented by a woman, other nations are symbolized by male figures. Uncle Sam embodies the United States, as when he calls men to the military ("Uncle Sam wants you"), and the personage of John Bull is taken to represent England. Less directly, male superheroes, such as Superman or Captain America, can be seen as flesh-and-blood stand-ins for the American nation. Fighting for "truth, justice, and the American way," Superman's strength and special abilities suggest, by extension, that America has these qualities and will always triumph over evil. The US and Superman are both good in opposition to evil, and can spring into action when needed. Both have "mild mannered," normal lives (as Clark Kent in the case of Superman), meaning that the nation/masculinity are not always super, and that their superhuman qualities in fact require that they not always be superhuman. Superman has a normal daily life, as do average Americans. A narrative about Superman, then, can also refer to the American nation, with masculinity playing a key role in that narrative, by providing the nation a gendered subjectivity that implies something about national characteristics. The Superman example suggests but one way in which masculinity and the nation relate, but such connections recur in numerous ways throughout cultures and raise important questions about the nation and gender as related social constructs. Consequently, I will focus in this chapter on some key questions about that connection, namely: Why does the nation dovetail so well with masculinity? What kind of overlap is there between the nation and masculinity? How is the nation masculinized? How is masculinity nationalized? And how is the gendered connection extended beyond the realm of the nation? While my focus in this chapter is the modern nation, often considered an invention of the nineteenth century, the idea of gendered analogy could be thought about with respect to other spatially defined geographies, such as the kingdom, the duchy, the city-state, and the empire. The same can be said for proto-nations that do not have a firm national identity or a government in any modern sense but are instead unified through the figure of a sovereign or through cultural factors, including early modern France, England, and Spain.

I might begin to respond to these questions by stating the obvious – that traditionally men have built and propagated nations, often to serve their own interests. Leaders of nations have more frequently been male than female, and since the image of the nation is closely connected to the gender of its leader or leaders, the masculinity of a president, prime minister, king, or tsar influences how the nation is perceived and how it perceives itself. One might gender a nation by analogy with the gender of its leader, or a leader may act in a certain gendered manner in order to gender the nation by analogy. Conversely, if a leader's gender is seen as not ideal, the nation's gender may be a source of concern by extension. Anxiety about the homosexuality of a king, for instance, might transfer into an anxiety about a nation's gender. Or, the desire for a new leader can be linked to a desire to remasculinize the nation. Ronald Reagan's taking over the presidency from Jimmy Carter in 1981 was seen by some as a remasculinization of a feminized America. Nations with female leaders, too, can reinforce this link as female masculinity can come to signify the nation. As the "Iron Lady," Margaret Thatcher in the United Kingdom may have had to be, or to act, masculine to become the leader of the country and to maintain a perception of a kind of national masculinity. On the other hand, a perception of the need for a masculine nation may mean that some see a female leader as an impossibility. Hillary Clinton may have lost her presidential election bid in 2008 in part because of a cultural anxiety about a feminized nation.

The military, as a traditional way in which the nation is built and strengthened, whether through conquest, defense, or warfare, can function metonymically for the nation. Historically speaking, of course, the military has been an all-male institution and serves as a coming-of-age institution for boys, so increasing the connections between the military and the nation can de facto help render the nation more masculine. Attacking another nation or going to war might be prompted, at least in part, by a desire to masculinize the nation or to dominate another nation imagined as feminized by military loss. And certain traditionally patriotic characteristics, such as courage and honor, are often viewed as inherently masculine traits, whether exemplified by a man or a woman. When key elements of the actual nation (such as the military) are considered as unwaveringly masculine, the nation by extension may be seen to assume that gender coding as well.

Modern citizenship might be taken as a kind of homosociality, particularly during periods in which women could not be citizens or could not vote. Groups of men – or one large group of men assumed to compose the nation – are banded together, in mutual love of their object of desire, the nation. This triangular relation means that, as in the case of homosociality in chapter 2, the nation is a way for men to create non-threatening links among themselves as well as a way to create a national body that they all desire. The classic homosocial triangle incorporates desire for the woman as well as desire among men, whereas this kind of national model suggests mutual, mediated desire for a woman-like nation as well as masculine homosocial desire that functions within the framework of the nation. An all-male military platoon in which the men fight together as one for the love of country could imply mediated desire for nation and for each other. It could also imply a mediation of masculine rivalry through the nation, such that it has the perceived effect of making men equal and beyond rivalry, thus of cementing masculine bonds. Their mutual love of the nation, however it is imagined to be, can be a way to create male harmony and thus to maintain male dominance when women are excluded from taking part in the nation. This kind of national homosociality provides one explanation for gendering nations as female, especially as erotically coded women (like Mother India or France's Marianne) who are meant to create mutual heterosexual desire among male citizens and create a bond of non-rivalry.

The nation is coded as masculine metonymically, then, because it is considered to be composed of male bodies or of physical elements coded as masculine. Perceptions of the masculine cultural character of the men of a nation may also engender the nation by extension. Some might apply stereotypes of Italian machismo or a hearty German constitution to Italy and Germany as a whole. But applying stereotypical masculinities to an entire country in this way suggests that the gender of a nation is in no way naturally linked to its physicality, but exists in the realm of representation. Indeed, many underlying similarities between the nation and masculinity – between the body politic and the body of the man – are commonly perceived or experienced. This link is possible because of a shared characteristic of masculinity and the nation: both are constructed through representation and discourse.

Under the influence of Benedict Anderson's influential book *Imagined Communities* (1983), it is a critical commonplace to think about how the nation is an imagined construct.[1] It is not an imaginary construct (nations do exist, of course, and they have physical effects such as war), but important aspects of the nation are imagined. America might, for instance, be imagined as "from sea to shining sea," but that well-known phrase does not mean that America is in reality contained between two seas. Are Alaska and Hawaii included? What about all the Americans living abroad or on American military bases elsewhere? And what about undocumented immigrants? The point is not that America is physically or geographically defined in a certain way, but that the country is imagined or discursively constructed through language and representation. Consequently, this imagined construct comes to *be*, or to stand in for, America in the minds of many. Phrases such as "from sea to shining sea" allow for the geography of America to be imagined as bound and contained in a certain way, in this case by two oceans. Discursive constructs can also imply other characteristics of the nation, as for instance, in this case, that America is an entire continent or a natural or inevitable entity because it stretches from one sea to another. This construct helps to establish seemingly natural borders when in fact the nation is not natural at all.

The nation may be constructed largely by men (particularly in periods in which women were excluded from participation in politics and government and could not vote), but it may also be imagined as all-male. A military composed only of men may be imagined as an embodiment or arm of the nation, but whether the military actually *is* all male is another question entirely. In these cases, actual physical aspects of a nation come to embody the nation. Those parts are selected and take on representational significance because they are viewed as possessing qualities that some want the nation to have (prowess, military might, or courage in the case of the military). Such selections mean that someone or something else that could potentially embody the nation does not and that the choice to represent the nation with one gender-coded image necessarily excludes many others. If an all-male military takes on that role, for instance, an all-female group is excluded from embodying the nation. If the actual military is mixed-sex but an all-male group is

---

[1] Benedict Anderson, *Imagined Communities: Reflections on the Origin and Spread of Nationalism* (London: Verso, 1991).

imagined to embody the nation, then the actual presence of women in the military is de facto rejected in the representational sphere. These kind of metonymic connections, then, always imply a choice to include or to focus on one representation along with a choice to reject others. Those rejected representations can say as much about the gender of the nation as the ones selected to embody it.

Perhaps the most common similarity between the nation and the male body is that both are imagined as limited and bordered. For Benedict Anderson, the nation tends to be imagined as limited (p. 7). We might imagine physical borders around a nation and a checkpoint where one has to show a passport to enter. We might assume that we are either in or not in a nation or that we cross the border. In that limited and bordered space, according to Anderson, the nation has ultimate control over everything: it has laws, government, law enforcement, and prisons. Nations may try to enlarge their territory, but that is only to move their borders to another place. As with the nation, it is impossible to imagine the male or the female body, or gender, or masculinity, without imagining something. The male body does not have meaning in itself, but takes on meaning in and through language or through the ways in which it is imagined to exist. As discussed in chapter 4, the male body tends to be constructed as bound, as not fluid, or as hard and impermeable. The borders of the male body are routinely and frequently established and reestablished as solid, and we might assume that masculinity ends at the edges of the male body. Because of this particular similarity between masculinity and the nation, there are recurring representations of nationalized bodies in which national and gendered representation function in tandem. Superman's hard, muscular body may be imagined as impervious to bullets or to other weapons, like the American nation which is also considered impervious to attack from the outside. In his book on masculinity and Nazi Germany entitled *Male Fantasies*, Klaus Theweleit discusses how fascism created an idea of the male body as firm and bordered (among other traits), very much in parallel with the way the nation was attempting to construct itself.[2] In the battle for the nation, an avoidance of femininity, and characteristics such as fluidity assumed to accompany femininity, create

---

[2]   Klaus Theweleit, *Male Fantasies*, vol. 2, *Male Bodies: Psychoanalyzing the White Terror*, trans. Erica Carter and Chris Turner (Minneapolis: University of Minnesota Press, 1989). See esp. chs. 2 and 3.

masculine subjectivity and the nation simultaneously. Attempts to construct a certain type of male body, then, can be closely intertwined with attempts to construct a certain kind of nation.

A further important commonality between nation and masculinity is that both can be considered ideological. Though any person might be assumed to have a nationality and a gender, these forms of subjectivity are not actual possessions, but are both ideologically constructed. Discourse is central to these constructs: in the same way that definitions of male subjectivities are discursive, the nation is constructed in and through discourse and especially in political discourse (speeches, government documents, civics textbooks, etc.). In this way, a person can function within or without one or both of these ideological constructs, and be aware or not aware of them in the first place. I may walk around as a French man or an Egyptian man, but I may take my gender and my nationality for granted and consider neither of them consciously or explicitly. Or, at a given moment, I may walk around unaware of the ideology of masculinity in which I function but aware of the ideology of nationality in which I think I operate. At such times, the hidden ideology may buttress the other. My conscious or expressed desire for my country to go to war (and my justification for war) may be prompted by a hidden or unexpressed masculinity that gets channeled into nationalism. I may want my nation to wage war in part because I perceive the enemy as effeminate or because I fear the perception of my home nation as effeminate, but without being able to articulate these perceptions. The converse of this phenomenon may be true as well: I may be aware of gender but not of nationality.

As key ideologically defined aspects of subjectivity, nationality and gender are often put in dialogue with each other since one can help prop up the other. Masculinity can help make nationality appear natural, as for instance if a nation's sending a group of men off to war is seen as a natural phenomenon, an extension of the male gene, a result of hormones, or part of what men do. But, in fact, war is not simply natural, so such beliefs about men imply that the nation is co-opting a certain vision of masculinity for the purpose of defining war as natural. Evoking a male desire, or need, or tendency to go to war or to act warlike (in military recruitment materials, for example) can be a technique to suggest that the nation, too, has a nature that makes it wage war. Conversely, a national ideology can be applied to masculinity to make it seem natural. If America is the land of freedom, then a man is justified in acting free if he is American. The national ideology in which he functions can mutate into a gendered ideology, which justifies leaving his wife and kids or having an extramarital affair. It may mean that he can decide to go live in Wyoming as a cowboy or that he can exercise his second amendment right to bear arms. Because masculinity and national ideologies overlap and influence one another, it may not be entirely clear when one influences the other. A nation at war may be at one point influenced by that nation's ideas of masculinity, but at another point that nation's ideas of masculinity may be influenced by the nation at war. It is often extremely difficult to know what the originary ideology is in this back-and-forth process of mutual construction. The process of engendering between the gendered subjects of the nation and the nation itself is dialogic, since each influences the other and since the nation creates masculinity at the same time as masculinity creates the nation. One of the ideologies may be assumed to be originary, but that assumption only hides the other's previous functioning.

Like masculinity, the related ideology of heterosexuality has a close relation to the nation which may be imagined or assumed to be composed of a series of male–female couples or to be constructed within the realm of heterosexual or heteronormative desire. Ideologies of nationalism can suggest a heterosexual ideology as well, with reference to family values, conservatism, or traditional marriage between a man and a woman. Representations of the nation may depict a heterosexual couple, a nuclear family, or a series of nuclear families. While heterosexual ideology can be distinct from the ideology of masculinity, it is impossible ever to fully dissociate them as masculinity may evoke or employ heterosexuality as one of its constituting elements. A man who adamantly believes that gay marriage should be banned because it is un-American reveals the overlapping of the two ideologies within the rubric of gender. A heterosexually coded nation can have the effect of effacing or excluding non-heterosexual people (gay, queer, transgender, transsexual) from the community, an exclusion meant to help define men and the nation as heterosexual as well as masculine. Furthermore, a specific type or form of heterosexual desire or love may signify imagined characteristics of the nation itself. Sheldon Lu studies transnational romances between Chinese men and Russian or American women in Chinese television dramas from the 1990s. For him, these recurrent elements of Chinese masculinity in the media are a way to "explore the possibilities, limits, fallacies, and fluid boundaries of national identity …

in the circumstances of an increasingly *trans*national, deterritorialized global economy in the post-Cold War era."[3] In this case, the sexuality and heterosexual desire of Chinese masculinity, has symbolic import for what the nation is and what it is becoming within the context of globalization. At the same time, the representation codes the nation as functioning within an ideology of heterosexuality and codes male heterosexual desire as a signifying element for the nation. If queer or transgendered subjectivities do not take on this allegorical function in representing the nation, attention should be brought to the characteristics of the nation that are not being represented and that are being hidden. As nations are founded on representational forgetting and hiding as much as on representation itself, the gendered elisions say something about the nation and the way in which it is represented or assumed to be.

Anderson explains that, as ideological constructs, nations and communities are distinguished from other ones by virtue of "the style in which they are imagined" (p. 6). A given nation imagines itself in a way that differs from any other nation's self-perception. But also, as Anderson writes, the nation "is imagined as a community, because, regardless of the actual inequality and exploitation that may prevail in each, the nation is always conceived as a deep, horizontal comradeship" (p. 7). That "style" may mean that the nation is imagined as a community of men, that national "comradeship" is coded as male or as masculine, or that (as per the discussion above) citizenship is considered to be inherently male or homosocial. That comradeship might also be imagined as heterosexual. Or, the ideology of masculinity itself can serve as one element of a given national community's imagined style: it might factor in heavily, it might factor in very little, or it might factor in at some times and not at others. Anderson's idea of "style" in a national context returns us to Judith Butler's ideas about gender as a "style." This coincidence of keyword in each thinker's work suggests that nation and gender function similarly, that neither is a deep-seated state of being but both are open to change. The gender of the nation is performed, just like an individual performs his or her gender, and the repetition of that national-gendered style comes to be seen over time as stable, as natural-like, or as inextricably characteristic of that culture.

---

[3] Sheldon H. Lu, "Soap Opera in China: The Transnational Politics of Visuality, Sexuality, and Masculinity," *Cinema Journal* 40, no. 1 (2000): 43–4.

The German nation may be coded as very masculine because of the repetition over a long period of time of connections made between Germans and masculinity, and those repetitions may lead people (both German and not German) to consider the German people as naturally masculine and to assume that a stable masculinity is part of their physicality or genetic makeup. The specific ways in which the nation is gendered, however, change over time as the styles of nation and masculinity respond to various sociohistorical factors that arise and to other previous gender constructs. Germany may be imagined as masculine because it is considered strong in war, but the specific codings of that masculinity are one way because of the specific events of the Franco-Prussian War in the nineteenth century and another way because of World War I in the twentieth century.

The gender of the nation is imagined and constructed in a number of ways by the people who have an investment in that nation, but it is also possible to consider how the nation constructs its men to have or to propagate a certain style. National discourse may implicitly or explicitly teach its men how to be masculine, a leader may transmit what a man is or should be (or what he should not be), or he may pass on a certain national style of masculinity. The original handbook for Boy Scouts (1910), an important aspect of early twentieth-century national discourse, aimed "to combat the system that had turned such a large proportion of our robust, manly, self-reliant boyhood into a lot of flat-chested cigarette smokers, with shaky nerves and doubtful vitality."[4] Ronald Reagan's or George W. Bush's personal cowboy style may have had effects on the style of the US's masculinity, as perceived at home or abroad.

Masculinity and the nation function by analogy, as one supposedly has characteristics like the other, but processes pertaining to both masculinity and the nation can also be analogical. Quebec's imagined independence from Canada might be represented as the maturation process of a boy becoming a man, or an African coming-of-age novel may be an allegory of European decolonization and the maturity of a new nation no longer under the watch of its parents. A narrative may position the two textual levels together in indistinguishable ways such that national and masculine process are textually indistinguishable and each

---

[4]   Cited in Mark Seltzer, "The Love-Master," in *Engendering Men: The Question of Male Feminist Criticism*, ed. Joseph A. Boone and Michael Cadden (New York: Routledge, 1990), 140.

maturity buttresses the other. These narratives help construct the nation as masculine, of course, but also as inevitable and natural because a boy's becoming a man is also seen as inevitable and natural.

When the nation and the boy come of age, they may be assumed to acquire power and independence, meaning that similarities between masculinity and nation can also be based on perceptions of power and ruling/sovereignty. As masculinity rules, so does the nation. Anderson points out that the nation is imagined as sovereign (p. 7). One assumption behind an imagined sovereignty is that a sovereign rules and rules over others. Consequently, the man that symbolizes the nation may have to have power over others to help the metaphor function. The male-dominated household has often been taken as metonymic for the nation: the man rules the household – the wife, children, and others – in the same way that the king or the leader rules the nation, as both may be considered to have power over others. The man who knows how to rule the house is like the man who knows how to rule the nation. The fatherland is ruled by a leader who is also symbolic father. For this reason, the ruler of a nation may have to convey sovereign masculinity, to follow this metaphorical order of things. With the analogy in place, his perceived ability to rule may depend in part on his ability to rule his actual household, by dominating or controlling his wife or by being a good father.

This ruling analogy can also be linked to the male self: the man who is able to dominate or to control the self, to remain moderate and to control his passions and desires has historically been considered able to transfer that self-rule to others. Simply put, the man who rules the self is justified in ruling the other. Consequently, in some sociohistorical contexts moderation has been a defining element of masculinity since the virtue permits self-control and justifies control of the other. Male power, then, is linked to questions of ruling because inner self-control permits external control. These ideas can be extended from an individual leader to the men of a given nation, or even to the nation itself in a more abstract sense. A moderate group of men defined nationally, culturally, or racially (whether the French, Western Europeans, or white Americans) can by extension justify their rule over a group of immoderate others (e.g., black Africans or New World natives, African-Americans). Their self-perceived masculinity implies that the cultural or national other needs to be ruled over, and as a result, such groups may be coded as effeminate, as out of control, or as woman-like. In this way, masculinity and the nation's power mutually reinforce each other's theoretical ability to rule the other. European claims to rule their colonies, then, can be seen as in parallel with masculinity's natural rule over the gendered other as both systems of domination make themselves out to be natural and inevitable.

The link between masculinity and the nation as powerful can be extended even further when the nation attempts to take over other nations or cultures and become an empire. The strength of an empire may be seen to resemble masculinity, in fact even more so than a single nation. The empire may be seen as strong, brave, dominating, controlling, hegemonic, or powerful. The Roman and the British Empires may be conceived of as more masculine than pre-empire Rome and Great Britain because the former rule over more territory than the latter. The idea of a small European country ruling over large numbers of Africans and Asians might evoke a strong sense of power and domination, and the smaller the mother country in proportion to its empire, the more masculinity may be evoked.

Masculinity may be one impetus for colonization or empire-building in the first place, but this association does not necessarily mean that women have no relation to colonization. They may take part in the actual process in various ways, and they may identify with or desire the masculinity of empire in ways like or unlike the way men do. Moreover, gendered representations of empire may be more complicated than a simple equivalency between hypermasculinity and empire. The famous image of Britannia as symbol of the British Empire could be considered in this light: is she meant to evoke heterosexual male desire on the part of her subject as per the homosocial model? Is she a form of female masculinity meant to appeal to both men and women? Is she a pure abstraction meant to imply that the concrete aspects of the empire are masculine? Or does she perform more than one function?

Other Gender, Other Nation

Whether on the level of the individual nation or of the empire, these kind of gendered oppositions between strength and weakness imply a dominated other who might function analogically as not powerful or as lacking in strength. The other can be an internal other, part of the nation itself (the Jew or the Native-American, for example). When the nation codes certain of its own citizens or those within its borders as non-masculine, the examples of racial constructs discussed in chapter 7 are not simply about the coding of a certain racial or ethnic group, but are also ways to construct or reconstruct a gendered nation. The most extreme examples of this kind of construct of the nation may be in fascism: Nazi Germany's attempts to construct the Jew as effeminate suggest, by implication, that the rest of the German nation or the nation without Jews is somehow inherently masculine or that its own race–gender analogy is purged of the effeminate. If Asian minorities in the US are coded as effeminate, some people may interpret this to mean that the white majority, and by extension the nation as a whole, has a masculine nationality by comparison.

Another nation coded in a certain way may also serve as contrast case, or a superpower may attempt to construct one of its colonies or part of its empire as other. US culture has coded French culture as effeminate in its imaginary, in part because French masculinity is regarded as effeminate, as a way to masculinize itself by opposition. These constructs allow American culture to justify ascribing certain stereotypical characteristics to French culture and to the French nation. If France is coded as effeminate but is not a woman, then it can not be militarily strong, for instance. Such codings, however, often imply the imposition of one nation's definition of masculinity onto another where it may not apply. An American may view French masculinity as effeminate because of, among other traits, its attention to clothing when, in a French context, an emphasis on dress is considered a culturally sanctioned form of masculinity and not necessarily effeminate.

This process of othering a nation may function on the level of sexuality, too, if the non-masculine nation is viewed as queer or if its effeminacy is linked to sexuality. Nationalized images relating to anal penetration might suggest the metaphorical superiority or the position of the rapist as on top. The British in colonial India, for example, symbolically represented their hegemony via images of anal rape between men. The suggestion of male rape may construct a certain kind of masculinity, analogically, without necessarily suggesting the homosexuality of the dominant nation, as with sexualities in prison, in which homosexual acts can function as a trope for control or power. Similarly, the nation attempting to masculinize itself might depict other cultures as linked to sodomy or to sodomites. Sodomy has, at various historical moments, been assumed to come from a certain culture or nation, suggesting that the group is inherently queer while the culture doing the coding is not. In the Renaissance, for instance, sodomy was often taken to have spread from Florence to outside Italy, and *florenzen* was a contemporary German verb meaning "to sodomize."[5] The words "buggery" and "bugger" are semantically related to "Bulgaria" because sodomy was thought to have been brought back from Eastern Europe during the Crusades. The implication may be that sodomy can be learned or picked up if one enters into a culturally different space, in this case the fringes of Europe, not far from the even more culturally other Turkish lands. This idea of the other as queer often assumes that sodomy or same-sex desire is localizable and containable, not widespread or universal as a practice or phenomenon. The imagined queer other that risks infecting a nation may be internal to the nation instead of external when homosexuality is associated with one part of the nation rather than another. Quebec might get coded as queer vis-à-vis a heterosexual Anglophone Canada, constructs that might make Anglophone Canada appear both more masculine and more dominant than its Francophone minority. The abject other might be seen as an infection, a kind of disease with respect to the body of the nation. Gay men with HIV-AIDS were regarded as problematic in the US at certain points because they symbolically infected the nation and threatened to spread the disease to the nation as a whole. Queerness of this national kind might be considered a problem in part because it does not help the nation reproduce, and because reproduction is often a key element in the propagation of national masculinities.

The binary oppositions between a nation and its gendered others function in larger, more diffuse terms under the umbrella of "orientalism," a term in wide circulation in the academic world since the appearance of Edward Said's monumental *Orientalism* in 1978.[6] Race and the nation are combined together as a kind of binary opposition viewed as much larger than one nation's relation to another or as one nation's relation to a given racial/ethnic group, but as groups of nations to other groups of nations or races. In an orientalist view of the world, strict binary oppositions are imagined between the East and the West. Consequently, non-sanctioned Eastern subjectivities are not heard as viable alternatives to the dominant, official voice of the West. Authentic

---

[5] See Michael Rocke, *Forbidden Friendships: Homosexuality and Male Culture in Renaissance Florence* (New York: Oxford University Press, 1996), 3.

[6] Edward W. Said, *Orientalism* (New York: Pantheon Books, 1978).

Eastern discourse is not taken into account on its own terms. Instead, national discourses attempt to stabilize the essence of the other and make the other into what the West wants it to be. Said talks about "constraints upon and limitations of thought" (p. 42) that make the oriental subject stable-seeming and the European subject the definer of discourse and thought. Accompanying the definitional binary oppositions are various other oppositions (p. 42). Implicit in an West/East opposition also lies civilized/uncivilized and culture/nature oppositions, by which the West is coded as more civilized and as more cultured than the East. A certain biology may also be ascribed to the Easterner to help prop up these cultural attitudes and to make them seem natural. The Cossack may be coded naturally savage or wild so as to make the Western European appear otherwise. The principle of binarism thus functions to separate, stabilize, and hierarchize East and West, along with the elements ascribed to each category, whether such oppositions are between Germany and Turkey, France and Indochina, England and India, or Russia and Mongolia.

Of particular interest to my discussion, however, is the binary opposition of gender, by which oppositions such as masculine/feminine, masculine/effeminate, or masculine/homosexual function as one constitutive element of the East/West binary and thus of Said's orientalism. The parallelism between gender and ethnicity also implies other oppositions linked to an imagined idea of gender. Issues around power and ruling are particularly important in this regard as the colonizing West codes itself as like a man who rules over women or his household, and, conversely, Eastern cultures come to be coded as feminine or effeminate. This kind of recurring analogy might mean, then, that an Indian man, in the eyes or discourse of a Westerner, is viewed or discussed as similar to a woman, whether physically or psychologically. Or it might mean that an Arab or Turkish man is assumed to be prone to sexual licentiousness (unable to control himself like a man should) or to homosexuality or sodomy. In *Colonial Masculinity*, Mrinalini Sinha has documented the complicated ways in which the Bengali in the late nineteenth century was viewed as effeminate and, conversely, how the Englishman was "manly."[7] While in no way stable, these types of oppositions are perceived as fixed and unchanging, not open to movement. A British man arriving in colonized India might have an image of

[7] Mrinalini Sinha, *Colonial Masculinity: The "Manly Englishman" and the "Effeminate Bengali" in the Late Nineteenth Century* (Manchester: Manchester University Press, 1995).

Indian men as feminized, a gender construct lying at the confluence of race and gender that influences how he comports himself with respect to Indian men and how he feels about himself and other Brits. These constructs might also justify the way in which he imagines British dominance over India, since, for instance, he might have the analogy in his head that the man dominates the woman as Britain dominates India. The colonizer might also see the "oriental" as childlike, as prepubescent, and thus as not having achieved masculinity and as not developed like the more mature European. This adult/child opposition resembles a male/female opposition since the child and the woman hold the same half of the binary oppositions by analogy, as both are dominated by the man. The binarism comes to define not just Eastern men, but the whole nations or cultures themselves. Various Arab cultures, for example, may be imagined as closely linked to woman, as in the stereotype of the harem or the veil, which can be taken to represent Arab culture as a whole. The woman imagined as ready for sex with the colonizer can embody the entire colonized nation, ready and willing to be penetrated and ruled over. That there is a close link between Eastern cultures and such feminine tropes implies a preconceived notion of how cultural alterity and gender dovetail, a notion defined not by contact with the cultural other.

I am discussing the nation here, in a chapter following one on race, but that does not mean that race is absent from constructs related to the nation or to orientalism. Orientalism may operate in large-scale terms that are hard to pinpoint, but it also functions more locally as one nation or race or ethnicity defines itself against another. The Englishman may be opposed to the Arab, for example, but the orientalist impulse might function within the nation itself. A masculinity coded as white can come to embody the nation, both literally and figuratively, through various figures that incarnate the spirit of the nation and its interests. White masculinized figures, then, can representationally run, construct, or embody the nation, meaning that race and the nation are difficult to extricate from each other and that it is hard to see where one stops and the other begins. Richard Dyer studies the phenomenon of the white male bodybuilder within the context of films starring bodybuilders (such as Schwarzenegger, Stallone, Van Damme).[8] In many of these cases, the muscular or toned white body serves a

---

[8] See ch. 4 in Richard Dyer, *White* (New York: Routledge, 2000).

neocolonial or nationalistic purpose. This purpose may be orientalist, colonialist, or racist (or some combination of the three), but, in any event, such films privilege a version of white masculinity and oppose it to another brand of racialized masculinity. The figure of Tarzan, for example, is white and buff unlike many of the natives he encounters, but he also masters the jungle, is superior to the natives and is helped by animals, a sign of how white Euro-masculinity naturally dominates unnamed foreign lands. While white masculinity may tend to signify national or ethnic dominance, it does not necessarily have to incarnate the ideal as other racialized masculinities can still serve the function. Some view Barack Obama, half black and half white, as a new embodiment of America, a representation of two American racial masculinities fused into a single male body. And as I will discuss in the next chapter, interracial male friendship might signify the ideal nation.

In all these cases, the relation between masculinity and the nation may be considered in terms of identification. A man identifies with the masculinized nation because he views himself – or would like to view himself – as masculinized as well. The same may be true for a woman who desires to masculinize herself. If America is coded as masculine, then my patriotism can affirm, or create, my link to masculinity and help masculinize me by association. In this way, the gendered nation functions psychoanalytically as a kind of parent whom the child takes as a role model in terms of gender. This identification may be encouraged by the nation and its supporters since it encourages nationalism or patriotism and strengthens the nation, and familial links may be created because this identification is like family (Uncle Sam is everyone's uncle, for instance). Along with the principle of gender identification, desire can be taken into account in these codings, since desire for the nation and desire for an individual are closely linked. Doris Sommer has famously discussed this issue in her book on Latin American literature, *Foundational Fictions*.[9] For her, the sense of love for the nation and the sense of erotic love can feel the same, meaning that the erotic and the patriotic can mutually influence each other. The man loves the woman as he loves his country. This parallel explains, at least in part, why the nation can be embodied by a woman: so that male heterosexual

---

[9] Doris Sommer, *Foundational Fictions: The National Romances of Latin America* (Berkeley: University of California Press, 1991). See especially ch. 1, "Love and Country: An Allegorical Speculation."

desire can be linked to nationality. In Revolutionary France, for instance, a number of female figures, often erotically coded, directly or indirectly represented the nation, and in France today the modern voluptuous figure of Marianne still embodies the nation. Heterosexual romances in certain texts can thus allegorize the desire for, or the love of, the nation, and the desire to found a family can parallel the foundation of the nation. A bare-breasted woman as symbol of the nation could be riding a fine line between maternity and eroticism, implying that the male citizen is both child and desiring man. In this way, images of woman as nation are abstract as she represents something besides herself. She might be the object of male heterosexual desire in the service of the construction of nationhood, or she might be the abstraction of maternity that will symbolically take care of her children, the citizens. Images of woman as the nation are not necessarily about woman, then, but are attempts to pull heterosexual men into the realm of the nation through representation. At other moments, identification and desire might both be at play in an ambiguous or fluid way. A national masculinity can certainly identify with a national figure that is not a man. Marianne may evoke the man's own maternity such that he sees her as what he wants to be and not just what he desires. His draw toward the nation can be predicated on his wanting to be like the representation of the nation and his feeling a commonality with it. By contrast, a classic national identity can also be based on desire. The white man who sees Tarzan embodying British hegemony may identify with that masculinity, but because the identification–desire binary is unstable, there may also be an element of homoerotic desire for the masculinity seen as powerful and handsome.

Undoing the Nation, Undoing Masculinity

So far, this chapter has focused on how masculinity and the nation dovetail with each other, operating under the assumption that they mutually reinforce each other. To masculinize the nation is to ascribe gendered characteristics to it, especially power, hegemony, and sovereignty. Conversely, such constructs provide masculinity with another way to appear to have these desired characteristics. But placing the constructs of nation and masculinity together is also a risky proposition since they do not always buttress each other or operate smoothly in

parallel. Rather, the analogies and connections made can also be indicative of an underlying anxiety about the nation, about masculinity, or
both. In other words, masculinity might be linked to the nation precisely because the nation needs to be buttressed by another incarnation
of power or because masculinity needs to be helped by the representational power of the nation. A nation that has suffered, or fears suffer-
ing, military defeat may use images of masculinity to revitalize or
revirilize itself. A nation just starting out may appropriate masculinity
to try to come of age. A man who fears castration or emasculation may
turn to patriotism or to more extreme nationalisms (fascism, right-
wing evangelism) to assuage his own anxiety about being a man. In all
these senses, masculinity and nationalism function as curative panaceas
for each other, at least theoretically. Because of the recurrence of the
links between masculinity and nationality, concern over the power or
virility of the nation can be readily projected onto concerns about the
masculinity of the boys or men of a nation, and, conversely, concerns
over boys' and men's masculinity can threaten the perceived health of
the body politic. The coding of forms of non-masculinity as anti-
nationalistic (e.g., the gay or Jewish man as foreign body) can also be
indicative of a similar anxiety of the nation, as the nation needs to masculinize itself by constructing a non-masculine other to divert attention from its own crisis of gender that may or may not be articulated
directly. Anti-Semitic images of the Jewish man as castrated point more
to other men's own anxieties about their gender, projected onto an
other, a projection that may be related to race, ethnicity, class, nationality, or some other element of subjectivity. In the case of colonization,
constructs of a colonized group as effeminate suggest issues around
colonizers' masculinity back in the home country or on the world stage
and have little or nothing to do with the reality of the colonized culture. The feminized oriental is thus a projection or a fear of a feminized
aspect within the male self, paradoxically revealing a need or dependence on his part. The English colonialist's image of a feminized Bengali
is in part a projection of an anxiety of his own fears of effeminacy, or of
his nation's anxiety of effeminacy. The lens of orientalism provides a
way to think about the imperial subject gazing on the colonized or
orientalized subject as both sexual same and other. Similarly, the oriental subject may be a projection of the colonizer's own homoerotic or
repressed desires. Constructing the other in a certain gendered way is
a way for him to live out fantasies or other issues in his own life. As Hema

Chari writes: "the East is not only projected as the other, but, more importantly, as the aberrant other to fulfill Western psychosexual needs and to sanction the phenomenon Said terms as 'orientalisms'."[10] The issue, then, is that the other cannot in fact be opposed or separated from the same because the other is a screen for projected fantasies and needs related to the self.

What this lack of a top/bottom binary means is that common associations between the nation and masculinity can work in the reverse direction as one subverts the other. If the borders of the male body and those of the nation can be representationally similar, then the subversion of the borders of the male body can represent the subversion of the borders of the nation. This link explains why nationally defined borders of various types represent the breakdown or fluidity of the male body or of masculinity, and why the male body's destruction can represent the end of national borders or of national power. Superman's death in 1992 could be taken as symptomatic of the decline of American hegemony in the world or of the fall of America as the world's great superpower. Even without this death, Superman's famous vulnerability to kryptonite means that American hegemony or dominance is not infallible or without weakness, allegorizing an anxiety of national–masculine weakness. In the film *The Three Burials of Melquiades Estrada* (2005), the fluid borderland between the US and Mexico serves as a setting in which the masculinity of the characters can be destabilized as well. In the French film *Indochine* (1995), the main male character's body is increasingly revealed throughout the film as France's hold over its colonies in Indochina is correspondingly loosened and eventually lost. The revealing of the vulnerable male body in the film comes to emblematize the end of France's colonial empire in Asia. The very idea of colonization or of taking over other countries to create an empire may suggest a desire to masculinize the nation and its citizens in the face of an anxiety of being an effeminate nation. Conversely, the fall of an empire can be seen to parallel a fall or end to masculinity. Narratives relating to failing or deficient masculinity in a postcolonial context, in the UK, France, or Russia for example, can be taken as representations of the nation after empire. One might ask of such texts: How does the

---

[10]   Hema Chari, "Colonial Fantasies and Postcolonial Identities: Elaboration of Postcolonial Masculinity and Homoerotic Desire," in *Postcolonial, Queer: Theoretical Intersections*, ed. John C. Hawley (Albany: State University of New York Press, 2001), 279.

end of empire affect or influence the representation of masculinities if empire had symbolized or implied virility?

These analogies between powerful masculinity and the nation that cultures attempt to maintain cannot ultimately remain stable ones that just circulate within culture unchallenged. America cannot always be Superman. Western masculinity does not simply reorder non-Western masculinity as effeminate. British masculinity does not simply create *ex nihilo* a brand of Indian or Bengali masculinity in the way it so desires. Indeed, the very presence of such analogies means that they are resisted, in much the same way that there is necessarily resistance against racial constructs or, in even larger terms, that constructs of power evoke resistance against them. These analogies produce counter-analogies, leading to a representational struggle between two series of associations. It makes sense, then, to examine in any discursive context the relations between hegemonic representation and resistance to them. Such resistance can be an attempt to flip the opposition, to remasculinize a group made to seem effeminate by dominant cultural constructs. Resistance to a colonizing power may include attempts to reconstruct the colonized as masculine, or as more masculine than the colonizer. This resistance may take the form of appropriating key aspects of the colonizer that contribute to its own representation as masculine (e.g., suit and tie). Or, it may mean a recoding of non-masculine aspects of the subjected culture and their transformation into masculine ones that may or may not be legible as dominant to hegemonic masculinities. In a culture where a suit and tie is not typical male dress, men may attempt to code their own clothing (which may seem dress-like and effeminate to some observers) as masculine.

But that relation can be even more complicated than an attempt to flip or recode the oppositions. For there can also be a constant oscillation between constructs and their resistance not predicated on a binary, but on an unstable series of back-and-forth gendered movements. A colonized or hegemonic subject, for instance, might find himself in a position of ambivalence with respect to constructs of national masculinity: he may internalize those constructs, in some ways, in some situations, or to some extent. On the other hand, he might reject them in some ways, in some situations, or to some extent. He may go about his life moving back and forth between accepting and rejecting them, much as any kind of ideology can be taken to operate. That dialogue can be private/internal or public/external, part of one's own individual psychological makeup or part of cultural attitudes and discourses. The oscillation can function vis-à-vis hege-monic masculinities as well: the male British colonizer may not always believe in the binary constructs of the national–gendered other put forth. He may, on some level, know that the constructs put forth by himself or by his cultural context are fraudulent and predicated on power more than on any inherent reality. Discourses of hegemonic masculinities can thus be scrutinized for signs of ambivalence, signs of consciousness of a fraudulent nature or of an anxiety about the verac-ity of the gendered associations. In other words, since masculinities make the other into a gender–national other as a way to reaffirm one's own gendered nationality, the signs or the traces of that original impetus or need to construct an other can be located. He might let slip his own fear of effeminacy, or see the other as the one who should be on top.

The complicated nature of this oscillation can be considered in another framework as well. In chapter 6, I discussed the idea that male subjects can invite or encourage women to approach masculinity but, ultimately, keep them from fully obtaining it, for example because of their lack of a penis (pp. 137–8). The butch lesbian may not ultimately be a threat to masculinity because she proves the desirability or value of masculinity without ever being able to truly attain it. This concept can likewise be transposed into the realm of the racial and the national. An African-American man may need to act white in order to secure a certain position in a company, for instance, but this racial adaptation may be considered never fully possible simply by virtue of his original race. Reactions to the racially mixed figure of Barack Obama could be considered in this light: to what extent is he allowed to approach or to achieve dominant masculinity? And to what extent is his not being allowed to achieve masculinity suggestive of another representation of masculinity that may be more or less masculine than simple white or black masculinities by virtue of its racial hybridity?

Like race and racial mixture, the category of the nation provides a related framework by which a man can be invited toward a nationally inflected masculinity without ever being given the possibility of reach-ing true or full masculinity, defined as that of the dominant group. The Bengali man during the age of British colonialism, for instance, may be invited to become like British masculinity in certain ways (education, language, dress), to affirm the desirability of that form of gender and thus to assume its desirability. The Bengali man can speak and dress like a European, but in the end his underlying non-white body keeps him from ever reaching the perfect state of masculinity. The nation, then, defines a certain other kind of masculinity as asymptotic, as approaching its cultural masculinity but never actually reaching it.

This model in the realm of gender resembles the way in which Homi Bhabha talks about mimicry in a colonial context as "almost but not quite."[11] For him, colonial mimicry suggests a resistance to colonial authority since colonial discourse is ambivalent about its own authority and always contains the possibility of internal rupture: "a model of representation that marginalizes the monumentality of history, quite simply mocks its power to be a model, that power which supposedly makes it inimitable" (p. 125). Mimicry thus has the effect of disrupting colonial authority by revealing its anxiety about its own power over the other. The hegemonic may have deep anxiety about its own rule, but mimicry may also lead to another anxiety, namely that the non-hegemonic masculinity will in fact take over as a better form of masculinity and that the very inability to become a fully hegemonic masculinity can be turned into a strength in itself. What if the black African man who is invited to become English but can never actually achieve Englishness ends up as more masculine than the colonizer because his in-between subjectivity is not a weakness but a strength? On the other hand, the invitation to cultural or racial similarity in the first place may be a way to reassure colonial masculinity of its hegemony in the face of its underlying anxiety of fraudulent rule. Watching the black African man become English may reassure the colonizer that, because the colonized wants to become like him, he should dominate even as he knows somewhere that colonialism is a racist endeavor. It is a way to justify, implicitly, the hegemonic by constantly repositioning itself as hegemonic.

Venturing Out: Space and Masculinity

One potential issue with the theoretical concept of a dominating culture's imposing a non-masculine coding onto colonized cultures is the simplistic assumption that the hegemonic imports gendered and

---

[11]   Homi K. Bhabha, *The Location of Culture* (London: Routledge, 2004), 129.

national constructs from home and imposes them onto other cultures. In fact, those constructs cannot simply be imported from another cultural context. For cultural and spatial movement reconstructs gender and masculinity, and, as a result, the home constructs may be transformed in unexpected ways when one goes abroad or into other cultural spaces. The move to a new space may unrepress certain desires that "civilized" or Western culture tends to repress. When a man goes to the colony or outside his home culture, he may experiment with alternative masculinities that he did not or could not consciously experience in his home country. The cultural context itself may permit gendered experiments that his former cultural context disavowed or that he perceived as disavowed. He may be more prone to homosexual acts or desires that he would never consider at home, for instance. Or, he may not import European masculinities or his unconscious fantasies with him intact, but new types of masculinities that he never noticed before may come to influence him in new spaces. This kind of gendered transculturation, in which the move to a new cultural space reconstructs subjectivity, means that cultural influences create a new gendered subjectivity that is a mixture of old and new. He may see how men act in that space and imitate them. He may be drawn to constructs of the other as non-masculine and want to imitate that gender construct. Or, it may be the case that he constructs new gendered forms by virtue of being constrained to follow new constraints. New gendered interdictions in a new cultural space may produce new and unexpected responses to them. If he feels that his gendered subjectivity is based largely on the need to rule the other in the colony, that very dictum may have a reverse effect and lead him to create or to desire a form of masculinity in which he is ruled over by someone. A British man who lives in colonial India may not be permitted to love interracially, but that very interdiction may produce the very desire that it forbids. He may have sexual fantasies in which these desires are played out. In short, masculinity does not remain a stable construct when a man moves to another context. A man who goes to a new cultural space cannot, on the other hand, simply disband all previous constructs of masculinity, as he necessarily maintains some of those he held in his original cultural context and as unexpected traces remain. The masculinity he remembers and the new masculinity with which he ends up are not mutually exclusive, and may in fact be conflicted in his mind as he tries to make sense of all of them. In the end, it may be the oscillation or the tension between previous and new masculinities – whether those found or those produced – that define transcultural masculinity.

This idea of transculturation applies to one's nation or to one's home culture, which does not necessarily equal nation. I can experience transculturation when I leave my home in one region for another part of my country. My masculinity is transformed when I leave my home city on the east coast to visit Los Angeles, or when I leave the city for the mountains. The masculinity of colonial Canadians necessarily changed when they moved to the western frontier of their own country because new cultural constructs reconfigured their gender (e.g., the absence of women, the necessities of daily life, close contact with other men). Even a move into a new local space can reconstruct masculinity. If that move is into an all-male space such as a prison or the military within one's larger cultural context, the move may still have gendered effects. If a man moves to a local woman-dominated or gay male space, it may be different still. The nation is just one type of spatial construct that defines masculinity, and when that space is left for another, gender is necessarily reconfigured.

Spatially defined changes in gender subjectivity can occur in non-physical or projected spaces as well. Utopian spaces or futuristic science fiction spaces may reconfigure gender, and masculinity in particular, by providing the possibility to reimagine masculinity without some of its current constraints. If those spaces are virtual, a man may construct a masculinity that he does not possess or see himself as possessing. A man who enters into a military video game might temporarily remasculinize the self as he has the experience of becoming a soldier or a ninja. Or, he may take on the role of a female character in a video game and reconstruct his masculinity as a man manipulating a female body, becoming a kind of gender hybrid or cyborg. A woman may experience a new virtual masculinity, too, by taking on the role of a male body and experimenting with muscularity or traditionally male traits or experiences. Virtual spaces, by definition other spaces, may allow for the expression of repressed desires or gender configurations that a man would not express under other non-virtual circumstances. On-line spaces like blogs, YouTube, or My Space, for instance, permit a certain kind of transculturation as men view text or image that they might not encounter in reality or as they make comments on-line related to gender that they may not otherwise make. The construction of a virtual masculine self without materiality may allow for the experience of a fully representational masculinity not necessarily bound by the constraints that form male masculinity in daily life. Out-of-body experiences may more easily lead to the dissipation of sex and of a subjectivity more fully based on gender and gender movement. At the same time, however, virtual experiences of gender may not permit one to ever fully leave the non-virtual world, meaning that virtual gendered becomings are in constant dialogue with non-virtual ones. A man may thus move back and forth between two kinds of gender experiences, such that the overall experience of gender is composed of the oscillation between them. The man who lies about aspects of his body and his gender in on-line dating is constructing another gender subjectivity, but his overall gender experience may be defined by a movement between that constructed self and his own anxieties about his body or his gender.

Bibliography

Even as there is really no definitive theoretical book on the topic, the relation between specific nations and masculinity has sparked a growing amount of research. For several examples, see the essays in Tamar Mayer London, ed., *Gender Ironies of Nationalism: Sexing the Nation* (New York: Routledge, 2000). For sample books on specific national masculinities, see Roy Jerome Albany, ed., *Conceptions of Postwar German Masculinity* (Albany: State University of New York Press, 2001); Xueping Zhong Durham, *Masculinity Besieged? Issues of Modernity and Male Subjectivity in Chinese Literature of the Late Twentieth Century* (Durham, NC: Duke University Press, 2000); Christina S. Jarvis, *The Male Body at War: American Masculinity during World War II* (DeKalb: Northern Illinois University Press, 2004); Lahoucine Ouzgane and Robert Morrell, eds., *African Masculinities: Men in Africa from the Late Nineteenth Century to the Present* (New York: Palgrave, 2005); Klaus Theweleit, *Male Fantasies*, vol. 2, *Male Bodies: Psychoanalyzing the White Terror*, trans. Erica Carter and Chris Turner (Minneapolis: University of Minnesota Press, 1989); Thembisa Waetjen, *Workers and Warriors: Masculinity and the Struggle for Nation in South Africa* (Urbana: University of Illinois Press, 2004).

On heterosexuality and queer nationalism, see Michael Warner, ed., *Fear of a Queer Planet: Queer Politics and Social Theory* (Minneapolis: University of Minnesota Press, 1993). See also Theweleit, *Male Fantasies*.

Probably more than any other kind of text, film has been the privileged locus for studying the relation between nation and masculinity. For an example of how film constructs a national machismo (in this case, in Mexico), see Sergio de la Mora, *Cinemachismo: Masculinities and Sexuality in Mexican Film* (Austin: University of

Texas Press, 2006). On Reagan's masculinized America, see Susan Jeffords, *Hard Bodies: Hollywood Masculinity in the Reagan Era* (New Brunswick, NJ: Rutgers University Press, 1994). This important book provides a model for thinking about how national obsessions and anxieties about masculinity relate to specific texts. Other examples include Mike Chopra-Gant, *Hollywood Genres and Postwar America: Masculinity, Family and Nation in Popular Movies and Film Noir* (London: I. B. Tauris, 2006); Andrew Spicer, *Typical Men: The Representation of Masculinity in Popular British Cinema* (London: I. B. Tauris, 2001).

An important book in the study of national masculinity is Susan Jeffords, *The Remasculinization of America: Gender and the Vietnam War* (Bloomington: Indiana University Press, 1989). While Jeffords's context is specifically post-Vietnam America, her model of thinking about historical masculinity has wide applicability to numerous national contexts, particularly ones in which a nation suffers anxiety from losing a war.

For sample discussions of textual parallels between the coming of age of a boy and of a nation, see Daniel Coleman, "Immigration, Nation, and the Canadian Allegory of Manly Maturation," *Essays on Canadian Writing* 61 (Spring 1997): 84–103; Jarrod Hayes, "Idyllic Masculinity and National Allegory: Unbecoming Men and Anticolonial Resistance in Camara Laye's *L'enfant noir*," in *"Entre hommes": French and Francophone Masculinities in Theory and Culture*, ed. Todd W. Reeser and Lewis C. Seifert (Newark: University of Delaware Press, 2008), 224–50. Hayes looks at how allegories and counter-allegories of nation and masculinity exist side by side.

On the father and the nation as parallel constructs (a tradition inherited from Aristotle), see Constance Jordan, "The Household and the State: Transformations in the Representation of an Analogy from Aristotle to James I," *Modern Language Quarterly* 54 (1993): 307–26.

On power, self-control, and moderation as defining elements of masculinity in the early modern period (but with connections to the pre- and post-modern), see Todd W. Reeser, *Moderating Masculinity in Early Modern Culture* (Chapel Hill: University of North Carolina Press, 2006). Michel Foucault's well-known discussion of power and the self in ancient Greek culture can be found in Michel Foucault, *The History of Sexuality*, vol. 2, *The Use of Pleasure*, trans. Robert Hurley (New York: Vintage, 1985).

For a study of how female bodies embody the nation and how they relate to masculinity and homosociality, see Joan B. Landes, *Visualizing the Nation: Gender, Representation, and Revolution in Eighteenth-Century France* (Ithaca, NY: Cornell University Press, 2001). Beyond Marianne in France, other nationalistic figures may be considered in their relation to the nation. The trope of Mother Africa, for example, provides a way to examine men's relation to national and African contexts.

See Florence Stratton, "The Mother Africa Trope," in *Contemporary African Literature and the Politics of Gender* (London: Routledge, 1994), 39–55. On masculinity and/as citizenship, see Anna Clark, "The Rhetoric of Masculine Citizenship: Concepts and Representations in Modern Western Political Culture," in *Representing Masculinity: Male Citizenship in Modern Western Culture*, ed. Stefan Dudink, Karen Hagemann, and Anna Clark (New York: Palgrave, 2007), 3–22.

The bibliography on colonialism and masculinity is rich. See, for instance, Robert Aldrich, *Colonialism and Homosexuality* (London: Routledge, 2003). For a study of masculinity on the frontier, see Adele Perry, *On the Edge of Empire: Gender, Race, and the Making of British Columbia, 1849–1871* (Toronto: University of Toronto Press, 2001). On eighteenth- and nineteenth-century adventure narratives and masculinity, see Richard Phillips, *Mapping Men and Empire: A Geography of Adventure* (London: Routledge, 1997). See also Philip Holden and Richard J. Ruppel, eds., *Imperial Desire: Dissident Sexualities and Colonial Literature* (Minneapolis: University of Minnesota Press, 2003); Nalin Jayasena, *Contested Masculinities: Crises in Colonial Male Identity from Joseph Conrad to Satyajit Ray* (New York: Routledge, 2007). For a case study in clothing and colonized masculinity, see Frances Gouda, "From Emasculated Subjects to Virile Citizens: Nationalism and Modern Dress in Indonesia, 1900–1949," in *Representing Masculinity*, ed. Dudink et al., 235–57. For a discussion of Said and gender, see Hema Chari, "Colonial Fantasies and Postcolonial Identities: Elaboration of Postcolonial Masculinity and Homoerotic Desire," in *Postcolonial, Queer: Theoretical Intersections*, ed. John C. Hawley (Albany: State University of New York Press, 2001). On whiteness and the colonial male body, see ch. 4 of Richard Dyer, *White* (New York: Routledge, 2000).

The colonial context of the Indian subcontinent has provided some of the most rich and explicit engagement with the study of colonial masculinity. The following discuss theoretical models of how to study masculinity in colonial contexts: Ashis Nandy, *The Intimate Enemy: Loss and Recovery of Self under Colonialism* (Delhi: Oxford University Press, 1983); Mrinalini Sinha, *Colonial Masculinity: The "Manly Englishman" and the "Effeminate Bengali" in the Late Nineteenth Century* (Manchester: Manchester University Press, 1995); Revathi Krishnaswamy, *Effeminism: The Economy of Colonial Desire* (Ann Arbor: University of Michigan Press, 1998), who views Indian effeminacy as "a process that reflects a continuous and contentious struggle to assert hegemony in the face of resistance" (p. 7) and whose introduction provides well-articulated critiques of Said in the area of gender.

For a sample study of how Bhabha's notion of mimicry can be considered in a specific context, see Meredith Goldsmith, "Of Masks, Mimicry, Misogyny, and Miscegenation: Forging Black South African Masculinity in Bloke Modisane's *Blame Me on History*," *Journal of Men's Studies* 10, no. 3 (2002): 291–307. See also Krishnaswamy, *Effeminism*.

For a sample study of transnational masculinity, see Dorinne Kondo, "Fabricating Masculinity: Gender, Race, and Nation in a Transnational Frame," in *Between Woman and Nation: Nationalisms, Transnational Feminisms, and the State*, ed. Caren Kaplan, Norma Alarcón, and Minoo Moallem (Durham, NC: Duke University Press, 1999), 296–319. See also Sheldon H. Lu, "Soap Opera in China: The Transnational Politics of Visuality, Sexuality, and Masculinity," *Cinema Journal* 40, no. 1 (2000): 25–47.

On masculinity and video games, see Derek A. Burrill, *Die Tryin': Videogames, Masculinity, Culture* (New York: Peter Lang, 2008).

9

Interracial Masculinities

In chapter 7, I discussed ways in which one racialized coding of masculinity contributes to constructing another. Stereotypes of excessive black male sexuality, for example, imply an idea of moderate or reasonable white masculinity, if it is assumed that black implies not white and if binary oppositions are taken for granted. This type of confluence of race and gender may be more common on a cultural rather than an individual level, since it may be easier to imagine binarisms of masculinity when one does not actually know the men involved. Thinking in broad, abstract terms about race and masculinity, without actually being familiar with the groups imagined, can be a prerequisite for the functioning of these constructs and for their stability. But actual interactions, or representations of interactions, between racialized masculinities can complicate such simplistic constructs. Once a white man and a black man become colleagues, friends, relatives, or lovers, gendered interactions may increasingly come to define subjectivity. In this chapter, I am interested in what happens to male–male interactions or relationships when men are coded as racially distinct and, in particular, how they are complicated or transformed by cross-racial interactions. How does race change those relations? How do race and gender relate in male–male interactions? What about race and sexuality? The analogies often made between race and gender mean that certain masculinities function as signs that are not simply racial or simply gendered, but that with their double codings, they take on new roles with respect to other masculinities. The analogies between race and gender discussed in chapter 7, then, influence male–male interactions in often unexpected ways, a number of which I will articulate here. My focus is on interracial masculinities in an American cultural context, although the models discussed can be considered in other contexts as well.

Interracial Male Bonding

While the frequency of actual interracial male–male relationships varies according to factors such as cultural context, a number of examples of interracial male friends can be found in Anglophone cultural production: Huckleberry Finn/Jim, the Lone Ranger/Tonto, Robinson Crusoe/Friday, and Ishmael/Queequeg (in *Moby Dick*). While not produced recently, these representations still circulate widely in US culture today. The interracial buddy movie is an important locus of this recurring construct, with recent American films such as *48 Hours* (1982), *Lethal Weapon* (1987), *White Men Can't Jump* (1992), and *Rush Hour* (1998). This kind of bonding across racial borders can be seen to function metonymically for a move toward a utopian world. Because the two men can be friends, they are in effect crossing over racial difference and thus over an important defining element of US culture, showing how America's racist origins can presumably be overcome. If hegemonic masculinity is seen as having had a major hand in slavery and other racist practices, then the recuperation of those practices must involve a reconfiguration of male–male relationships, and of masculinity more generally. A man's ability to trust, to have intimacy with, or to relate to another man codes the relation as falling outside constructs of masculinity as non-intimate, racist, and homophobic. In addition, the freedom implied in male interracial relations, a symbolic move out of the cultural bondage of racial inequality, dovetails with the all-important idea of freedom often ascribed to American masculinity. The image of two male buddies doing what they want, outside the constraints of marriage, children, or even women in a larger sense, symbolizes a form of non-sexual and non-committal love that symbolically frees both men and nation from what ties them down. Government or other institutions may also be rejected in favor of masculine freedom. So while masculinity may emblematize the nation for various reasons (as in chapter 8), in this case it is male–male relationships that stand in for the nation by (re)imagining it in a new way. The relationship between Tonto and the Lone Ranger, for example, may be taken as metonymic for a certain America in which the white man and the Native-American man work together as one and in which racism and racial tensions do not exist. *Huckleberry Finn* (1884) may be the great American novel for many, in part at least, because it depicts a black–white relationship that overcomes, in a very explicit way, racism against black men. The raft on the Mississippi river could been seen as an alternative or utopian national space in which relations between males reposition a cultural and racial divide and gesture toward a new era of racial–gendered practice. This imagined recuperation of America's racist past is not just an element of the late nineteenth century, however, as numerous films function in a similar way. Melvin Donalson documents a number of mixed-race, male–male relationships from the 1930s through the early twenty-first century in US film, many of which attempt to represent this kind of harmonious relationship.[1]

Unlike some actual racial relations, then, this kind of relation suggests a non-problematic bond, free of tension, in a very specific gender configuration. The symbolic import of this representation may be culturally attractive for reasons related to interracial harmony and help fulfill an anti-racist agenda, serving as a microcosm of a gender utopia that reflects a desire for a new cultural context in a larger sense. In some cases, it may reflect real-life relationships and serve as a case study in how masculinity does in fact contribute to a racist-free culture. Masculinity, in this case, provides a convenient avenue for a new agenda precisely because of its perceived importance and its representational force. Male relationships can have such symbolic import in part because other racialized configurations are excluded from playing that utopian role. Depending on their context, male–female interracial love and interaction may present an issue because of the threat of miscegenation and a racially mixed child. Two racially distinct female friends may not have the same representational force as two male friends either. Women may be perceived as already connected to other people and, for this reason, female interracial connections cannot a priori stand in for the recuperation of racial difference and a racist past. Or, in male-dominated cultures, female friendship may be less visible than male friendship, traditionally seen as the more valued and visible kind. These exclusions do not mean that these relations are unable to represent larger cultural relations, only that they may be less likely to do so culturally.

If female friendship is excluded in this model, the potentially optimistic coding of male friendship as a national, cultural, or racial ideal should also be interrogated as to how (or whether) it ignores or effaces

---

[1]   Melvin Donalson, *Masculinity in the Interracial Buddy Film* (Jefferson, NC: McFarland, 2006).

racial inequality and the cultural history of racism. Ideally, racial and gendered progress should incorporate an understanding of past issues and struggles as well as look forward to a new future. These kinds of relations should be examined on a case-by-case basis to determine if they are hiding America's racist past and suggesting that the possibility of two racially diverse buddies has always, and can always, exist. For the idea of buddy narratives embodying a utopian potential or a new history that rewrites the past can be founded on less progressive actions such as hiding or reorganizing racism. Donald Bogle has called this American cultural phenomenon a "huckfinn fixation," with Twain's novel as the epitome of the obsession.[2] In his articulation of the model, a "good white man" who rejects societal norms becomes friends with an outcast, "a trusty black who never competes with the white man and who serves as a reliable ego padder" (p. 140). This fixation may allegorize "the white liberal American's dream of lost innocence and freedom" and give the white man the "spirituality" he has lost in society (p. 141). For Bogle, this representation reaffirms white male hegemony since the black man serves as the sidekick to reconfigure or reaffirm the white man's masculinity, not to establish a friendship based on equality. In her important book *American Anatomies*, Robyn Wiegman discusses this model in theoretical terms, critiquing the fixation for the same reason. For her, even though contemporary interracial bonding narratives tend to place African-American men within the visible category of the masculine, as the friend of the white man, "such a reconfiguration is not necessarily evidence for a part of the process of meaningful social change."[3]

Interracial masculinity in American culture may be represented most commonly through black–white relations, because the major racial rupture to be remedied is generally seen as a result of slavery. Yet, this model could be extended to incorporate other racial or ethnic configurations as well. In a North American context in which north–south immigration is an issue, a Latino–white masculine friendship may embody an American incorporation of Latino culture into a culture perceived as white if the friends function harmoniously under the direction

---

[2] Donald Bogle, *Toms, Coons, Mulattoes, Mammies, and Bucks: An Interpretive History of Blacks in American Films* (New York: Continuum, 2001), 140.

[3] Robyn Wiegman, *American Anatomies: Theorizing Race and Gender* (Durham, NC: Duke University Press, 1995), 118.

of the white friend. Or, more optimistically, if the friendship is one based on equality, it might signify a dialectic mixture of the two ethnic categories into a national melting pot. In other cases, white–Asian male pairs or two non-white men could play similar symbolic roles for American culture. In cultural contexts outside the US, the racial or ethnic configuration of the buddies may be entirely different, reflecting a given national or cultural obsession about interracial connections. The very idea of interracial masculinity as metonymic for national utopia is itself a culturally coded phenomenon, however, and may or may not exist in non-American contexts in which heterosexual love or familial relations might be more likely to serve the function. In such contexts, one might examine the significance of the absence of interracial masculinities with respect to the nation, asking why intimacy between two men cannot serve or embody the nation's progress. This idea of masculine harmony could also be expanded outside the context of race and ethnicity per se and into the realm of male–male difference. Two men who may simply be different in some visible way but who are close or intimate may allegorize an ethnic gap that is turned into a unity. They may both be white, for example, but be different types – physically or personality-wise. One may be blond, the other dark-haired, or one tall and the other short. In such cases, it might make sense to ask why that form of difference embodies national harmony instead of a more racialized version. Is difference in coloring between two white men, for instance, a way to evoke and contain racial difference without actually having to have recourse to the more thorny question of race?

Whatever the racial configuration, this kind of relation often suggests a mentality of "you and me against the world" as the two men struggle against larger cultural forces. Huckleberry Finn and Jim are faced with a series of racial, prejudicial encounters as they journey along together. In the film *Rush Hour*, a Hong Kong and an African-American man join forces to fight a common enemy, who turns out to be white and British. Their friendship could be taken as an interracial struggle against white, Western hegemonic empires represented by the United Kingdom. On the other hand, the cultural strife may be located within the relationship itself if the friends attempt to establish harmony in their friendship but remain unsuccessful in so doing. In this way, the evocation of the possibility of interracial friendship, along with its subsequent failure, represents a nation in which racial harmony cannot take place as the rivalry or struggle between the men embodies or symbolizes a larger cultural or racial struggle. The ultimate failure of what should be possible or even probable in any culture (male–male friendship) can present a pessimistic but eye-opening portrait of a culture's inability to bond internally. In other cases, the relation between the two men may begin as antagonistic or seem impossible and then move beyond impossibility, imitating a cultural interdiction against interracialism that is overcome through male bonding. In *Rush Hour*, the two men end in solidarity as friends, but their beginning is rough and introduced as so culturally impossible that the men cannot trust each other at all.

Despite the transformative or utopian potential of these relations, it is important to determine what gendered presentations subtend the model. Male friendship may be problematic because women are excluded, because the man of color is the white man's inferior, or because a racist past is hidden, and masculine harmony may be predicated on other gendered exclusions that are less than progressive. This national ideal plays itself out here in male–male relationships, and not in the presence of women, raising the question of whether utopia can be represented only by men. The image of the Lone Ranger and Tonto in some undefined geographical context may be dependent on the idea of a womanless West, and, by extension, on the absence of heterosexual desire. If interracial heterosexual male–female love is a problem in this context, male–male relationships mean that issues related to reproduction are not evoked. Symbolically or actually dispelling women, then, also dispels the threat of different races reproducing with each other and establishes the non-reproductive nature of the masculine bond. On another level, male–male relations should be interrogated to determine whether one of the men functions as a symbolic woman and stands in for the absent or expelled women. The interracial couple may be composed of two male bodies (sexed male), but in fact function symbolically as a male–female couple (gendered male–female). Race may operate analogically as a sign of gender, and the non-white subject may function as the wife-like sidekick to the white man. Consequently, one of the men may be located representationally in an undefined space between race and gender. As Leslie Fiedler writes in a ground-breaking essay on *Huckleberry Finn* entitled "Come Back to the Raft Ag'in, Huck Honey!": "The notion of the Negro as the unblemished bride blends with the myth of running away to sea, of running the great river down to the sea."[4] Twain evokes the possibility, if not the actual idea, of an interracial marriage, but without the need for a man and a woman and without a heterosexual couple. Tonto may function symbolically as the Lone Ranger's sidekick-wife, with analogies between the Native-American male body and women/effeminacy/feminization subtending the coding. In this way, the expulsion of women from the all-male relationship may be a way to permit the creation of a woman-like, racially coded man whose "marriage" to another man represents a kind of domestic and, by extension, national bliss. So, despite the freedom symbolically accorded to a male friendship, the possibility of heterosexuality or heteronormativity is not fully disbanded but reformulated into another guise. As the nation will need heterosexuality to encourage reproduction, the new racial guise can symbolically evoke it just enough to keep any anxiety of its total absence at bay. But at the same time, because it is not actually a heterosexual marriage or couple, the threats of racial intermingling and of racially impure children can be avoided. The utopian idea of America is evoked as neither entirely masculine, nor entirely heterosexual, creating a new racial–gendered coding all its own.

This model can have the effect of (re)virilizing white masculinity when it codes the non-white man as *like* a woman. In *Lethal Weapon*, the white detective Martin (Mel Gibson) is widowed, but in a certain sense his relation with his new African-American partner Roger (Danny Glover) fulfills some of the functions of a heterosexual romance. At one point, for instance, Roger brings Martin coffee in bed in the morning, and Roger's teenage daughter's crush on Martin can be seen as a transfer of his own homosocial crush on his partner. In the final scene of the film, the two men embrace in the rain as if they have become one through their common crime-fighting experience. These kind of scenes have the effect of making Martin into the symbolic man in the duo, thus the viril "lethal weapon" of the title of the film.[5] In other contexts, the man of color may be the "lover" for another man of color. In *Rush Hour*, when the African-American and Hong Kong pair

---

[4]   *The New Fiedler Reader* (Prometheus Books, 1999), 9. The essay was originally published (without the citation above) in *Partisan Review* 25 (June 1948): 664–71.

[5]   Wiegman discusses the complicated race–gender representations at play, especially how the black man remasculinizes the white man in the film, and how the "lethal weapon" is the white male body. See *American Anatomies*, 139–45.

of buddies together defeat their common enemy, the Asian man (played by Jackie Chan) literally kisses his friend to thank him for his help but also to signify that their relationship is like that of a heterosexual couple, his character functioning as the woman kissing his/her hero. In such cases as these, the feminized man may help the other man masculinize himself by opposition, or the heterosexual-like relationship may function as a sign of unity between the two men of color.

This similarity between heterosexual romance and male–male interracial relationships can also suggest the specter or threat of homoerotics or homosexuality. In chapter 2, I discussed how male–male relationships tend to display an anxiety on some level, implicitly or explicitly, of homoerotics or homosexuality. Part of the issue around this anxiety is that similarity between men can evoke the possibility of homosexuality. Jokes about the homosexuality of Batman and Robin, Simon and Garfunkel, Ernie and Bert, or other male pairs regularly seen together in popular culture require not only that they both be men and that they do something together (e.g., fight crime, form a pop music duo, live together), but also that they both be white or be perceived as racially similar. Because homosexuality is often linked to sameness in the realm of sex and gender (a man plus a man), racial sameness may be a precondition for the threat of homosexuality. A couple like Batman and Robin may be likely to evoke the idea of homosexuality because their age difference evokes possible pederasty, but also because they are both white. With racially distinct male pairs, however, the same homophobic threat may be less likely to be perceived. Despite their own age difference, Huck and Jim, for instance, are probably not perceived in the twenty-first century as potentially homoerotic in the same way as Batman and Robin. The relation between two racially distinct men may be perceived as less potentially homoerotic than one without racial difference. This representation results in part from cultural miscegenation: although it is a question of two men, and not a man and a woman, the interdiction on heterosexual interracial love may still carry over into male–male relations and dispel the possibility of the two men having sex, or desiring each other erotically. In short, because the two men are racially distinct, in the cultural imaginary they will never have sex. So while other male–male relations require triangulation and a woman as mediator in order to dispel a homoerotic threat, this kind of relationship may not necessitate a third term since race already serves the function of displacing desire outside the threat of the homoerotic. On the other hand, however, these kinds of relations may need to evoke women or heterosexual desire at some point in a cursory way to render it clear that homosexuality is not a possibility, even as homosociality may be. In a buddy narrative, a wife, a girlfriend, or a female object of desire may appear early on so that the men's heterosexuality be established or assumed, and then the narrative may move on to focus on the men's relationship.

Alternately, it may not be racial difference that dispels a homoerotic threat, but non-racial forms of difference that evoke the concept of racial difference. In a male–male duo, in which one man is fair and blond and the other dark, the difference in coloring may suggest difference and thus dispel potential homosexuality, perhaps referring to a racial coding (blond hair as white-like, brown hair as black-like). This kind of difference in coloring recurs in male–male buddies, in television shows such as *Starsky and Hutch, Bosom Buddies, Sesame Street* (Ernie and Bert) or in films such as *Butch Cassidy and the Sundance Kid*. Differences in body type might also serve a similar function, as with Laurel and Hardy or Ernie and Bert (tall versus short) and suggest that two physically different men can never enter into homosexuality because they are dissimilar physically. Consequently, the use of physical characteristics or traits to create differences in male relationships might be considered in symbolic relation to gender and sexuality.

Racialized Triangles

In the approach articulated above, race or some aspect of difference may take over for the female mediator in Sedgwick's model in order to dispel a homoerotic threat. But in other cases, two men may relate in a more classic triangulated relationship in which racial codings are an integral aspect of how homosociality functions. I will discuss several different types of triangles in which race and gender function in tandem. These models are all racialized revisions of the standard model of triangulation discussed in chapter 2. The model is not always thought about in relation to race, so rethinking the model is a way to revision the model itself.

One such triangle consists of two racially distinct men and one white woman as mediator. In this model, the two men desire a mutual object, but their desire is predicated on racial rivalry, unlike the harmonious model of masculinity in which mutual desire creates homosociality. Or, more precisely, their desire is predicated on the concept that mutual desire can equalize racial hierarchy when the non-white upgrades to white status through the medium of the desired object. By desiring, attaining, or loving the white woman, the non-white man imitates white masculinity in the framework of desire and may gain access to white privilege or to whiteness itself. Heterosexual desire and racial imitation thus becomes a means to transform racial subjectivity. Frantz Fanon, in his important book on colonial subjectivities, *Black Skin, White Masks* (1952), can be read as articulating a model of race and gender in this vein, an approach which has been discussed in terms of masculinity and triangulation by Gwen Bergner.[6] For Fanon, the black man in a colonial context attempts to become a white man by desiring the white woman: "By loving me [the white woman] proves that I am worthy of white love. I am loved like a white man. I am a white man."[7] In this model, the ultimate goal of *being* a white man takes place through the medium of the white woman whose status as standard object of heterosexual desire makes her a means to a masculine end, a kind of phallus that the black man needs, thinks he needs, or is told he needs, in order to become another kind of man. This kind of re-racializing through desire could be seen as a way to masculinize the black male body when it is symbolically castrated or seen as lacking. To acquire the phallus through a white woman, then, evokes a nexus of racially and gender-coded factors that operate in tandem.

The question of how homosociality functions in this racialized model might be posed since the relation between the two men may be predicated more on homosociality or more on racial rivalry. On the one hand, the desire for the white woman might be a way to acquire whiteness through homosociality with the white man (and homosociality through whiteness), but on the other hand, it suggests a latent racial rivalry in which racism and racial hierarchy position the white man as the black man's rival and the black man as the white man's rival. In the latter perspective, the model can create rather than disrupt homosociality. For despite their racial difference, the male subjects may in

---

[6] See Gwen Bergner, "Who Is That Masked Woman? or, The Role of Gender in Fanon's *Black Skin, White Masks*," *PMLA* 110, no. 1 (1995): 75–88.

[7] Frantz Fanon, *Black Skin, White Masks*, trans. Charles Lam Markmann (New York: Grove Press, 1967), 63.

the end bond over their desire for the white woman in a way they may not be able to with a non-white woman because the white man sees white women as the only possible objects of desire. Like homosocial triangles more generally, interracial homosociality is misogynist in nature when the two men employ women as objects to create their own bond.

From another perspective, desire for the same object can be taken as a mediating force that deconstructs any possible homosociality when the men's relation functions more through rivalry than through homosociality. This relation can serve to create or to reinforce an imagined rivalry when the non-white man is imagined as the white man's competitor in terms of desire for the white woman. The white man may imagine the black man's desire, for example, in the form of fear of raping the white woman. This supposed mutual desire, turned into a threat, allows the white man to save her from him and to make the black man his rival. In this way, the white woman as well as the black man both become pure objects, imagined in a certain way for ends related more to hegemonic masculinity than to desire per se. This racist model might lead, in certain cultural contexts, to lynching, castration, or other punishments for the black man for his desire. Robyn Wiegman discusses this model, revealing how this racist rivalry can also include a homoerotic element as lynched black men's genitals/testicles were passed around in certain nineteenth-century contexts.[8] The white man's seeing desire on the part of the racial other, then, may also be a way to deflect his own fluid homosocial desire for a black man. Texts in which a love triangle with two racially diverse men plays a central role can be considered from this perspective. In such representations, it is important to examine the reasons for interracial heterosexual desire as well as how the men's own relationship defines their desire for the same woman. In Shakespeare's *Othello* (1622), for instance, in which a white man (Othello) and a Moor (Iago) both love the same white woman Desdemona, the love triangle can be thought about from the perspective of the two men's homosocial bond as well as their rivalry.

A further permutation of this model to consider is a triangle in which the woman as mediator is racially distinct from the white man, but racially similar to the other man. This approach is particularly relevant

---

[8] See Wiegman, *American Anatomies*, 99, who is also interested in the feminization of the lynched black man.

in a colonial context in which the European or Western colonizer desires the woman in the colony and feels the need to protect her from the men who live there. If British colonizers in colonial India imagined that they were saving Indian women from Indian men, the mutual desire for the women on the part of the British and Indian men may suggest that the triangle also includes an element of rivalry between the racially distinct men. A relevant construct to consider would be how Americans viewed or represented the invasion of Afghanistan in 2001, and whether the military was viewed as saving Afghan women from their male dominators, allowing them to free themselves of their veils. In these cases, the white man's desire for the non-white woman could be as much about his own relation to the Afghan men as to the Afghan women as his fighting in the country could be construed as a large-scale homosocial rivalry.

Womanless Triangles

Another way to imagine racially coded triangles is without actual women as mediators, but with signs or tropes of women playing the role of intermediary. In this model, women may tend to function as tropes anyway, not as actual women, because they serve a function for masculinity. But the representation of woman can be even one more step removed from female subjectivity. When not actually present, woman – or the idea of woman – may be completely invented so as to dispel any homoerotic threat between men and to permit a non-problematic homosociality. Within the context of European travel narratives, for example, men may come to the Americas womanless, but invent love triangles by means of an imagined woman back home that does not actually exist. They may project sex or gender onto the land or territory, rendering the land womanlike, as a kind of physical mediator of male–male desire and rivalry. Colonial men can together give human traits to, and desire, the gendered land (e.g., mountains, lakes, valleys) as a displaced projection of mutual desire for woman. Similarly, as we saw in the last chapter, invented nationalized figures of women can mediate a national homosociality, but virtually anything can be made to play the role of woman when given female traits.

If woman can be transformed into a sign that still plays the female role in the triangle, then it is also possible for that mediating role to be held by a man coded in a certain way under certain circumstances, sexed male but gendered otherwise. In chapter 8, I discussed ways in which colonized masculinities might be perceived as other for coloniz-ing masculinities. A European may perceive an orientalized Middle Easterner or Indian as feminized to a large enough extent that he serves as a mediator of desire between men. The French writer Gustave Flaubert, while in Egypt, wrote back to his male friend about a male dancer he saw while abroad: "we have seen male dancers. Oh! Oh! Oh!" and then described the dancer's erotic/effeminate dance.[9] This kind of comment between men may not be as possible in a European context: the racial coding of the dancer may be what allows for Flaubert to express his apparent desire or titillation and, by extension, to bond with his friend through the dancer. Finding him attractive can be a way for two Frenchmen to make the Middle Eastern man an object and to place him outside the realm of gendered representation. Such a con-struct of a feminized man as mediator of desire may be a way to render the male colonized subject as lacking subjectivity, a racially coded object of exchange between real men. The desire for another man may not be sexual in nature, at least in the way "sexual" is generally under-stood, but be based on a more fluid kind of desire that can be expressed when the other man is womanlike. To call it homoerotic is not entirely accurate since it may be desire for a specific, racialized, ethnically coded gender presentation. Instead of the colonizer and the colonized as homosocial rivals, as in the first model above, white men may create a homosocial bond with other white men if non-white men in the colony are desired on some level by the colonizing men.

If this interracial male–male relation is not necessarily perceived as homoerotic and thus not problematic in certain contexts (colonial ones, for example), it may be because the man leaves his home country and sees another culture's way of doing gender, which opens up a space for him in which alternate or new forms of desire are possible. In his letter to his friend cited above, Gustave Flaubert later mentions his own desire for sodomitical acts while in Egypt: "Traveling as we are for educational purposes, and charged with a mission by the government, we have considered it our duty to indulge in this form of ejaculation" (p. 84). Part of the reason for "seeking" sodomy is the cultural context

---

[9]   *Flaubert in Egypt: A Sensibility on Tour* (London: Bodley Head, 1972), 83.

in which "[o]ne admits one's sodomy, and it is spoken of at table in the hotel" (p. 84). The concept of transculturation, by which one's subjectivity changes because one goes to a new cultural space, applies here in terms of desire: a man's heteronormative desire in his home culture or country is transformed into something new when he goes to another cultural space and, perhaps particularly, to a non-Western space in which he is already a dominating or colonizing power and thus in a position of strength from which to experiment. But transculturation does not mean that a man becomes entirely other, in this case, that a straight man turns gay. Rather, his desire and his gender can be queered or mutated in complicated and unpredictable ways that reconfigure triangulation as experienced in his home culture. This kind of reformulation of triangulation is just one specific way in which masculinity more generally is transculturated when moved to another cultural or national space, as discussed at the end of the previous chapter.

A final womanless model of triangulation can be articulated when the three positions of the triangle are held by three racially distinct men and one man plays the symbolic role of woman. In this case, the mediator of desire between two men functions analogically as a non-man, thus allowing for his mediating function. This mediation might be based not on desire for a common object, but on mutual hate toward a common racially coded enemy. In this sense, it is through a common object perceived as mutual threat that the two men forge a homosocial bond that may normally be difficult to construct because of interracial difference or rivalry. The mediator is not, then, an object of exchange per se, but he plays a similar role, in the sense that he exchanges the two men's relationship. This anti-racial hate which creates desire between the haters resembles the mechanism by which two men bond misogynistically even as they may desire the same woman. The threatening object can be racially distinct from the two other men in order to create an interracial harmony between two men who are racially distinct, especially when they are members of groups that have historically not been buddies. Brian Locke analyzes what he calls the "Orientalist buddy film," in which an Asian peril is mutually combated by a black and a white man.[10] These films allow the black and white men to bond as buddies in the face of a threat perceived as foreign,

---

[10]   See Brian Locke, *Racial Stigma on the Hollywood Screen from World War II to the Present: The Orientalist Buddy Film* (New York: Palgrave Macmillan, 2009).

alien, or somehow other (as the Asian man is taken to be in the films that Locke studies). In this case, preexistent cultural constructs of effeminate Asian men may allow for them to better serve as racial mediators. Such an other may be racially, ethnically, or nationally coded depending on the kind of bonding taking place. This kind of triangle, then, functions similarly to the "huckfinn fixation" model with which this chapter began: here, two men bond in the face of a third common enemy to whom they react together, but they may do so to reconstruct symbolically a new idea of nation as utopian and racially harmonious.

Bibliography

The interracial buddies question was first evoked, in terms very different from those of modern gender studies, by Leslie Fiedler in his ground-breaking "Come Back to the Raft Ag'in, Huck Honey!," *Partisan Review* 25 (June 1948): 664–71. In his later book, Fiedler adds the possibility of the mother to the equation: "the bulwark of woman left behind … the wanderer feels himself without protection, more motherless child than free man. To be sure, there is a substitute for wife or mother presumably waiting in the green heart of nature: the natural man, the good companion, pagan and unashamed – Queequeg or Chingachgook or Nigger Jim." See *Love and Death in the American Novel* (New York: Stein and Day, 1966), 26. For a sophisticated reading of this model, as well as the larger issue of how and why race and gender are categorized together, see Robyn Wiegman, *American Anatomies: Theorizing Race and Gender* (Durham, NC: Duke University Press, 1995). While not the center of the analysis, Sedgwick does refer to race in her introduction in Eve Kosofsky Sedgwick, *Between Men: English Literature and Male Homosocial Desire* (New York: Columbia University Press, 1985), 9–10.

For more on racial triangulation, see Susan Fraiman, "Geometries of Race and Gender: Eve Sedgwick, Spike Lee, Charlayne Hunter-Gault," *Feminist Studies* 21, no. 1 (1994): 67–82. On interracial friendship in film, see Melvin Donalson, *Masculinity in the Interracial Buddy Film* (Jefferson, NC: McFarland, 2006), and Donald Bogle, *Toms, Coons, Mulattoes, Mammies, and Bucks: An Interpretive History of Blacks in American Films* (New York: Continuum, 2001). Brian Locke addresses the triangulated model of white–black–Asian in *Racial Stigma on the Hollywood Screen from World War II to the Present: The Orientalist Buddy Film* (New York: Palgrave Macmillan, 2009). See also his " 'Top Dog,' 'Black Threat,' and 'Japanese Cats': The Impact of the White–Black Binary on Asian American Identity," *Radical Philosophy Review* 1, no. 2 (1998): 98–125.

Fanon's discussion of the colonized black man's relation to the white man and woman has been influential in the study of masculinity. See Frantz Fanon, *Black Skin, White Masks*, trans. Charles Lam Markmann (New York: Grove Press, 1967). For a reading of racialized homosocial triangles, see Gwen Bergner, "Who Is That Masked Woman? or, The Role of Gender in Fanon's *Black Skin, White Masks*," *PMLA* 110, no. 1 (1995): 75–88.

On the Flaubert passage cited and other orientalist homoerotics, see Joseph Boone, "Vacation Cruises; or, The Homoerotics of Orientalism," in *Postcolonial, Queer: Theoretical Intersections*, ed. John C. Hawley (Albany: State University of New York Press, 2001), 43–78. See also Hema Chari, "Colonial Fantasies and Postcolonial Identities: Elaboration of Postcolonial Masculinity and Homoerotic Desire," in *Postcolonial, Queer*, ed. Hawley, 277–304; Ashis Nandy, *The Intimate Enemy: Loss and Recovery of Self under Colonialism* (Delhi: Oxford University Press, 1983), 9–10.

10

Unstable Time: Masculinity in History

So far in this book, the emphasis has been on synchronic approaches to masculinity in which gender is considered as a snapshot at a given moment in time. In chapter 1, however, I discussed how masculinity can be seen as constantly moving across time and as different from one moment to the next (see pp. 45–9). A man or woman might conform to a construct of masculinity at some moment, but over the course of even a short period of time, it is impossible to remain in the same gendered position. No one can maintain any kind of masculinity because time passes, even as one may perceive or experience a gender core that transcends time. From this perspective, masculinity cannot be considered essential or natural, and temporality can serve as a de-essentializing tool for gender. A construct of masculinity that exists in one unit of time can return later, in a possibly unexpected moment, rendering time's relation to masculinity disjointed and complex. Whereas a man may appear continually masculine, for instance, he may from time to time experience anxiety about his gender – a remnant in part of previous events from his life that still affect him in unpredictable ways.

The relation between masculinity and stages of life provides a case study to consider this question of unstable time. It is often thought that the aging process over a period of time tends to change masculinity. It might wax in adolescence and wane in old age. But such changes are a result of the ways in which cultural discourses represent the links between a given age and masculinity. Because those discourses are incoherent and ambiguous, one stage of life cannot univocally map onto a type of masculinity. A man in his twenties is not always considered more virile than a man in his thirties, for example. One culture or time period may consider a certain age as more virile or masculine than another, while in a different context those ages may be coded very differently. In addition, chronological movement over a lifetime does not imply a linear or direct relation to gender, in part because ages are partially composed of other ages. Manhood and boyhood, for example, are not absolutely distinct. In fact, aspects of boyhood may be a key definitional component of one's manhood, and aspects of manhood might partially define one's boyhood. The idea that a boy becomes a man reflects an overly simplistic view of temporality, one in which two periods of life can be totally discrete. In a man's own experience, memories of former masculinities, ones perhaps from another phase of life, may be part of how his current gender subjectivity is articulated, whether because he wants to distance himself from them or because he wants to relive them. A man's childhood relationship to his mother may influence how he conceives of his masculinity as an adult. The presence of female masculinity over the course of a woman's life cycle raises similar questions. Transsexual masculinity is also constructed and reconstructed in time, albeit in ways possibly unlike male or female subjectivity. Male-to-female transsexual subjectivity can be defined by the continual rejection of one's earlier masculinity and, conversely, female-to-male subjectivity by an accelerated or gradual move toward masculinity and retrospective attempts to locate it within one's boyhood. Or, transsexual subjectivities can be uneven, characterized by continual back-and-forth movements from one temporally defined gender construct to another. The point here is that, like gender, time itself is an undulating concept, and in the same way that self and other cannot be totally discrete, temporal blocks cannot be regarded in full isolation from others, and the unstable relation between those blocks – in which gender subjectivities are contained – can be what defines gender.

Temporality has a mutating effect on masculinity with respect to individuals, but it does something similar from a historical perspective, since no cultural definition of masculinity remains static over the course of time. The figure of the knight organizes a set of gendered characteristics for the middle ages, but how a knight is defined in one century is different in another. And within a given century, definitions of the knight change and fluctuate. Historical periods might create certain definitions of masculinity that are maintained as partially cohesive for a certain period of time, but those definitions inevitably change as time moves on. Such changes might be reflected in beliefs or attitudes (what a knight is or should be, for example), or in the behavior of actual knights (what they actually do). In the Butlerian terms outlined in chapter 3, I might say that a given style of masculinity is necessarily replaced by a new one in time. While styles of gender may change from minute to minute, or from second to second, methodologically speaking, some temporal coherence has to be assumed in order to study these cultural attitudes or behaviors.

Thinking about masculinities in historical terms contributes to the larger goal of disbanding simplistic or essentialist notions of masculinity. Cross-temporal comparison of our own gendered context with that of previous periods has the effect of making our own notions of masculinity appear historically situated and not transhistorical. Our own presentness is framed as we see our gender constructs as relative. Forms of alterity, against which masculinity is defined, change over time, meaning that, in the same way that what is coded masculine changes, what is not considered masculine changes too. A twenty-first-century North American might think of male homosexuality as a key type of alterity for masculinity, but by looking back at other cultures in which homosexuality either existed very differently (e.g., before "homosexuality" as a term or concept existed) or was not coded as negative or as unmasculine (in ancient Athens, for instance), the very relation of masculinity to that form of alterity comes to seem relative as well. There can be no natural or essential opposition between masculinity and male homosexuality, and even when operative in culture, the specificities of the opposition look different in each context. Definitions of masculinity necessarily change as their relation to women, effeminacy, race, ethnicity, class, and numerous other forms of subjectivity are transformed. One way to approach doing a history of masculinity, then, is to start with the assumption of historical difference and the absence of transhistorical masculinities. This approach to constructs of masculinity relies on an assumption of historical rupture, an assumption that the past is different from the present, and, consequently, that historicized masculinities are radically unlike those in other time periods. An important definition of masculinity in one period might make no sense in an earlier or later context (and, by implication, a current definition may make no sense in the future). A man seen as highly virile in contemporary culture may be viewed as the epitome of masculinity. He may affirm and reaffirm his masculinity by conquering women and having sex with as many as possible. He may be considered exceptional because of the frequency with which he can "get it up." But in other periods, this specific idea of virility may instead appear anti-masculine. In the

Renaissance, for instance, under the influence of ancient philosophy and culture, moderation was a key definitional element of masculinity and, as a result, the ideal man was supposed to be guided by this virtue in his sexual dealings. If the hypervirile modern man could be transported back to Renaissance Europe, he might appear to their eyes as not ideal at all. Likewise, a Renaissance moderate man transported forward to contemporary American culture might appear as less virile than in his own time period. As a result of historical difference, past masculinities can be counter-intuitive to us as moderns: a moderate man may or may not appear to conform to twenty-first-century notions of masculinity, and excess may not de-masculinize a man but in fact be a trait that defines his masculinity.

A moderate form of masculinity may have disappeared as a key definition of gender to be replaced by other forms predicated instead on excess or on "going for the gusto." In these kinds of gender shifts over time, masculinities can be defined by their breaks with, or rejection of, previous forms of masculinity. Recent calls to remasculinize men, for example, are partly in response to perceptions of excessive effeminacy or queerness that have supposedly destroyed masculinity and sexual distinction. One recent example of this phenomenon is the "retrosexual" – a reaction against the morphology of the "metrosexual," usually defined as a heterosexual and stylish man with some traditionally feminine traits. This new brand of masculinity is oppositional as it tries to call men into a new era in which the retrosexual is more masculine than the metrosexual. The very name of the new morphology is based on a linguistic rejection of the previous form and on an attempt to move back ("retro") to a time when men were presumably men and sexual distinction was supposedly clearer. Fear of effeminacy or emasculation fuels the development and propagation of numerous constructs of masculinity that are distinguished from former ones.

But can we really say that modern masculinity is simply unlike previous masculinities, that masculinities simply change and morph over time into something new, leaving past definitions behind? Does a new form not have a relation to the past from which it came? If we compare the metrosexual to earlier constructs of masculinity, it is obvious that this form of masculinity is a new one crafted for various reasons related to the sociohistorical context in which it arose (e.g., a reaction to the cultural presence of gay masculinity, and to a global marketplace in which the ability to mold or craft oneself is prized). But at the same time, the metrosexual does not spring out of nowhere, nor does it simply appear because of contemporaneous social factors. The metrosexual could instead be considered to morph out of a lengthy Western tradition in which certain definitions of masculinity focus on self-construction and its close relation to art and aesthetics and to fashioning the male body. Early modern masculine morphologies, such as the courtier, or more modern morphologies, such as the dandy and the gentleman, have paved the way for the possibility of the metrosexual by rendering certain characteristics acceptable or valued. While modern eyes might now find the courtier effeminate and far from a paragon of masculinity, the courtier's effeminacy could in fact be a way to represent himself as subject to a sovereign, and consequently the courtier was a brand of masculinity in which effeminacy was often a perfectly acceptable – if not desirable – element. The courtier as figure, then, creates or propagates the possibility of masculinity's effeminacy. Once this idea is established as a possibility, it is easier for later morphologies of masculinity to evoke this kind of approach to effeminacy. In the nineteenth century, the dandy can appropriate such traits because the terrain has already been prepared for them. In turn, the figure of the metrosexual is possible, in part, because the dandy has paved the way for it. And other masculine definitions yet to be articulated will be possible in part because of the metrosexual and his predecessors. The relation between the Southern or English gentleman and these earlier morphologies could likewise be considered. The point, then, about historical approaches to masculinity is that, while a new morphology might arise for various contextual reasons and seemingly appear out of the blue, key elements of that masculinity can have a direct or indirect relation to elements that predate it. Morphologies can explicitly evoke previous masculinities, or they may not be linked to them in any explicit way.

Another way to express this idea is to say that a new morphology of masculinity does not mean that previous ones are unrelated to it since there may be some key aspect of masculinity that the new morphology transforms. The figure of the metrosexual may be new, but the idea of the masculine incorporation of feminine traits is far from new. While the ability to wage war has not really disappeared from masculinity over time, the specific ways in which morphologies of masculinity relate to war and battle have changed over time and current definitions of military masculinity are dependent on previous ones. The medieval morphology of the knight is quite different from the image of the

Napoleonic soldier, who is quite different from the American soldier fighting in Iraq. Yet all of these forms of masculinity are centered on the ability to wage war in a certain sociohistorical context. So while the specific way in which masculinity is represented changes over time, a given aspect of masculinity may not change from one definition to another and from one era to another. This recurrence does not mean, however, that war defines all masculinities across time or that it is an important construct in all cultures, only that some recurring morphologies are closely related to it.

There is another issue around historical continuity and change. I said, above, that over time masculinities necessarily change. But this does not mean that no form or vestige of previous forms of masculinity is circulating in culture along with newer forms. To take one of my previous examples, the moderate man is a key definition of masculinity in early modern Europe and not so central to modern definitions of masculinity in the US, but there are nonetheless moments today in which the notion of moderation defines masculinity. We may know men that are moderate and reasonable whom we might consider masculine because of (and not despite) their moderation. The construct of the man of reason, for instance, who keeps his emotions in check and does not act excessively in terms of his emotions might be considered masculine under certain circumstances. The notion of moderation as a definitional element of masculinity might also manifest itself today because various constructs of non-masculinity are linked with excess, such as women (e.g., the nymphomaniac or the hysterical woman) or homosexuals (e.g., the gay man who sleeps with a different man every night). Racial codings might also factor in: the supposed sexual excess of the African-American man might be a way to discount him from the category of masculinity. These excessive codings, which circulate in complicated ways in Western culture, point to an underlying assumption that masculinity, in certain guises at least (heterosexual, white), is not excessive and thus is moderate. So while moderation might be an important definition of masculinity in early modern Europe and while that definition might be much less widespread in twenty-first-century American culture, it nonetheless does circulate and remains one element of how gender and masculinity function. Masculinity might be ideal when moderate in some cases and when excessive in others. My point here is that contradictory forms of masculinity are always simultaneously in cultural circulation, and that relations between supposedly archaic or outdated definitions of masculinity operate alongside or against common or accepted ones.

These contradictory forms, one more current and one less so, can define one's subjectivity, and may or may not be experienced as contradictory. A man might operate under the assumption that excess is a key aspect of his subjectivity (more muscle is better, more sex is better, more money is better), but have moments in which moderation governs his gender. On the other hand, contradictory definitions can be defined by the tension between them. The man who cannot decide if he should act gallantly or aggressively may feel caught between two definitions of masculinity, one of which may have been more widespread in another era. A man may also be snared in an outdated masculine construct, unable or unwilling to change as he remains within a gendered framework that was more widespread in a previous time. The masculinity of a man who continues to act like a knight as the institution of knighthood is on the wane, may be constituted by the very attempt to maintain that gender subjectivity in opposition to his cultural context. The sociohistorical reasons why an outdated masculine construct came into existence may no longer be operative, but the construct itself may be held over and adapted to new circumstances.

In the end, then, we can look for both continuities and ruptures as we think about constructs of masculinity in our own era and move backwards to locate ways in which the past might see things differently. But at the same time, we are seeking ways in which the past continues into the present in complicated or unpredictable ways. This historical approach to gender, one based on instability between past and present, is in many ways the temporal equivalent of the approach to binary oppositions discussed in chapter 1. The relation between masculine and non-masculine is unstable, and the masculine is in the non-masculine (and vice versa). Similarly, one form of historically defined masculinity contains elements of a previous form within it, even if that form is seemingly rejected.

Historical masculinities can be approached discursively, using many of the ideas about discourse discussed in chapter 1. Morphologies of masculinity are conveyed in certain types of discourse, are constructed in certain ways, and are transformed in specific ways and for specific reasons over time. In *How to Do a History of Homosexuality* (2002), David Halperin has taken this kind of discursive approach to the study of male homosexuality in Western historical contexts, examining how various types of what we tend to place under the umbrella of "homosexuality" operate in complicated and overlapping ways. What are called "peder-asty" and "friendship" might seem like very distinct morphologies of same-sex sexuality, but in fact they have certain commonalities and overlaps, even as they operate in ways that might not always make intu-itive sense. In the introduction to his book, Halperin provides the example of how ancient Greek pederasty, which might be assumed to be contained within an ancient socio-historical context, in fact tran-scends that context and functions as a discursive form of gay male sub-jectivity, with which moderns may identify in certain ways.[1] This presence of a previous type of sexuality does not mean, however, that many men actually practice pederasty (though a few may, and some may fantasize about it), but it does mean that it still operates as one discur-sive definition of same sex sexuality. A man might define himself as "queer," "gay," or "homosexual," thus through a sexual subjectivity that is historically very modern, but he may also have recourse at certain moments and for certain reasons to previously dominant sexual subjec-tivities such as the ancient pederast, the premodern sodomite, or the nineteenth-century invert (a woman in a man's body). Modern and premodern discursive categories together constitute his subjectivity, and the same can be said of cultural conceptions of sexual subjectivity. My discussion of historical masculinities as relational and overlapping is greatly indebted to Halperin's approach to male homosexuality, even as his categories are very unlike the categories of masculinity that interest me here.

Halperin locates the major discursive categories of what we might currently call "homosexuality" across time in the West, including effemi-nacy, sodomy, friendship, inversion, and homosexuality itself: "there are histories to be written of at least 4 different but simultaneous categories or traditions of discourse pertaining to aspects of what we now define as homosexuality" (p. 109). Categorizing each of these discursive tradi-tions requires asking a series of questions, for example, "Is it an orienta-tion?" or "Does it involve gender-deviance?" (p. 135). There are major differences between male homosexuality and masculinity that make the way they should be approached historically very different. If we take "what we now define as masculinity" in lieu of homosexuality here, it would be hard to posit historical masculinity as four categories or discur-sive traditions. Masculinity is unlike male homosexuality because it is

[1] David Halperin, *How to Do a History of Homosexuality* (Chicago: University of Chicago Press, 2002), 15.

often more prevalent and harder to categorize, and, because masculinity is often hidden, it may be harder to categorize into discrete types. In the Foucauldian model, homosexuality would be more present than masculinity, in part because discourse tries to make the former out to be a problem. To pathologize homosexuality requires that culture define it, know what it is, and stabilize it. While discourses of homosexuality are undoubtedly slippery too, discursive constructs of masculinity may be even more so when they are meant to represent a norm and to remain hidden. It would be difficult, if not impossible, methodologically speaking, to list a handful of categories of masculinity in the same way. Instead, it may make sense to alter Halperin's model and consider key discursive traits of masculinity that have recurred over time, and to break those traits down into their attendant categories or morphologies. For it is largely positive masculine traits that tend to be localizable, more discursively present, than specific categories of men.

I might thus suggest some clusters of Western masculinity along with more specific definitions or morphologies that could fall under their umbrella. First, I might propose a model of masculinity in which some kind of incorporation of perceived feminine characteristics factors in heavily. As discussed earlier in this chapter, the metrosexual is one such example, but that morphology may have been preceded by the dandy, the gentleman, or the premodern courtier. These various morphologies are both related and unrelated, and the connections amongst them defined by a complex interplay of continuity and difference. The athlete might be another key cluster, a construct predicated on athletic prowess and the primacy of the body as definitional elements, whether a professional athlete in some modern sense (a pro football player, a bodybuilder), or an ancient Greek discus thrower. A modern bodybuilder has an overlapping but also distinct relation to the construct of the ancient athlete as well as to other premodern morphologies. The military man might constitute another cluster, whether the modern soldier in Iraq, a member of a Napoleonic legion, a knight, or an ancient foot soldier. Other clusters might include: the male provider or breadwinner, be it the ancient Roman *pater familias* or the successful modern American father with a large house, good job, minivan, beautiful wife, and kids; the self-sufficient man who needs no one and is defined by his position outside a normative societal context, which might include the bachelor, the rebel, the cowboy, or the maverick; the man of the mind for whom the rejection of the body defines gender (the Cartesian man of reason, the philosopher, the lawyer, or the judge). In all of these cases, the question of continuity and rupture within the cluster (as discussed with respect to the metrosexual) could be asked. While this list is sketchy and incomplete, my goal here is not to lay out every possible historical morphology of masculinity (which would hardly be possible given the scope of this book and the complexity of gender), but to think about the idea of historical categories. The lacunae or disagreements with these categories that will necessarily arise suggest the complexity of masculinity, when considered historically. In no way are these complete categories defined only in themselves. Questions around race, ethnicity, class, and the nation would have to be factored in as well. How, for instance, does the figure of the samurai relate to the cluster of the military man?

While we all know men that fit some of these categories (perhaps perfectly), few actual men fit into one category that defines their entire subjectivity. Instead, these categories are more commonly mixed up in individual men. The breadwinner may also be a man of reason, or the military man may be a breadwinner too. Similarly, within discursive contexts, these morphologies and clusters of masculinity necessarily overlap in conflicting and contradictory ways. The dandy may at times incorporate, be dependent upon, or act like the soldier or the man of reason, which are seemingly very different morphologies. Though the dandy may be defined in a seemingly stable way, definitional movement or the ability to morph into other masculinities may also define him as one element of the morphology itself. Or, acting in a way that another morphology is assumed to act may serve to highlight his dandy-like traits by opposition.

When examining historical or diachronic masculinities, one might consider not only discursive clusters or morphologies, but also experiences or practices of masculinity (what one does) and how they change over time. Like these categories, masculine practices reflect both continuities and ruptures in time that function in complicated ways. The skilled use of a lance, for instance, might transform into the practice of using some other kind of weapon, or might transform into the use of a lance for recreational jousts. But discourse and practice are not inseparable. Discourse influences practice, and vice versa. Men may actually act moderate in practice and consequently construct the moderate man as ideal in certain discursive contexts. Conversely, discursive constructs may inspire certain men to act or want to act moderate. One of the reasons why discourses of masculinity change over time is that practices themselves change, and a construct of masculinity in part reflects changing practices and is retroactive in nature. The metrosexual – or the main characteristics of the metrosexual – already existed before the figure was codified in a handbook. Conversely, discourses of masculinity have an influence on practices. If the ideal man is healthy and well built, and that ideal is propagated by discourse over time, men are more likely to practice masculinity in that way and to change how they practice gender over time. Men may receive *The Metrosexual Guide to Style* as a gift from their girlfriends and alter their gendered practices over the course of time. On the other hand, a discourse of masculinity may move a man to act in a contrary way, just as a practice may influence him to create a counter-discourse that responds negatively to that practice. In the end, however, discourse and practice may be hard to distinguish or separate out, even as the history of masculine constructs is ultimately composed of both of them.

Bibliography

Work in queer and gay studies has provided sophisticated ways to think about gendered and sexual subjectivity in history, some of which have influenced my thinking in this chapter. See especially ch. 4 in David Halperin, *How to Do a History of Homosexuality* (Chicago: University of Chicago Press, 2002). See also a classic queer theory text that influenced Halerpin, Eve Kosofsky Sedgwick, *Epistemology of the Closet* (Berkeley: University of California Press, 1990). See also Carla Freccero, *Queer/Early/Modern* (Durham, NC: Duke University Press, 2006); Jonathan Goldberg and Madhavi Menon, "Queering History," *PMLA* 120, no. 5 (2005): 1608–17; Valerie Traub, "The Present Future of Lesbian Historiography," in *A Companion to Lesbian, Gay, Bisexual, Transgender, and Queer Studies*, ed. George E. Haggerty and Molly McGarry (Malden, MA: Blackwell, 2007), 124–45. The discussion here could be considered in relation to female masculinities as well. On morphologies of female masculinity, see the suggested readings in chapter 6. On transsexuality and temporality, see, for instance, Judith Halberstam, *In a Queer Time and Place: Transgender Bodies, Subcultural Lives* (New York: New York University Press, 2005); Jay Prosser, *Second Skins: The Body Narratives of Transsexuality* (New York: Columbia University Press, 1998).

Index